Praise for *Skyscraper Jails*

"In this view of New York City politics from the street, Jarrod Shanahan and Zhandarka Kurti cut through the double-speak of carceral humanism that elites used to turn the Campaign to Close Rikers into a plan to build new skyscraper jails. Real estate developers and politicians make New York City hospitable to more jails, but so do the philanthropists, nonprofit service providers, professors, and architects who celebrate modern and even 'green' jail design. But Rikers is not just a toxic complex of buildings. Rikers is built on the toxic social relations of capitalism. This, as Shanahan and Kurti tell us, is what we must confront."

—**NAOMI MURAKAWA**, author,
The First Civil Right: How Liberals Built Prison America

"I urge you to embrace the insurrectionist antiliberalism so generously unfurled in *Skyscraper Jails*. Blending grounded analysis, critical storytelling, and historical study, Shanahan and Kurti identify the emergence of a 'progressive,' twenty-first-century counterinsurgency regime in New York City and beyond. These pages demystify the coalescence of philanthropic, nonprofit, academic, and Democratic Party actors and social media influencers who have weaponized the terms of 'social justice' and 'abolition' to advance reformist expansions of carceral warfare. *Skyscraper Jails* is an indispensable tool for identifying new and old enemies of serious liberationist praxis—a painful though necessary task in this moment of proliferating cooptation, opportunism, and confusion."

—**DYLAN RODRÍGUEZ**, Critical Resistance founding collective
and Distinguished Professor, University of California

"*Skyscraper Jails* is an invaluable resource for anyone looking to fight carceral state expansion from a deeply rigorous, anticapitalist, and revolutionary standpoint. Kurti and Shanahan show how our struggles can be documented, studied, and written about in ways that offer tangible lessons for the future. And for abolitionists committed to bringing about the closure of Rikers and reclaiming the city, *Skyscraper Jails* is necessary reading on the specific liberal contexts and organizations from which the borough based jails plan emerged and which continue to have profound impacts on policing, incarceration, and social control in New York City."

—**MON MOHAPATRA**, organizer,
Community Justice Exchange and No New Jails NYC

"I have fought against jails in my community for years, and I have lived this history. *Skyscraper Jails* has the audacity to expose the truth about nonprofits and how they have sabotaged our work as revolutionary abolitionist organizers. This book is a must-read for anyone who wants to be involved in the hard work of breaking down prison walls and fighting to build another world."

—**LISA ORTEGA**, organizer,
Community in Unity and Take Back the Bronx

"Jails are instruments of crisis management, class containment, and counterinsurgency. In their examination of New York City as a laboratory for neoliberal governance and innovations of carceral violence, Jarrod Shanahan and Zhandarka Kurti interrogate the alliance of philanthropic, nonprofit, and governmental forces attempting to rescue the legitimacy of incarceration through deploying the vernacular of social justice. At once a sober assessment of the terrain of struggle and a searing argument that, whether decrepit island or gleaming tower, jails are central sites of racialized class war, *Skyscraper Jails* lays out the urgent stakes of this central battle for an abolitionist future."

—**JUDAH SCHEPT**, author, *Progressive Punishment: Job Loss, Jail Growth, and the Neoliberal Logic of Carceral Expansion* and *Coal, Cages, Crisis: The Rise of the Prison Economy in Central Appalachia*

SKYSCRAPER JAILS

THE FIGHT AGAINST JAIL EXPANSION IN NEW YORK CITY

JARROD SHANAHAN
AND ZHANDARKA KURTI

HAYMARKET BOOKS

CHICAGO, ILLINOIS

Published in 2024 by
Haymarket Books
P.O. Box 180165
Chicago, IL 60618
www.haymarketbooks.org

ISBN: 979-8-88890-264-6

Distributed to the trade in the US through Consortium Book Sales
and Distribution (www.cbsd.com) and internationally through Ingram
Publisher Services International (www.ingramcontent.com).

This book was published with the generous support of Lannan
Foundation, Wallace Action Fund, and Marguerite Casey Foundation.

Special discounts are available for bulk purchases by organizations
and institutions. Please email info@haymarketbooks.org for more
information.

Cover design by Eric Kerl.

Printed in Canada by union labor.

Library of Congress Cataloging-in-Publication data is available.

10 9 8 7 6 5 4 3 2 1

*Dedicated to the abolitionists fighting to break
down prison walls in NYC and beyond.*

If I know anything at all,
It's that a wall is just a wall
and nothing more at all.
It can be broken down.

—Assata Shakur

CONTENTS

CLOSING RIKERS
TIMELINE OF EVENTS

August 2014: The US Department of Justice releases a scathing report, based on its own investigations, on the violence in Rikers.

October 2014: A group of formerly incarcerated people form #ResistRikers and hold their first rally outside the jail complex.

March 2015: Following increased calls for action to address the violence on Rikers, Bill de Blasio and then Department of Correction commissioner Joseph Ponte announce their fourteen-point plan.

June 2015: Kalief Browder, who spent three years on Rikers awaiting trial, commits suicide in the Bronx.

June 2015: The Campaign to #ShutDownRikers is formed at a rally celebrating the life of Kalief Browder.

February 2016: In her State of the City address, New York City Council speaker Melissa Mark-Viverito calls for reforms to reduce the population on Rikers Island with the goal of eventually shuttering the jail complex.

March 2016: The Independent Commission on New York City Criminal Justice and Incarceration Reform (known as the Lippman Commission) is formed.

April 2016: JustLeadershipUSA launches its #CLOSErikers campaign with a rally at city hall.

March 2017: Bill de Blasio and Melissa Mark-Viverito announce a ten-year plan to shut down the Rikers Island penal colony.

April 2017: The Lippman Commission releases its report *A More Just New York City* and calls for closing Rikers and replacing it with smaller jails in the city's five boroughs.

June 2017: The de Blasio administration releases *Smaller, Safer, Fairer: A Roadmap to Closing Rikers Island*, a blueprint for closing Rikers that includes improved safety protocols, reduced capacity, and reduced isolation for prisoners.

February 2018: Flanked by New York City Council speaker Corey Johnson, Mayor de Blasio announces the four borough-based jails to replace Rikers Island.

September 2018: No New Jails NYC (NNJ) abolitionist group is founded.

October 2019: De Blasio and Johnson agree to close the jail complex by 2026 and open four new jails at a total cost of $8.7 billion. The city council approves the deal a week later.

May 2022: New York City ramps up construction of a new jail in Queens, sparking protests from residents.

October 2022: A federal monitor that had been tasked with investigating progress at the city jails concludes that "nearly every facet of the jails' operations, procedures, and practices needs to be dismantled and reconstituted."

September 2023: Demolition begins in Chinatown to replace the Tombs with the tallest jail in the world.

PROLOGUE

The book you hold in your hands was produced by the unique historical moment in which the symbols, rhetoric, and tactics of social justice activism, including prison abolitionism, were successfully deployed in support of one of the most ambitious and massive jail construction projects in recent memory. Responding to activist energy and public demand to close the Rikers Island jail complex, the #CLOSErikers campaign, fueled by millions of dollars from the philanthropic sector, promised to end the violence on Rikers—by replacing the last penal colony in the nation with the tallest jails in the world. This plan was accomplished by an equally novel and complex constellation of jail boosters, representing a sophisticated division of labor bridging the old money of big philanthropy with so-called social entrepreneurship, social justice nonprofit organizations, nonprofit service providers, Democratic politicians, social movement politics, and the New York City real estate industry.

This is far from a local story, although it begins, like so many experiments in austerity and social engineering have, in New York. Under the guise of criminal justice reform, cities around the country are building new carceral institutions and sparking opposition movements in response. As we complete this book, one of the most important and exciting struggles is currently unfolding in Atlanta, Georgia, where a robust social movement is opposing the proposed construction of what threatens to be the largest police training facility in the country. These struggles, and many others we can anticipate in the coming years, are fertile ground for renewed organizing efforts against white supremacy, austerity, and, we hope, capitalist society itself.

Our own interest and commitments to this project are grounded in our backgrounds in mass movement politics. We became acquainted with each other during the Occupy Wall Street movement, and we remained active in street-level politics through the protests in response to murder of Trayvon Martin in 2012, the post-Ferguson wave of street militancy in 2014, the George Floyd rebellion in the summer of 2020, and several smaller campus, workplace, and community campaigns in between. Some of these campaigns were explicitly anticapitalist, while others we hoped to make so.

Observing New York City politics from the vantage point of the street, we became increasingly interested in the central role that police, courts, and jails play in managing the city's daily life—especially with regard to the working-class communities of color that are structurally excluded from New York's fabled prosperity—alongside the social movements that episodically arise demanding, in the words of an old slogan, *everything for everyone*. We also noticed the distinctly anti-police character of struggles like the Black Lives Matter movement and the George Floyd rebellion, which focused on cops, courts, and carceral facilities to launch an attack on the racist violence and oppression that holds American capitalism together. We took particular inspiration from the anti-police street militancy—and networks of care and social reproduction underlying it—seen in the summer of 2020, which served as the basis for our book *States of Incarceration: Rebellion, Reform, and America's Punishment System.*[1]

Like most New Yorkers, we first heard about the #CLOSErikers campaign in 2016. Zhandarka was undertaking extensive fieldwork in the South Bronx for a dissertation critically examining the experiences of Black and Latinx youth with lower courts and probation. Jarrod was beginning a sustained historical study of the Rikers Island penal colony, based on an experience he had with short-stay incarceration there following the 2014 post-Ferguson street movement, which would become *Captives: How Rikers Island Took New York City Hostage.*[2] Jarrod was also recruited off the street to participate in #CLOSErikers as a "formerly incarcerated leader." He didn't really feel like his experiences made him much of a leader, and was ambivalent about getting involved with a project with such deep ties to seasoned counterinsurgent nonprofits like the Ford Foundation, and asked Zhandarka for advice. She counseled, "As long as they want to shut down a jail, they're our friends, but as soon as they want to build a new one, they aren't." Heeding these words, and cherishing the opportunity to see such a unique political constellation from the inside, Jarrod got involved with #CLOSErikers for roughly half a year, until it pivoted, as Zhandarka had feared, to advocating for new jails.

We recognized in the campaign for these new jails much of what we had been studying in isolation and began collaborating on critical assessments of the skyscraper jails plan and the intricate nexus of criminal justice reformers, politicians, and nonprofit organizations supporting it.[3] We also participated, as both researchers and agitators, in the abolitionist opposition to the new jail construction No New Jails NYC (NNJ), an experience that shaped the present study immensely—as did our membership in a vibrant intellectual community of abolitionists, activists, militants, and street fighters, whose hard-won insights can be found throughout *Skyscraper Jails.*

The NNJ campaign was exciting to us because it articulated a political position that brought together some of New York City's radical grassroots groups in opposition to the city's liberal elites and attempted to connect the fight against jails to other potential fault lines of working-class discontent. The campaign underscored how the city had committed to the funding and construction of new carceral facilities while abandoning its responsibility to meeting the basic needs of working-class New Yorkers. This message found resonance far beyond the usual activist milieus. Despite its uphill challenges and internal limits, NNJ shook the bipartisan pro-jail consensus that has dominated New York—and American—politics since the 1980s and created an alternative radical position that the jail boosters had to seriously contend with. In our view, NNJ earnestly grappled with the need for public-facing radical activism as they engaged with an initiative that affected everyday people, dedicated themselves to study alongside struggle, and attempted, in however limited a fashion, to form a mass-level organizational capacity that could abet the revolutionary transformation of society.

As of publication, skepticism that the skyscraper jails will result in the closure of Rikers—a key argument made by NNJ members in 2019 and hotly disputed by the jail boosters—is becoming conventional wisdom among the boosters themselves. In 2023, Board of Correction executive director Martha King evoked "the strong likelihood that, rather than closing Rikers and opening four borough jails, New York City will have an expanded jail system that includes Rikers." Oddly enough, King cites this sad fact as further evidence of why a "no new jails" position remains untenable.[4] We can't help but see things the other way around. At the same time, activists continue to struggle against the skyscraper jails, albeit with a diminishing chance of stopping them.

Nonetheless, we do not pretend to know with any certainty whether the penal colony on Rikers will ever close its doors for incarceration, be it for city prisoners, supposedly mentally ill unhoused people presently targeted for forcible detention by Mayor Eric Adams, undocumented people, or others especially vulnerable

to human cages.[5] Nor do we know if the skyscraper jails will in
fact open—though at present, the plan appears to be proceeding
full-speed ahead. As this struggle unfolds, however, we believe
that a close study of the skyscraper jail construction plan holds educational value for anyone, whether or not they live in New York,
seeking to understand important changes occurring among the
interrelated phenomena of capitalist crisis, state governance, the
nonprofit industrial complex, mass incarceration, criminal justice
reform, prison abolitionism, and mass movement politics.

The importance of building anticapitalist movements that
are independent of parliamentary politics and the nonprofit industrial complex remains the crucial task for twenty-first-century
revolutionaries and activists. We are buoyed by the recent wave
of pro-Palestinian protests which have made opposition to Zion-
ism and settler-colonialism the baseline for building solidarity. All
leftists should take heed from their principled activism and make
prison abolition a basic tenet of our organizing and coalitions, up-
lifting the righteous *no compromises* ethos of Palestine solidarity.

The idea for *Skyscraper Jails* came from a passage in prison
scholar Judah Schept's *Coal, Cages, Crisis*, an excellent study of
a carceral expansion plot in rural Appalachia. "It is important to
recognize the contributions of various actors within the county
and region," writes Schept, "who worked to create hospitable material and ideological conditions to recruit and site the prison."[6]
We began what follows by applying this simple premise to the
New York story, hoping to document what we found for activists
fighting the construction of carceral facilities elsewhere. Along the
way, we discovered that our study also shed light on the nature of
American capitalism in crisis and the ever-changing terrain of reform and rebellion unfolding amid its intrinsic chaos. The result is
a short book written for those who seek to understand the present
world, in order to build a new one.

It should be no secret that we are opposed to the skyscraper jails and the organizations and individuals who have campaigned so tirelessly for them. We believe that incarceration throughout New York City—and not just on Rikers Island—is nothing short of a grave humanitarian crisis calling for swift and radical redress. It is very likely that as you read these words, real people are suffering on Rikers Island. We advocate any means necessary to bring this suffering to an end, within or outside the law. As abolitionists, we believe the immediate interests of incarcerated people are in sync with long-term strategies for human emancipation. Therefore, we reject the notion, popularized in recent years around the skyscraper jail debate, that opponents of the new jails are thereby indifferent to the plight of people presently caged in the old ones. Let us state at the onset that our position remains, as it has been all along: Close Rikers now, no new jails!

INTRODUCTION

HISTORY IN THE MAKING

The crisis consists precisely in the fact that the old is dying and the new cannot be born; in this interregnum a great variety of morbid symptoms appear.

—Antonio Gramsci, 1930

On October 17, 2019, the New York City Council passed a "historic vote" in favor of an $8.3 billion plan to close down the Rikers Island jail complex by 2026 and to replace it with skyscraper jail buildings in Manhattan, Brooklyn, Queens, and the Bronx. In the spirit of compromise, this staggering price tag had been reduced from an original proposal of $11 billion (though it has since ballooned back to $10 billion thanks to inflation).[1] In the eyes of many progressive city council members, the gravity of this vote lay not in the unprecedented height of the new proposed buildings, destined to become the tallest jails in the world, nor in the immense scope of the jail construction project, the most elaborate single carceral-expansion effort in the city's history. Instead, they believed history was being made in the steps these new jails represented toward reforming mass incarceration and achieving social justice.

"We're on the cusp of a new, more humane era for our city," proclaimed the council's liberal speaker, Corey Johnson.[2] Another avowed progressive, Mayor Bill de Blasio, took it a step further.

"The era of mass incarceration," he declared with stunning finality, "is over."[3]

While the vote was dutifully disrupted by the abolitionist group No New Jails NYC, another group of ostensibly left-wing activists in the audience briefly caused a disturbance by unfurling a banner *in support* of the new jail construction. A chorus of progressive organizations, including the New York Civil Liberties Union, lauded the resolution.[4] Meanwhile, the names of Kalief Browder and other tragic casualties of Rikers Island were evoked on the council floor in defense of building more human cages like those that claimed their lives.[5] One council member speaking in defense of the skyscraper jails even cited the work of veteran abolitionist organizer Mariame Kaba, an outspoken critic of the plan.[6]

What accounts for the enthusiasm among so many in the so-called progressive New York City community for a project that dissenting abolitionists correctly observed would constitute "the tallest skyscraper jails in the world"?[7] Answering this question requires us to engage with the local, national, and international characteristics of our capitalist society in crisis and to place incarceration *at the center* of the story of twenty-first-century capitalist life.

In recent years, the deadly and dehumanizing jail complex on Rikers Island has become the crumbling avatar of the racial and class violence at the center of mass incarceration. Despite progressive reform efforts that have reduced the jail population at Rikers by 233 percent from its peak in the 1990s, race and class disparities in New York City jails have worsened.[8] A report released by the Data Collaborative for Justice at John Jay College of Criminal Justice compared racial disparities in New York City jails across a five-year period (2016–21) and found that in 2021, Black and Latinx people made up almost 90 percent of jail admissions despite constituting only 52 percent of the city's general population.[9] The report also found that Black people were jailed 11.6 times more than white people in 2021, up more than double from 2016.[10] The Rikers Island jail complex also serves as the city's largest mental health facility—nearly half of all those detained have some kind of mental health diagnosis.[11] Since 2020, the number of people detained with serious mental health diagnoses has nearly doubled, reaching a monthly average of nearly 1,200 people, with no new services added to accommodate them.[12]

The city has looked the other way as detainees, disproportionately Black, Latinx, and people battling mental illness, experience horrifying pretrial conditions, including widespread brutality and abuse. Those unfortunate enough to be incarcerated there even described Rikers as a "torture island" scarcely different from Abu Ghraib.[13] Reports gathered by independent monitoring confirm this sentiment. The monitors, appointed in the settlement of *Nunez v. City of New York*, a 2011 class action lawsuit filed by Rikers detainees, for years have kept track of use of force by staff and have produced annual reports that document the deadly violence inside the jail complex. And then the COVID-19 pandemic hit Rikers, making nearly every aspect of incarceration there worse.

While human caging on Rikers Island has been opposed by those locked up there since the penal colony's founding in the late nineteenth century, nowhere in the city's history has there existed the political willpower to close the jail that we see today. For much of Rikers Island's existence, city elites have responded to the horrors of the jail as they respond today to every social crisis engulfing New York City, from the precipitous decline of mass transit to homelessness and drug overdoses. They willfully ignore the crisis, or when that fails, they push a narrative that off-loads the blame of the crisis squarely on individual—not systemic—failings, whether the scapegoat is brutal guards, out-of-control youth gangs, or lack of funding to improve infrastructure. But today, the violence unfolding in Rikers Island is too politically costly even for city elites who have spent the past six decades turning New York into a model of twenty-first-century business-friendly governance.

Jails like those on Rikers Island have not always existed. Modern capitalist society has normalized the idea that jails should be the appropriate response to "criminal" behavior, without questioning why and how certain forms of behavior are criminalized or why it is that the poor and the most marginalized are the primary targets of our society's brutal punishment regime. The very history of the jail can be traced to the advent of capitalist social relations, which created two classes with diametrically opposed interests: one class that owns the means of production (the capitalists) and one that has to labor to survive (the workers). The wealth of contemporary capitalist societies was accrued on the backs of enslaved people and Indigenous people subjected to genocide, forced labor, underdevelopment, and theft of land. The attendant creation of working classes all over the world required the use of barbaric punishments and draconian laws operating alongside the expropriation of land and traditional sources of livelihood as part of a history "written in the annals of mankind in letters of blood and fire."[14] The jail was an early tool of this process.

The history of capitalist exploitation and plunder thus runs parallel to the history of prisons and jails. Early carceral institutions sprang up alongside factories and were tasked with disciplining workers who refused, or were structurally unable, to go quietly into the industrial workforce, as well as women who refused to follow the dictates of the patriarchal family.[15] Ever since, the threat of incarceration in jail and prison has been a tool wielded by the elite to discipline the poor and working class to accept wage discipline, rooted in the principle of "less eligibility," by which conditions in jails and prisons must be more unpleasant than even the worst life for a wage laborer on the outside.[16]

As Friedrich Engels noted in his seminal work *The Conditions of the Working Class in England*, capitalist exploitation creates wretched living and working conditions for workers. And the presence of a racial division of labor all but ensures that the so-called races on the lower end of the class ladder will disproportionately bear the burden of this "vulnerability to premature death," which as Ruth Wilson Gilmore reminds us, is the very definition of racism.[17] The state does not decry capitalist exploitation as "social murder," to use Engels's memorable words.[18] Instead, the main targets of the state's crime-control strategies and punishment remain the poor and anyone who either disrupts or does not adhere to the imperatives of capitalist order.

As the work of scholar John Irwin demonstrates, jails mark and discipline those who are perceived as undesirable populations, or "rabble," by the police and legal system and those who are increasingly alienated by society's social and economic transformations, especially those living in cities that have been transformed by the return of intensive capital investment dubbed "gentrification."[19] In short, carceral institutions are *central*, not ancillary, to class struggles unfolding in the United States and around the world. As Jack Norton, Lydia Pelot-Hobbs, and Judah Schept put it, "The jail is everywhere."[20]

In recent years, jail populations across the US have grown exponentially, fueled by various local and national transformations. For instance, top-down reforms attempting to downsize state prison populations like that of California's Public Safety Realignment Act shift a portion of the state prison population to local county jails.[21] In rural regions of the United States in particular, jails have increasingly assumed the burden of treatment for mental health and substance abuse. This is especially the case in areas where community mental health care services and medical providers are scarce. For instance, counties in rural Tennessee, a region that has witnessed the highest rate of hospital closures, have decided to ignore this public health crisis and instead fund the building of new jails.[22] As a result of these and other transformations, rural jails now detain people at twice the rate of urban jails.[23] In addition, the prevalence of cash bail has driven the rise in jail populations because of the simple fact that most detainees are too poor to afford bail. Contrary to what law-and-order pundits claim, most people incarcerated in local jails have not been found guilty of anything besides being poor, and often of being Black or Latinx, in America. They languish awaiting adjudication that can take years or else waste their time on short-stay incarceration for minor offenses not serious enough to warrant a state sentence. In 2023, 87 percent of people in Rikers Island were pretrial detainees.[24] These statistics are reflective of general nationwide trends—in 2023, an estimated 83 percent of people were held pretrial.[25] As a result of these developments, a far greater number of people churn daily through local jails than through state prisons. For example, in 2023, close to half a million people entered prison, whereas seven million people were admitted into local jails.[26]

The jail churn demonstrates that these carceral facilities serve no social good except to temporarily quarantine the social problems that society is unable, or unwilling, to solve in a setting that takes people who have suffered trauma, addiction, houselessness, mental illness, and other scourges of life on the bottom rungs of the labor market, and makes their dire situation even worse. Jails are also less likely than prisons to have programming for incarcerated people, educational or otherwise, thus highlighting their warehousing not rehabilitative function.[27] From time to time, the conditions inside jails garner public attention and scrutiny that initiates a game of Whack-A-Mole, whereby officials move to address the conditions in one jail, usually by closing it down, only to be confronted by another set of issues that justify the building of new jails. And this is the history of Rikers Island.

A HISTORY OF FAILED REFORMS

Rikers Island was named after Abraham Rycken, a Dutch settler who purchased the island from the colonial government in 1664 following its theft from the Lenape tribe. It was for generations thereafter a small family farm in an obscure pocket of the East River. During the Civil War, the island was used as a military base to train Union soldiers and served as a haven for Black New Yorkers fleeing the racist violence of the Draft Riot. Following the war, the land was primarily used as a garbage dump.[28]

Contemporary accounts of the island's history emphasize one member of the Riker family, Richard, who worked as a recorder for the city's main criminal court in the mid-1800s and is commonly misidentified as the island's namesake.[29] At that time, New York abolitionists had won the end of slavery in the state, the ban of the Fugitive Slave Act, and the extension of due process in the form of a fair hearing to fugitives from slavery. Richard Riker used his position and power as part of a larger ring of city officials, including judges, lawyers, and police officers, dubbed the Kidnapping Club by local abolitionists, to reverse these gains by rubber stamping the removal and return of accused runaway slaves without trial.[30] The historical coincidence of the island's name reminds us of the anti-Black history of the US government, the capitalist market, and many enduring social institutions. But the Richard Riker story has also inspired the unfortunate idea, promoted by the #CLOSErikers campaign, that there is something metaphysically evil about Rikers Island apart from the fact that it contains a large number of human cages. From the premise that Rikers has a unique "dark history" that explains its present-day inhumanity, the solution can easily become "new cages somewhere less haunted and hence less racist."[31]

The real history is a bit more banal but no less dark. City Hall purchased Rikers, an estimated eighty-seven acres, in 1884, at a time when New York City was becoming one of the most densely populated cities in the nation. Accounts of slum life and the poverty and violence that underpinned it, especially among the city's immigrant populations, shocked middle-class reformers, who in turn devised the social-engineering programs to uplift the so-called deserving poor. But banishment remained the preferred method of social control reserved for the city's unwanted populations, and it included detention on Blackwell's Island and in the Manhattan Tombs. In response to the growing scandal around this practice, Rikers was explicitly purchased as part of a great reform initiative: separating out supposed criminals from ordinary poor people in the various asylums of Blackwell's Island to prevent the contamination of the latter by the former.[32]

The city first began increasing the size of Rikers Island in the late 1890s, using city prisoners—working in dangerous and disgusting conditions—as forced laborers, to off-load the city's garbage and excavation from the subway system, swelling the island's mass to the 440 acres it boasts today. This transformation proved the viability of Rikers Island to city officials looking to expand the city's carceral capacity. Initially, the city ferried prisoners from the Blackwell's Island penal colony to work as convict laborers. Many of these prisoners were locked up full-time in the island's earliest jails beginning in 1903, initiating 24/7 incarceration on Rikers Island that continues to the present day. From these earliest days, the forced laborers of Rikers Island regularly took proactive steps to free themselves from the stinking landfill as the island's first captives had done—by swimming across the treacherous East River current to freedom, and in the process, taking decisive steps to end incarceration on Rikers, if only for themselves.[33]

The grueling labor these prisoners were subjected to on Rikers was carried out in the service of criminal justice reform. Since 1884, the city had endeavored to relocate its prisoner population from the decrepit Blackwell's facilities to a state-of-the-art jail on Rikers Island. Rikers, then, was born as a reform. From the outset, the architects tasked with building Rikers sought to build an efficient model jail. But the willpower to execute these plans would not exist until decades later when Progressive Era reform ideologies gained more mainstream prominence.[34] Most importantly, Rikers was going to replace Blackwell's, a former pastoral island turned into "a lounging, listless madhouse," as Charles Dickens remarked in his 1842 visit to the so-called lunatic asylum, which formed an integral aspect of the carceral archipelago.[35] Blackwell's was not only an embarrassment to city elites and a standing rebuke to their legitimacy as preservers of order but also a financial burden. The land on Rikers was promising, especially since prisoner labor had increased its land value by transforming the area from a landfill into an urban farm. One penal colony was soon replaced by another.

Much of Rikers Island's infrastructural expansion—including its original 1934 penitentiary, multiple other jails still in use today, and the 1964 bridge that connects the island to the mainland, enabling the housing of pretrial detainees on the island—was carried out under the auspices of criminal justice reform. Its original penitentiary was overseen by stars in the field of progressive penology, to great celebration in national reform circles. Of course, these new jails were built to solve the problems of the old ones, only to become notorious in their own right, leaving would-be reformers clamoring to replace them with *still more jails*. According to the philosophy of rehabilitation penology that the New York

City Department of Correction (DOC) professed until the 1970s, new jails were even intended to serve a positive social function, improving both prisoners and society at large by addressing the individual problems that supposedly led to incarceration. However, such progressive reform efforts only helped to preserve the jail system's legitimacy and justify its expansion over the course of the twentieth century.[36] Today, a similar cohort of progressive reformers seek to replace the sprawling jail complex with a network of borough-based skyscraper jails.[37]

In many ways, today's reformers are not that different from their historical counterparts. In the nineteenth century, as philosopher Michel Foucault examined, prison reformers decried public forms of punishment and embraced prisons as more humane and efficient institutions capable of regulating and disciplining the poor.[38] But this transformation from a punishment aimed at the body to one aimed at the soul was neither inevitable evolution nor simple human progress. As the historian David Rothman argues, the birth of totalitarian institutions like the prison was not just "an automatic and inevitable response of an industrial and urban society to crime and poverty."[39] Instead, the success of the prison reflected the power of reformers to frame social crises in a way that legitimized jails and prisons as the best way to handle disorder.

Despite its obvious resonance with centuries of carceral history, however, we must emphasize that the story of the skyscraper jails is not a mere case of "history repeating itself." Anyone seeking to make meaningful change in the present must not lose sight of the novelty of today's reformers, and the unique political and economic circumstances they inhabit.

A CRISIS WITHIN A CRISIS

For much of its history, the US state has turned to policing and carceral institutions to manage the contradictions inherent in a capitalist society driven by stark divisions of race and class. But the punitive policies that were rolled out in the second half of the twentieth century represent a distinct phenomenon in the history of punishment under capitalism that has drawn the attention of scholars and activists alike. Every year it seems that a new book comes out to try to explain why such a punitive path was taken and to study this system's consequences on both the nearly six million Americans under its control and American society in general. Despite these various and often conflicting interpretations, few would deny that today mass incarceration is the most blatant example of class and race domination in the United States.

We develop our own understanding of mass incarceration from Marxist and radical scholars who trace its roots as a response to deep crises of the 1960s and 1970s, including the challenge that Black-led revolutionary movements posed to capitalism, the system-wide economic crisis of capitalist rule and the class insecurities it unleashed.[40] We argue for a structural and historical interpretation of mass incarceration that places the phenomenon squarely at the center of the transformations of the American capitalist state—how it rules and manages increasingly sharp class contradictions engendered by the very nature of capitalist development itself. We insist that you cannot cleave off spectacular "injustices" from that total ensemble of social relations that produces them; far from an unfortunate stain on an otherwise great nation, mass incarceration is, to borrow a memorable phrase from Black militant H. Rap Brown, as American as cherry pie.[41]

We find the present crises have been developing for decades, beginning at the end of the postwar boom. To anyone living in 1968, no matter what side of the political divide they belonged to, the status quo seemed untenable. A growing segment of American society was fed up with politics as usual and articulated political visions that embraced a far more expansive human potential than was possible under the prevailing capitalist social order. Urban riots on the heels of the passage of civil rights legislation guaranteeing equality under the law challenged the illusions that the problem of institutional racism could be resolved through parliamentary politics. Declining rates of manufacturing profit and capital flight from American cities coincided with increased demands for wealth and prosperity, including from traditionally marginalized groups. In short, by the 1970s, the social, economic, and political arrangement that shaped the relationship between the capitalist state and the dictates of global capitalism was unraveling. The prison build-up, then, responded to problems central to how capitalism works, or more precisely, doesn't.[42]

The capitalist state, as the Italian theorist and revolutionary Antonio Gramsci reminds us, is first and foremost a social formation that organizes society in a way that is amenable to the accumulation and reproduction of capital.[43] The form the state takes under capitalism, rooted in liberal ideas of universal suffrage, political representation, and individualism, hides its explicit class interests. Between the 1930s and 1960s, the state in both the United States and the United Kingdom became a major intervening force in the economy and thus was able to resolve crises temporarily and save capitalism from itself through the creation of Keynesian welfare policies, effecting modest wealth redistribution through public spending and employment, and the incorporation of organized labor into the legal mechanisms of the state. From a ruling-class perspective, this was an acceptable-enough framework for capitalist accumulation in the so-called First World, until it wasn't.

By the late 1960s, this tenuous arrangement had entered into severe turbulence, and with it what meager social welfare capacity remained. In the following chapter we will explore in more detail this transformation through the vantage point of New York City, which in a few short decades transformed from a model social welfare city into a neoliberal nightmare. For present purposes, this crisis of the state is important because it rendered older forms of class domination obsolete and, as Stuart Hall and his colleagues persuasively argued in *Policing the Crisis*, moved "the operation of the state away from consent towards the pole of coercion."[44] Following Hall, it is within this crisis of state legitimacy and hegemony that we must place the rise of law-and-order politics and punitive policies that led to what we today call mass incarceration. We view the present crisis of mass incarceration as the result of this earlier stopgap measure coming apart.

Stuart Hall was one of the first scholars who attempted to understand how the political right used the racialized category of crime to frame the larger capitalist crisis. In Britain, Hall and others at the University of Birmingham Centre for Contemporary Cultural Studies (CCCS) noted the emergence of a moral panic over "mugging," which tended to be portrayed by the media and politicians as rampant Black-on-white street-level assault. When Hall and his associates looked at the numbers, however, they were not convinced that mugging had exploded into an epidemic in a short amount of time. Instead, they argued that the issue was a symptom and byproduct of the crisis of British and global capitalism.

To explain the panic around mugging, Hall and his colleagues explored how the major recession in the 1970s led to high rates of unemployment and civil unrest, signaling a loss of faith in the British government like the one we see today in the United States. In the face of this legitimation crisis, the ruling class needed a scapegoat to shift the blame onto, and they found it in a supposed increase of street robbery committed by Black youth. The media, for its part, seized on the opportunity to breathlessly sensationalize the issue, and right-wing politicians fanned the flames and demanded more punitive responses, including more policing. Amid the reality of economic insecurity, which often does, in fact, spur antisocial behavior among desperate working-class people, a ruling-class initiative emerged to remake the public sector in terms favorable to fiscal austerity, prefiguring the neoliberal order to come. The politics of crime control, including the role of the media and politicians and the popular embrace of law and order, therefore revealed much more than a supposed rise in crime statistics—this complex configuration pointed to an important new terrain of class struggle in England.[45]

The majority of arguments made by Hall can easily be extended to the United States. There, the political demand for law and order was promoted by an increasingly hardened right-wing segment of the American ruling class who capitalized on the social, political, and economic crisis facing ordinary Americans and framed the problem as one of crime and disorder.[46] For example, one of Richard Nixon's 1968 campaign ads argued that the main problem facing America was not poverty, structural racism at home, or the war in Vietnam—it was crime.[47] As the camera panned over images of disorder, including protests against the Vietnam War, Nixon warned those who threatened traditional American values to "recognize that the first civil right of every American is to be free from domestic violence." Another famous ad featured a middle-class white woman walking in the street alone at night as a narrator recounted statistics on violence. The ad ends with the narrator proclaiming, "Freedom from fear is the basic right of every American; we must restore it."[48] Both ads reveal the extent to which Nixon saw the antiwar left and Black people as internal enemies, a fact admitted later by Nixon's domestic policy chief John Ehrlichman.[49]

Nixon's famous courting of America's "silent majority" of white people to oppose racially coded street crime was the US equivalent of the cross-class alliance between working-class and elite white people that Hall saw unfolding in England around the same issue.[50] Amid the very real threat of urban rebellions, this new political coalition challenged the legislative wins of the civil rights era and promoted a reinvigorated focus on Black crime, which was successfully conflated with revolutionary politics.[51] The "hybridized monster" of law and order, in Foucault's words, found a particular opportunity in the 1980s with the devastating impact of crack cocaine on working-class communities of color.[52]

As Jonathan Simon has argued, in America, "crack was mugging on steroids."[53] It fueled a moral panic about inner-city crime that generated a wave of punitive policies that expanded the capacity of the state to punish and filled America's jails and prisons. Like "mugging" in England, the crack epidemic in the United States revealed the deep racialized insecurities that plagued cities in the wake of deindustrialization and other local transformations engendered by the global capitalist crisis. The moral panic about the crack epidemic successfully won ordinary Americans over to support coercive state measures to punish illicit drug use, especially by appealing to the racially coded ideology of protecting suburban children from the contamination of the so-called Black drug.[54]

But the turn to "tough on crime" was not limited to the crack epidemic. Throughout the 1980s and 1990s, various other moral panics, tied to youth gangs and street crime, helped to reinforce popular support for punitive policies that built up the system of mass incarceration we have in place today. As Naomi Murakawa reminds us, we cannot simply blame conservatives for the rise of the American carceral state.[55] Liberals also supported "tough on crime" and advocated for law-and-order policies that created mass incarceration. Crime policy, which was rooted in larger transformations in the economy and in the particularly sharp contradictions of race and class divisions within an advanced liberal democratic society, became safely lodged as an important mode of governance, with deep lasting impacts.[56]

Mass incarceration in the United States, as scholars Jack Norton and David Stein have vehemently argued, was always about a whole lot more than supposed increases in street-level crime.[57] As Ruth Wilson Gilmore has demonstrated, the nexus of local, state, and federal punitive policies was not simply a response to the rise of street-level crime but a stopgap measure to remedy the crises attendant to the loss of employment and tax revenue from deindustrialization, the lack of desirable outlets for domestic capital investment amid declining rates of manufacturing profit, the radical challenges to capitalist society from below in the form of mass movements, and the bipartisan consensus that large-scale public spending, necessary for the circulation of private capital, must favor the so-called security state. Gilmore calls this fateful confluence "the prison fix." And the resolution of these crises with the hothouse expansion of America's carceral state was not predetermined; it played out within the contested terrain of politics at the thorny intersection of race and class.[58]

Which brings us to the present day. Debates among US elites about the future of mass incarceration are actually about how a contemporary advanced liberal democratic society, riven by brutal inequality and yoked to the chaos of the global capitalist market, ought best to shore itself up against potentially terminal turbulence and find a way forward in the novel terrain of the twenty-first century. Importantly, mass incarceration has tipped the delicate balance between coercion and consent—which is central to ruling-class domination—more toward the former than the latter, engendering a whole host of problems and headaches for the ruling class. This explains why in the present moment a bipartisan consensus of liberals and conservatives, in tandem with philanthropic foundations, corporations, and social entrepreneurs, have thrown their political weight and considerable resources to reform America's behemoth punishment system. "Among the crises police interventions contain," write Ruth Wilson Gilmore and Craig Gilmore, "are legitimation crises, during which the foundations of the racial capitalist state apparatus shake and crack."[59] While would-be reformers of the system come to their work from different ideologies, and often with different preferred outcomes, the imperative to restore this legitimacy stands at the heart of all carceral reform efforts spearheaded by elites.

It is important to situate such crises, which most often manifest themselves at the local level, in the very composition of transnational capitalist social relations. Marxist political economist David Ranney calls the present morass "a crisis of value" on a global scale. This means that, amid declining rates of profit, there are far too many claims to the value produced by working people. Claims include literal deeds held by investors and financiers but also extend to working peoples' demands for housing, living wages, health care, and a clean environment. In short, the functioning of the market and state demands far more value than actually exists; the result is a serious challenge to the future viability of capitalism itself. "For the capitalist system, the only way out of this is to destroy some of these claims and change the way capitalism functions."[60]

While this conjuncture can be the opportunity for heightened class struggle, when the ruling class is firmly in the driver's seat, the objective becomes narrower: "destroying labor's claims on value."[61] This is a recipe for austerity at best, and at worst, for the actual destruction of labor power through policing, incarceration, and war. And while US militarism and monetary policy have served to shield Americans from the worst of the crisis, even these great crimes are now delivering diminishing returns. Some of the most obvious signs of our contemporary crisis have been the 2008 Great Recession and the rise of right-wing movements in the United States and the world over, including the election of Donald Trump in the United States and the passage of Brexit in the United Kingdom. These instances have led some to argue that we are currently experiencing a fundamental political crisis, or a "black swan" event that challenges previous modes of thinking and renders them obsolete.[62]

The hostility of the contemporary market to everyday people has been made particularly acute by the inflation crisis, a direct corporate offensive on the claims to value made by American consumers that scholar Phil Neel has called "the knife at your throat."[63] But the most common symptom of the crisis is the perennial downward grind of austerity as state institutions fall apart, as more and more working-class people fall through the cracks, and as life gets meaner and more unpleasant, bespeaking the origin of "austerity" in the Greek word *austērós*, which means "bitter" or "harsh."[64] In recent years, a plethora of social movements have arisen contesting this economic arrangement, creating a visceral sense of a society escaping governability. These include Trump's Make America Great Again movement and its overtly fascist fringe, which has flirted with extra-parliamentary politics like the January 6 attack on the Capitol; left-wing street movements like Occupy Wall Street, Black Lives Matter, and the loose agglomeration of antifascist activists called antifa waging street fights with the far right; and a number of riots, flash mobs, organized looting operations, and other pre-political rejections of the status quo that, rightfully or not, have created a common public perception of a social order teetering on the brink of chaos.[65] The fact that much of this dissident activity takes police as their direct object of antagonism and attack demonstrates an acute sense of the role the cops play in keeping the whole order propped up.[66]

Occupy and Black Lives Matter, in particular, have called attention to the social carnage wrought by capitalism in crisis, including the ways in which the state has off-loaded its responsibility for basic social reproduction to poor communities themselves. Social reproduction, according to theorist Tithi Bhattacharya, means:

> the activities and institutions that are required for making life, maintaining life, and generationally replacing life. I call it "life-making" activities. Life-making in the most direct sense is giving birth. But in order to maintain that life, we require a whole host of other activities, such as cleaning, feeding, cooking, washing clothes. There are physical institutional requirements: a house to live in; public transport to go to various places; public recreational facilities, parks, after-school programs. Schools and hospitals are some of the basic institutions that are necessary for the maintenance of life and life-making. Those activities and institutions that are involved in this process of life-making we call social reproduction work and social reproduction institutions.[67]

The present crisis of social reproduction cuts at the heart of the matter. As the incarceration rates ballooned, working-class Black and Latinx women disproportionately bore the added burden of having to support loved ones behind bars while continuing to raise their families on the outside.[68] And if this wasn't enough, the state shirked its responsibility to basic social welfare and off-loaded it to private nonstate and third-party agencies, a process known as *devolution*, resulting in widespread finger-pointing over whose responsibility it is, if anyone's at all, to provide people's basic needs.[69] But for the large part, elites didn't care about what was happening on the margins of society in the 1980s and 1990s, because they were too busy enjoying the triumph of American economic expansion. And then the crash of 2008 hit.

The Great Recession of 2008 called into question the ability of neoliberalism to secure financial stability for the system. Neither austerity policies nor neoliberalism in general has been able to reverse the profitability crisis, hence its continuation to the present day.[70] Austerity measures, and the pairing of state repression and organized abandonment these measures engender, are not capable of producing a sustained modality of governance across time; they can merely buy time, with diminishing returns, until the next crisis erupts. "Neoliberalism's delegitimation and dismantling of welfare state capacities reallocates racial capitalism's accumulation crisis," write Ruth Wilson Gilmore and Craig Gilmore, "by taking resources from institutions, programs, streets, households, and lives, throwing all into permanent crisis. Crisis, then, is organized abandonment's condition of existence *and* its inherent vice."[71] What does this all mean for the system's legitimacy and for the struggle ahead?

For the US state, the path forward amid these challenging conditions is made more complex by the growth of a global ruling class comprised of powerful transnational corporations or TNCs, which has no particular loyalty to any one nation-state, much less the short-lived global hegemony of the United States—appearing today to be in secular decline.[72] While this global ruling class is united around its main political objective to accumulate, it remains divided on how to do so.[73] "The transnational capitalist system is an economic reality," writes Don Hamerquist, "but initiatives toward transnational state structures are still in their infancy and are highly contested, although a range of transnational financial and economic institutions are operating beyond public scrutiny."[74] This means that despite the alarm bells of conspiracy theorists about such "globalists" operating coherent international governance, no serious class-conscious global elite has yet emerged that is capable of stemming disasters like climate change. Instead, we inhabit a potentially transitional moment, characterized by even more nearsighted statecraft than usual.

In crisis moments, then, individual states, including superpowers like the United States, must manage the violent disorder attendant to capitalist social relations with an increasingly narrow, and often self-defeating, set of options. In recent decades, this arc has bent away from wealth redistribution and the old Keynesian model and toward austerity and repression, which have in turn catalyzed widespread social disorder and resistance from below. While many activists simply demand the reversal of this trend, it remains a dubious proposition, given diminishing rates of profit, globalized capital, and societies increasingly held together by sheer repression, that traditional Keynesianism could actually return in advanced capitalist states, even if political elites desired it (which, by and large, they do not). Controversy over the way forward for mass incarceration must be understood within this context.[75]

World-historical objective factors have always steered the development of American prisons, from the rise of capitalism and industrialization, to the decline of American industry, and to the present inability of the neoliberal state to sustain consensus and stability. But the growth of the carceral system has not been an automatic process; within these crises, organized blocs of social actors have taken action and shaped its unfolding. In advanced liberal democracies, we find, then, the kind of Orwellian doublespeak in which the construction of jails can be justified by language of popular opposition to mass incarceration. One such ideology to emerge in recent years is what revolutionary scholar

James Kilgore dubbed "carceral humanism": the repackaging of jails and other repressive social institutions as beneficial social services for those trapped in their meshes.[76] It is, in the words of researcher Jasmine Heiss, "a state project that has embraced carceral institutions as the only legitimate manifestation of care."[77]

We should take carceral humanism and other suspicious ideologies as a sign of change in how the US state secures consent. In recent years, popular mass movements like Black Lives Matter have called into question the legitimacy of America's punishment system at the local, state, and national levels. This was felt quite powerfully in New York City. But while it is easy to imagine these movements opposing a static social order, this is a mistake. As revolutionary thinkers Don Hamerquist and Dave Ranney remind us, the carceral state is not "a determinate state of affairs."[78] This means that the ruling class is far more indecisive about what it will take to resolve the deepening crisis than activists give it credit for, and that the various governing mechanisms throughout the United States can hardly be reduced to a monolith called "the state."

Accordingly, we must also take seriously that pure repression is not the only avenue the ruling class is willing to pursue to maintain the capitalist order, at least domestically. Other important roads are its promotion of reform and its fashioning of new modes of governance, sometimes with the aid of social movements themselves. Elite responses to the George Floyd rebellion run a wide gamut from the pure repression championed by President Trump to the complex schemes of capture and recuperation we explore in the following chapter, which seek to use the movements as incubators for innovation favorable to the ruling class. Similarly, the various so-called criminal justice reform initiatives we see unfolding across America reveal the willingness of some US elites to dispense with some of its most overtly brutal means of controlling the poor and to shore up legitimacy by promoting a more humane capitalism.

As scholars Jack Norton, Lydia Pelot-Hobbs, and Judah Schept warn us, in the current political terrain, many projects of carceral expansion are no longer cloaked in the rhetoric of "tough on crime" but instead in the language of benevolent reform. It is, therefore, easy to lose sight of how jails and mass incarceration remain integral aspects of class war.[79] In New York City, as we will see, elites proposing to downsize and eventually close Rikers are working simultaneously to gain greater legitimacy for carceral institutions and to help engineer new methods of class-based coercion and control, which they hope will enjoy more popular consent than the presently discredited ones. However, the solution they offer is, much like mass incarceration itself, just another stopgap measure to stave off the next catastrophe.

A MORAL IMPERATIVE

Amid these epochal changes in the political-economic configuration of New York City and the broader world, opposing Rikers Island has become an urgent "moral imperative" for many New Yorkers, including a vocal contingent of the island's survivors.[80] Beginning in 2015, a well-organized and cash-flush coalition of nonprofit organizations, Democratic politicians, city developers, and criminal justice reformers, clearly sensing the momentum emanating from both above and below, argued that Rikers should, and could, in fact be closed in the near future—but that this would require the expansive construction of skyscraper jails to take its place.[81] These jails, their boosters argued, would restore the legitimacy of the punishment system while stabilizing the growing crisis in how the city government administers the lowest tiers of its workforce. In the process, New York's leading role as an innovator of business-friendly governance could be safeguarded for years to come.

A small cohort of politicians and paid nonprofit organizers constituted the core of this campaign, bespeaking, in turn, the growing pressure among political elites to rein in the embarrassment of Rikers and the campaign's dependency on the appearance of grassroots politics. But #CLOSErikers nonetheless tapped into widespread public sentiment against the penal colony and the demands for a new direction in the city's punishment system. A 2016 march on Rikers, for instance, drew thousands of people from across the city to a far-flung residential section of northern Queens. Participants, including the authors, marched behind banners, waved protest signs, and chanted against mass incarceration, reminiscent of street activity in previous years around the deaths of Oscar Grant and Trayvon Martin, the Ferguson and Baltimore rebellions, and the Black Lives Matter movement.[82]

Behind this social movement rhetoric, the boosters of the skyscraper jails framed themselves as pragmatists, especially in relation to the abolitionists who opposed them. But not all reformers understood the new jails as a Faustian bargain. In fact, the activist organizations promoting the new jails, led by the nonprofit juggernaut JustLeadershipUSA (JLUSA) and an independent planning group called the Lippman Commission, touted plans for cutting-edge, humanistic jail facilities resembling the fabled Norwegian and Swedish facilities more than those of Rikers Island, engendering something akin to what we might call *carceral enthusiasm* for the possibility the new jails represented. While the reader will be correct to detect some ambivalence on our part about how sincere the jail boosters are about their humanistic vision, we have wagered that it is politically important to distinguish between progressive reformers and those who simply want the same old cages, even if the final result is the same.

Regardless of their sincerity, the jail boosters were doubtless shrewd marketeers. They partnered with progressive architects, scholars, and small samples of formerly incarcerated people, using the pageantry of "participatory action research" to oversee former prisoners helping to design the cages that would hold others in the future. The scholarship of progressive jail boosters and architects past and present was cited extensively as evidence that these jails would be a marked departure from those that preceded them. The result was elaborate, brightly colored public relations material: jail booster propaganda, resembling the popular video game *The Sims*, depicting large-scale human caging as harmless, sanitary, and even fun, complete with video game consoles in the guards' break rooms. Simultaneously, the jail boosters significantly downplayed the actual height of the skyscraper facilities, portraying them as slight, a mere four stories tall, in this highly effective, and utterly obfuscatory, carceral agitprop.[83]

Many observers were, however, not convinced. Abolitionist critics pointed out that the city had made no binding resolution to shutter the island but only to build the new jails—and anyway, they believed that the correct path lay in the immediate closure of Rikers and its replacement with nothing, which was the demand of the original abolitionist Campaign to Shut Down Rikers.[84] And it wasn't just the radicals voicing skepticism. Council member Carlos Menchaca, explaining his vote against the resolution, noted "nothing in the plan that guarantees closing Rikers" and added that he did not trust the mayor, who would ultimately make or break the plan's execution.[85]

Even many of those who supported the jails, including former DOC commissioner Martin Horn, a proponent of previous iterations of this plan stretching back decades, were skeptical of the city council's timeline, which called for shuttering the island's final jail by 2026. Technocratic observers additionally cast doubt on the plan's reliance on halving the city's jail population, from roughly 7,000 to 3,500.[86] The *New York Times*, which, as usual, had largely served as stenographer to the jail boosters, tapered its coverage with doubt that the plan could be pulled off. Conservative politicians and the unions representing Rikers's uniformed staff similarly denounced the viability of closing Rikers at all, in the name of keeping as many jail beds as possible to ensure law and order—and keeping their jobs.[87] And the rumbling had already begun among residents living around the new jail sites, who protested the sites alongside abolitionists.[88]

In short, even as the media reported, quite wrongly, in October of 2019 that a decisive vote had been cast to shut down Rikers once and for all, it seemed the only voices of unqualified optimism came from longtime advocates of the plan—or the politicians who had staked their careers on it. And as Menchaca astutely observed and abolitionists noted with great apprehension, the actual execution of the plan would not be the domain of Bill de Blasio, himself an initial skeptic who had been dragged quite publicly into supporting it. Responsibility instead fell to the ruling politicians of an uncertain future.[89]

Hindsight would soon reveal that the skeptics were, at the very least, half right. Following the exaltation of the council's supposedly historic vote, it would be over a year before anything resembling a legal mandate to shutter Rikers was put in place: the February 2021 Renewable Rikers Act. This measure stipulated the biannual transfer of jurisdiction of DOC jails on Rikers to the Department of Citywide Administrative Services (DCAS), culminating with the closure of the final jail by August 2027, a noticeable postponement of the original closure date.[90]

The first transfer came in July 2021, when DOC turned over the James A. Thomas Center (JATC), the original 1935 Rikers Island penitentiary. Of virtually no value to DOC, JATC had been in notorious disrepair since the late 1960s and out of use entirely since 2000, enjoying one last hurrah as a setting for the 2002 mobster comedy *Analyze That*. Six months after JATC's closure, DOC followed with some unused land. Then, in its most substantive commitment to date, the department pledged to turn over the more modern Otis Bantum Correctional Center (OBCC) in the summer of 2022. This would be an important test of the enforceability of the city council's plan. And when the time came for OBCC to change hands, DOC simply refused.

"We are not in the position to transfer OBCC to DCAS," Commissioner Louis Molina remarked. By way of justification, he simply added, "It would not be logical for us to have a facility transferred to DCAS when there's a possibility in the future we may need that." The logic was impressive in its simplicity: DOC would not turn the building over now because in the future it could be needed. Could the department simply flout its legal obligation like this? The Renewable Rikers Act stipulated that "the mayor shall transfer charge over every portion of Rikers Island that the mayor determines is not in active use for the housing of incarcerated persons, or in active use for the providing of direct services to such persons."[91] So arbitration defaulted to the mayor.

Unfortunately for those seeking a speedy redress, the mayor who had overseen the 2019 vote and proclaimed the end of mass incarceration to be at hand had by this point long returned to civilian life. In his place stood a new breed of Clintonian Democrat named Eric Adams, a state senator and former New York cop and a firm believer in law and order, who campaigns openly for the cops and courts to send *more* people to jail. Even though he handed in his badge fifteen years ago, Adams never stopped being a cop. As a politician, he has been a vocal opponent of defunding the police, telling media outlets that the issue is not relevant to working-class communities of color but instead is being led by young white professionals.[92]

Even as he embraces law-and-order rhetoric, Adams has a complicated relationship to policing. He often recounts the time when he and his brother were beaten up in a Queens police precinct, shaping his lifelong ambition to reform racist police practices. As an officer, he joined the Black fraternal organization, the Guardians Association, and in 1995 helped form another internal reform group, 100 Blacks in Law Enforcement Who Care. His criticism of racism within the NYPD helped to draw a lot of support from working-class Black and Latinx New Yorkers who bear the brunt of aggressive policing practices. Yet, Adams did not forsake his allegiance to law and order. During his campaign, he showed up at shooting scenes to promote the need for more police to solve the problems of crime. Amid a raging COVID pandemic, his campaign videos stoked fears of crime and called for the unmasking of shoppers in stores experiencing retail theft.[93] He even planned to remake his controversial 2011 ad in which he instructed parents how to search through their own homes to look for "contraband," including guns, drugs, and any other illegal paraphernalia their children may have hidden.[94]

As mayor, one of Adams's first public fights with the new city council was over its decision to end solitary confinement on Rikers.[95] Adams is coy about directly opposing a plan that has the putative blessing of the law. But he has expressed clear doubt that closing Rikers is possible, citing the financial cost of the plan and the rising numbers of jail detainees, which, by his estimation, complicates the viability of depopulating the city jails down to the 3,500 population necessary for closing Rikers.[96] Adams feigns as if his office has no control over the policies that are increasing the number of detainees on Rikers. Instead of supporting measures that would lower the jail population, the mayor has done the opposite, even sidestepping the Mayor's Office for Criminal Justice (MOCJ), the agency which was put in charge of the plan to close Rikers.[97]

In place of the previous mayor's rhetoric declaring mass incarceration to be over, Eric Adams has provided vocal and unabashed support for the coalition of police, guards, real estate interests, and business-friendly law-and-order politicians who provided the political base for the rise of mass incarceration in New York City in the first place.[98] The zeitgeist supportive of progressive penology, the philosophy that is supposed to be guiding the new facilities' operation, seems today like ancient history. Meanwhile, construction on the skyscraper jails continues uninterrupted.

THE MASK OF PHILANTHROPY

Central to the story of the skyscraper jails are nonprofit organizations and the foundations that fund them. While these institutions can adopt a variety of ideological perspectives, we focus primarily on what we call liberal foundations and the nonprofits they support. These organizations promote a vision of society based on the ideals of classical liberalism, grounding a respect for individual advancement (including the individual overcoming of social disadvantages like poverty and racial prejudice) in an abiding conceit that "free" capitalist markets are the only legitimate social system. Like police, prisons, and every other institution presently structuring our social existence, foundations and the nonprofit agencies they finance have not always existed. Before examining the distinct role liberal foundations play in advocating for the skyscraper jails, it is helpful to recall their basic history.

The type of philanthropic activism we find today in the nonprofit sector isn't new. "A part of the bourgeoisie is desirous of

redressing social grievances in order to secure the continued existence of bourgeois society," Marx and Engels wrote in 1848, at
a time when private philanthropy was still largely the dominion
of local church parishes and disorganized, wealthy individuals.[99]
Within fifty years, the philanthropic sector would be developed
to largely mirror the increasingly ornate capitalist firms from
which it sprang, becoming more organized, bureaucratic, and
coordinated. And it was always political. An important point of
political organization for the nascent nonprofit sector came in the
charity organization movement of the late nineteenth century, as
proto-nonprofit organizations like the Charity Organization Society and the Association for Improving the Condition of the Poor
fought to keep the provision of social services to working-class
people a matter of revocable private charity, not public entitlement. Their intent was to preserve class deference, reform society
within terms beneficial to their own interests, and defeat the leftist
notion that the wealth of the earth belonged to everyone.[100]

The organizations we today call nonprofits, meaning tax-exempt voluntary organizations providing charity, education, and
other services, have existed in some form since colonial America,
when local churches assumed some of the responsibility for helping meet the basic needs of the poor to survive.[101] Philanthropy
was recognized by economists and early industrialists as a remedy
to the contradictions of the free market, which needed workers,
but did not want to bear the cost of supporting them day in and
day out, especially when they were not needed. Elites consistently
claimed that guaranteed subsistence would produce indolence and
entitlement to the bounty of the earth. Instead, the needy had to
demonstrate deference to their superiors, and, as many elites still
insist today, the means of subsistence provided to them must be a
revocable privilege, not a right. These dual imperatives lay at the
root of modern charity.[102]

As the classical economist Adam Smith famously quipped in his book *The Wealth of Nations*, "It is not from the benevolence of the butcher, the brewer, or the baker that we expect our dinner, but from their regard to their own interest."[103] This captures Smith's main argument that economic altruism is unnecessary in a competitive market system, since, over time, the fulfillment of self-interest would lead to a more equal society. Yet, as Marx argued, Smith often contradicted himself and also recognized that the free market system and the very nature of competition sometimes created an imbalance of power that charity could correct in the short term. Beneficence, or charity, Smith argued, was "the ornament which embellishes not the foundation that supports the building and which it was, therefore, sufficient to recommend, but by no means necessary to impose."[104] Smith saw charity and benevolence, in general, as a counterbalance to free market competition, and this is the main liberal view of charity that remains in place today.

By the end of the nineteenth century, private philanthropy became an important anchor of the charitable sector in the United States. Industrial capitalists like Andrew Carnegie articulated the need for philanthropy to balance the inequality produced by the free market.[105] Carnegie's economic altruism hid the fact that the wealth he gave back was accumulated through the exploitation of his workers. This is why philanthropic organizations deal largely in "twice-stolen wealth," in Ruth Wilson Gilmore's words, meaning money first stolen from the workers who produce surplus value and then withheld from taxes.[106]

The organizations we call foundations—large financial trusts endowing various nonprofit institutions with the requisite funds to operate—also emerged from earlier practices of privately sponsored charity and acquired formal legal structure between the late nineteenth century and first half of the twentieth century, paving the way for the organizations that today enjoy the legal status of 501(c)3.[107] The United States is the only country in the world that allows its charities to receive tax-deductible contributions from US taxpayers. While early tax-exemption regulation began in the early 1900s, it was not until the Internal Revenue Code of 1954 that the 501(c) structure we know today was established. In response to the demands of the Civil Rights Movement of the 1960s and the Great Society programs of Lyndon Johnson, the American capitalist state relied more on nonprofits to manage the social welfare state. Different from the New Deal, the Great Society programs of the 1960s provided funds directly to nonprofit organizations to manage urban povertyandinequality.[108]

Contemporary foundations and nonprofits are a distinct product of the early twentieth century. In this period, rapid industrialization and urbanization wrought social crises far beyond the meager administrative capacity of nineteenth-century states, and the social pitfalls of advanced industrial capitalism were matched only by the massive profits reaped by its robber barons. To mitigate the violent unfolding of capitalism's contradictory tendencies in this period, partisans of the so-called Progressive Era represented the emergence of a new ruling-class fragment of university-trained professional administrators working in fields like public health, urban planning, law, medicine, education, and penology. They sought to rationalize social development—and perhaps alleviate the suffering of the poor in the process—all within parameters favorable to sustained capital accumulation in a small set of hands.

These efforts, and those of the state to regulate big philanthropy's power, produced today's nonprofit sector and constellation of liberal foundations.[109] It is particularly worth emphasizing that progressives, whether as politicians, jail administrators, or activists organized in nonprofits like the Osborne Association, played an outsized role in the construction and expansion of prisons, courts, and supposed alternatives to incarceration in the early twentieth century, just as religious and secular reformers were instrumental in the birth of the prison a century earlier.[110] We have elected to call the nonprofit institutions that today promote the expansion of the carceral state, under the guise of reform, "carceral nonprofits."[111]

Many of the magnates who start foundations don't have much interest in what the foundations actually do. John D. MacArthur famously told his foundation, "I am going to keep making it, you guys will have to figure out after I am dead what to do with it."[112] Pioneering liberal foundations like Russell Sage (founded 1907), Rockefeller (1910), and Carnegie (1911), which are today synonymous with complex schemes of social engineering, owe their origins as much to dodging taxes on profits and generational wealth transmission as to the innovative ruling-class activism in which they have distinguished themselves.[113] The Ford Foundation had a similar origin, founded in 1936 to evade New Deal taxation. Amid the early stirrings of the 1960s urban crisis, Ford was refashioned to reshape the social terrain in terms more favorable to the progressive wing of the ruling class, which seeks to mold the unfolding of social change in terms amenable both to capital accumulation and to a business-friendly simulacrum of social movement politics.[114]

In many ways, the Ford Foundation pioneered big philanthropy's investment in social movement politics. As the Black Freedom Struggle simmered in the 1950s and early 1960s, the Ford Foundation was particularly engaged in engineering the outcome of Black struggle toward supporting Black politicians, businesses, and property owners loyal to the US ruling class.[115] This was accomplished through pumping funds into organizations and leaders deemed safe for business interests, like the National Urban League and the Congress on Racial Equality, and by working to isolate those deemed too radical, like the Student Nonviolent Co-ordinating Committee (SNCC). Simultaneously, Ford cultivated leadership friendly to US business interests throughout the rapidly decolonizing Global South. A prominent Cold War agency, Ford worked in close coordination with the State Department and the CIA, using this same criterion of selective funding to push back against socialist leaders promoting redistributive policies in some of the most resource-rich, but wealth-poor, nations in the world.[116]

As Black militant Robert L. Allen concluded in 1969, "the Ford Foundation has shaped itself into one of the most sophisti-cated instruments of American neocolonialism in 'undeveloped nations,' whether at home or abroad."[117] The Ford Foundation's involvement in the Civil Rights and Black Power movements also drew a lot of criticism from the law-and-order coalition, and by 1970 the organization shifted to funding liberal police reform, including a $30 million grant to establish the Police Foundation.[118]

Another key organization in the orbit of the skyscraper jail campaign is the Vera Institute of Justice, which is not a foun-dation but a nonprofit recipient of funds.[119] Since the 1960s, Vera has played an important role in local and national criminal justice reform, lending its technical expertise to local counties, states, and national projects with the aim of fixing the criminal justice system and making it more efficient. Vera was founded in New York City in 1961 by journalist Herbert Sturz, who would serve almost sixty years later on the Lippman Commission, and wealthy businessman-cum-philanthropist Louis Schweitzer. The group was founded to stem a spike in postwar incarceration and to invigorate a sluggish city response to expanding carceral capacities that embroiled the jail system in bad press and pre-cipitated a sharp decline in public confidence. Mayor Robert F. Wagner subsequently granted Vera an office in the criminal court building to start the Manhattan Bail Project, Vera's first major initiative. A year later, the Ford Foundation funded the program.[120] With Ford's assistance, Vera was transformed from a foundation to a nonprofit organization.[121]

In these early days, Vera also played a role in Mayor John Lindsay's efforts to defeat militancy in working-class Black and Latinx communities by co-opting leadership and preparing for the full-scale repression of urban rebellion.[122] Vera was also an early model for a number of contemporary foundations and non-profit organizations that provide reentry services, basic "alternatives" to incarceration, and diversion programs that are materially and ideologically invested in community supervision—displacing the site of punishment and control into these same working-class communities, as unemployment rose and as city, state, and federal governments withdrew public funding.[123] It is not an exaggeration to say that Vera and other nonprofit organizations serve as the research and development arm of the punishment system, assiduously working to promote its transformation during moments of legitimacy crisis. Sadly, the reforms these organizations have been innovating since at least the 1960s have proven utterly inadequate to halting mass incarceration.[124]

Mapping the dense webs of big philanthropy and the non-profit sector may sound a bit like a conspiracy theory. But these efforts are remarkably well documented, often in the words of the funders themselves. As scholar Michael Barker remarks in the indispensable *Under the Mask of Philanthropy*, "Is it really so far-fetched to believe that our planet's wealthiest liberal elites have conspired together to maintain their power?"[125] It's a shame that so much of the American public focuses its considerable ingenuity in fashioning conspiracy theories out of virtually thin air when there are so many real conspiracies impacting the lives of millions of people playing out in broad daylight.

We turn now to one such story.

CHAPTER I

SHUT DOWN RIKERS

This happens every day . . . it's got to stop.
                                    —Kalief Browder, 2013

n 2012, the US Department of Justice (DOJ) opened an investigation into what it subsequently dubbed a pervasive "culture of violence" on Rikers Island. Stories of brutality and oppression, exceeding even what New Yorkers had come to expect from the notorious city jails, had been emanating from Rikers in recent years, in particular, from its male juvenile facility, the Robert N. Davoren Center (RNDC). In 2008, the beating death of adolescent prisoner Christopher Robinson drew attention to a power-sharing arrangement known as "the Program" under which RNDC guards deputized leading gang members to run the cell blocks themselves. This regime was nothing short of totalitarian, rooted in a strict system of rank with powerful cliques of prisoners holding a monopoly on resources, terrorizing the prisoners deemed weakest, and meting out sadistic violence alongside extortion. The Program had the full blessing, and active cooperation, of guards supposedly employed to ensure the rights of all prisoners. When the scandal subsided, a mere two guards had been sent to prison, and a steady stream of reports suggested that little had changed in the RNDC.[1]

On August 4, 2014, the DOJ released a scathing report documenting the findings of its nearly two-year investigation.

Corroborating the fears of those who believed the bad old days of the Program had not come to an end, the DOJ found that casual violence and intimidation structured daily life in juvenile facilities at Rikers, carried out by prisoners and guards alike, evidence of which was deliberately and systematically purged from the official record. Assaults, the DOJ found, were far more common than they appeared on paper; guards routinely instructed assaulted prisoners to "hold it down" and not report the violence, even if this meant not receiving medical treatment for injuries. Simultaneously, guards cooperated to fabricate incident reports exonerating one another of violent acts, or else made these "use of force" incidents disappear. Prisoners requiring medical treatment reported, with stunning regularity, that they had slipped and fallen in the shower. Incriminating evidence simply vanished.

This was not the actions of a few rogue guards, as the Department of Correction had argued of the Program. The DOJ clearly specified that this modus operandi functioned with the support of officials up and down the chain of command. It may as well have been part of the staff handbook.[2] At the end of 2014, the DOJ joined the lawsuit *Nunez v. City of New York*, a class action suit filed in 2011 by Rikers prisoners alleging a pattern of violence amounting to unconstitutional conditions in the penal colony. This brought considerable federal scrutiny to Rikers and resulted in a court-mandated monitor to investigate and document DOC's attempts to provide constitutional conditions. However, forcing any substantive change to the city system would prove far more difficult than simply recording its failure to materialize.[3]

In the months following the DOJ's initial report, a young man named Kalief Browder stepped into the public eye and brought these findings to life. Profiled by *New Yorker* journalist Jennifer Gonnerman, Browder narrated the Kafkaesque nightmare of being falsely accused of robbery at age sixteen and subsequently languishing for three years in RNDC, fourteen months of which he spent confined to a 7-foot-by-12-foot cell in solitary confinement. All the while prosecutors requested delay after delay in his case, and the already flimsy charges against him fell apart, unbeknownst to him or his public defender. Meanwhile, Browder experienced many aspects of the Program still at work, including violent predation by prisoners and guards working in cooperation. Refusing to be cowed into following this regime, Browder came into regular conflict with prisoners and guards and wound up spending over seven hundred days of his time in solitary confinement. During this entire time, the prosecutor attempted to force him to plead out, which he refused to do, even after he was offered a sentence of "time served" that would free him immediately. Browder's story was one of refusal: he refused to be coerced by the Program, refused to respect the violent rule of the guards, and refused to allow the violence of Rikers to force him to plead guilty to something he hadn't done, as prosecutors and judges have often relied on in New York City.[4]

By the time the state admitted it had no case—the witness, whose story never made sense to begin with, had left the United States and had broken communication with the prosecution—Browder had suffered severe emotional and physical trauma and had attempted suicide at least five times. During one attempt, he was pulled down from a makeshift noose, composed of torn bed sheets, as he had observed another prisoner do. His rescuers were, however, Rikers guards, who immediately assaulted him, throwing punches, and subsequently accused him of attacking them. In another instance, a guard watched as he tore his sheets to make a noose and taunted him to go through with it. Following his release, and Gonnerman's profile, Browder became a symbol of the barbarism of Rikers and the race and class violence at the core of

New York City's punishment system. Browder put a human face on the statistics and horror stories to which the public seemed inured. But the trauma of his time at Rikers proved impossible to shake. Two years after his release, after several abortive attempts, Browder took his own life, using the method he had learned at Rikers.[5]

Remarkably, the Justice Department report, and Gonnerman's story, did not simply join the countless documented Rikers travesties about which nothing has ultimately been done. A decisive event that unfolded in the months between them explains why. On August 9, 2014, a Black teenager named Michael Brown was walking in the street in his hometown of Ferguson, Missouri, when he was accosted by a white cop who ordered him to "get the fuck on the sidewalk." Like Browder, Brown refused the position of deference imposed on him. But disrespect from a Black teenager was too much for this adult man in uniform to bear. The cop confronted Brown, demanding he submit. Accounts vary about what happened next, but in the end, the unarmed Brown lay dead, with six bullets in his body.[6] If the political implications of Brown's death were not immediately clear to the local Black community, he was left uncovered in the street for four hours, in what was widely compared to a lynching. When Brown's body was finally removed from the street, some mourners, led by Brown's mother, set up a makeshift memorial of candles and flowers on the spot where he had fallen. In response, multiple local cops ran it over with their cars. One cop stood by while his cop dog urinated on it.[7]

Brown's murder significantly escalated political momentum that had been building since the 2010 police murder of Oscar Grant in Oakland and the 2012 murder of Black teenager Trayvon Martin by a Florida vigilante. Martin's death, and the state's initial unwillingness to charge George Zimmerman, the man who shot him, spawned the hashtag #BlackLivesMatter. It became a rallying cry around a steady stream of police and vigilante killings of unarmed Black people, coupled with miscarriages of justice like the twenty-year sentence given to Marissa Alexander, a Black survivor of domestic violence, under the same Florida court system that subsequently acquitted Martin's killer. The callous chokehold death of Eric Garner at the hands of a gang of New York City cops in 2014 inspired both outrage and what would become an important call to action for the fledgling movement: Garner's final words, "I can't breathe."

The response to Brown's death in Ferguson, however, was of a different magnitude than what this nascent activist network had yet seen. As self-styled Black leaders, including President Barack Obama, vainly urged calm, the low-slung, diffuse suburb became the site of protracted rioting, expropriation, skirmishes with the cops, and the ransacking and arson of a gas station that was rumored to have called the cops on Brown. Meanwhile, even in the more traditional demonstrations, protesters confronted the heavily militarized cops with a gesture that turned nonviolence into offense: refusing orders to disperse, the courageous ranks placed their bodies on the line, and with hands in the air, chanted "Hands up, don't shoot."

The Ferguson rebellion unleashed a movement of heightened street militancy across the United States, though nowhere in the country seems to have matched the tumult of its point of origin, which included episodes of anonymous live fire in both directions. These chaotic days of snake marches, highway blockages, skirmishes with the cops, and episodic rioting culminated with massive mobilizations around the courts' failures to indict the cops who killed Garner and Brown. Additional police murders, like those of Akai Gurley in New York City and twelve-year-old Tamir Rice in Cleveland, amplified the protests against police violence.

Baptized in plumes of tear gas, the Black Lives Matter movement (BLM) had entered the American mainstream.[8]

NEOLIBERALISM IN NEW YORK CITY

BLM marched, quite literally, onto a political-economic terrain already shaken by crisis, and New York was no exception. Recent conflicts around policing and incarceration in New York City are inextricable from the tumultuous development of the city's neoliberal mode of governance, and reflect its uncertain future. Since its advent in the United States in the 1970s, neoliberalism has spelled the privatization of public services and spaces, cuts to as many social expenditures as possible, and greater reliance on cops and prisons for the function of social reproduction vacated by living-wage manufacturing employment and so-called welfare state spending. Meanwhile, international monetary, trade, and labor policies keep the wages, benefits, and social power of working people in check, while debt assumed by state and private consumers alike functions to keep consumption going, however untenably. This arrangement transfers the worst symptoms of capitalism's chaos into the lives of working-class people, particularly those with the least social power. In the United States, these people are disproportionately Black and Latinx and were already uniquely singled out for management by repressive state agents.[9] The issue of mass incarceration in particular, with its key component of aggressive policing, allows us to see clearly how global political shifts play out in everyday life for millions of Americans.

Unlike other major American cities, which were dominated by large-scale manufacturing, midcentury New York was supported by a diverse economy, including many small-scale manufacturing companies, a thriving garment industry, and a growing retail and service sector. These trades had considerable union density, as did the city's growing public sector. High rates of taxation, rooted in soaring manufacturing profits following World War II, and high rates of unionization, unthinkable by today's standards, fueled the expansion of a welfare state unprecedented in the United States, before or since. This included free public universities, quality health care, and affordable public housing. "The New York labor movement," historian Joshua Freeman argues, "led the city toward a social democratic polity unique in the country in its ambition and achievements."[10]

New York City had been the laboratory of many New Deal reform efforts, including the passage of the Temporary Emergency Relief Administration, which created the first-ever unemployment relief agency in the city and the country. Yet by 1975, amid white flight, capital flight, tax rebellion, and a decline in the profitability of American manufacture attributable to automation and growing global competition, the city could no longer afford the basic services that working-class New Yorkers had secured—at least, not without pushing for more substantive redistribution of wealth and power than the ruling class would tolerate. When the government was unable to cover its expenses, private creditors staged a coup d'état. As a condition for floating the city the funds it needed to continue operating, Wall Street effectively took over the city budget and restructured its public sector for decades to come, in terms favorable to the elite and disastrous to working people.[11] In a classic crossroads of *socialism or barbarism*, New York's elites imposed barbarism. The municipal government of "Moscow on the Hudson" was abruptly repurposed as a militarized engine of private profit. This is how the city's neoliberal order came to be.[12]

"Let New City lead the way," Jonathan Lippman wrote in a key document for the skyscraper jail campaign, "as it has done so often in the past."[13] Lippman is quite correct. The neoliberalization of New York City was the local incarnation of a global story, in which the city pioneered reshaping societies around the world in terms more favorable to their ruling classes. To put it somewhat simplistically, Pinochet's Chile was the testing ground in 1973, New York City followed, and so went the world.

Though it was partly carried out on the local level, neoliberalism simultaneously was the global elite's response to a broader international crisis in which there were more claims on the surplus produced by working people than there was surplus value itself. As profit margins tightened, elites responded not by sacrificing their own future wealth but by promoting the restructuring of local economies such that they would diminish the claims on value made by everyday working people.[14] The most extreme form of neoliberalism is the physical destruction of unwanted workers themselves, common in wartime. While few American politicians, even among the Reaganites, were willing to become the version of themselves parodied in the Dead Kennedys song "Kill the Poor," large numbers of unemployed workers, in Black and Latinx communities in particular, were relegated to the second-class citizenship of criminals and treated accordingly, even when they had done nothing wrong. The effect was a dramatic reduction in what working people could demand from both the private sector and the public sector, with the latter now almost solely serving the former's interests.

New York City's fiscal crisis, therefore, provided not only a rationale for the cutback and privatization of social services but also a justification for the dramatic expansion of the city's capacity to lock people in cages, most of which were located on Rikers Island. This was not automatic but was accomplished through a coalition uniting right-wing politicians like Edward Koch—a former liberal who found his political footing as a race-baiting, law-and-order austerity hawk—with rightward-drifting white voters, small business owners, big capital, and, most decisively, activist fringes of police and correction officers' unions, which supported the dismantling of the rest of the public sector in exchange for increasing their own power over the city. And as went New York, so went the nation, albeit with notable local specificities.[15]

Amid this buildup, important acts of resistance arose challenging the authority of New York City to cage the poor. These acts often emanated from prisoners themselves, who regularly engaged in direct actions and rebellion, as well as in heroic escapes. A high-water mark of struggle came in the late 1960s and early 1970s when scores of Black and Brown Power activists were jailed throughout the city as part of a national crackdown on militant organizations, helping spark the rise of an organized movement demanding the freedom of political prisoners—and all prisoners. Vociferous rebellion behind bars, in New York City and nationwide, coupled with increasingly organized support on the outside, engendered an enduring Prisoners' Rights movement and the birth of a movement to end incarceration everywhere, known as abolitionism.[16]

These righteous movements, and the prisoner rebellions that propelled them, would earn a host of reforms for New York City's prisoners—including religious freedom, methadone treatment, freedom of visitation and correspondence, enhanced legal appeals, and minimum standards for jail conditions (however loosely enforced).[17] But the decisive end of New York City's postwar welfare state in the mid-1970s and its replacement with rule by cops and guards, organized through their unions and acting at the behest of Wall Street, saw the hothouse expansion of incarceration on Rikers Island in the 1980s and 1990s, a central part of the neoliberal order still with us today. Efforts to overhaul or abolish the New York City jail system today are weighed upon immensely by this ponderous history.[18]

A PUBLIC RELATIONS DISASTER

A microcosm of the city itself, Rikers has been continuously beset by crises, yielding creative responses by elites. The recent campaign to move the city's jails off Rikers Island was not the first. In the early 1980s, a proposed sale of Rikers Island to the state prison system, brokered by Vera Institute of Justice founder, Ford Foundation and Open Society darling, and pioneering "social entrepreneur" Herbert Sturz, was scuttled at the last minute by Koch because of the proposal's hefty price tag. The plan was not to end incarceration on Rikers, or even to close down any of its jails, but simply to change the jurisdiction of the keepers. The plan bore many similarities to the recent effort to replace Rikers with borough-based jails, with which Sturz was also involved.[19] This was not the only plan that Sturz hatched in his new position. He also pushed for the creation of a Juvenile Justice Agency that would coordinate the detention of NYC youth, closing down Spofford, the notorious youth detention center in the Bronx, and replacing it with state-of-the-art detention centers near the courthouses.[20] But the city failed to close Rikers and replace it with smaller jails across the boroughs. Instead, the city added four thousand new beds in anticipation of more detainees.[21] And as the abolitionist adage goes, *if they built it, they will fill it.*

Another attempted DOC escape from Rikers, coupled with an ambitious jail expansion at the borough level, was promoted by DOC commissioner Martin Horn between 2005 and 2008. This plan also bears more than passing similarities to the borough-based jails purported to replace Rikers. Horn's plan was defeated largely by community opposition, which involved a bloc of abolitionists that included organizers Pilar Maschi and Lisa Ortega, who fought the construction of the borough-based jails in the Bronx that were supposedly meant as the first step in making Rikers redundant. Like Sturz's proposal, Horn's was not a plan that would end caging but one that would simply move cages elsewhere. Coming as it did in the borough with the weakest historical ties to the halls of power, its impressive defeat did not augur well for the remaining borough-based jails.[22] When Horn needed backup from politicians and civil institutions to support his jail reform scheme against abolitionist opposition, the cavalry was nowhere to be found. Simply put, not enough people with proximity to power thought that anything so drastic had to be done about Rikers Island.

Meanwhile, Mayor Rudolph Giuliani's tenure in the 1990s ushered in a "revanchist" war to take back New York's streets in the name of private property and profits, as geographer Neil Smith has argued.[23] Giuliani is perhaps most famous for hiring William Bratton as the NYPD's chief of police, who would go on to expand policing's reach into working-class Black and Latinx communities through broken windows policing practices, namely stop and frisk. The support for crackdown of quality-of-life offenses would continue with the subsequent three-term mayoralty of businessman Michael Bloomberg, which began in 2002. The Bloomberg era was an extended victory party for the real estate speculators who eagerly carved up the city, backed by the unchecked might of veritable armies of cops and jail guards enjoying a post-9/11 cult of badge worship that would endure for over a decade. Yet, as the first decade of the twenty-first century drew to a close, it was increasingly difficult for even the willfully ignorant to miss the disastrous effects of decades of probusiness, law-and-order governance in the lives of New York's working people.

Activists openly opposed this mode of governance. The 1990s and 2000s saw back-to-back struggles against racist police violence, including marches and demonstrations calling for the prosecution of police brutality cases like those involving Anthony Baez in 1994, Anthony Rosario and Hilton Vega in 1995, Abner Louima in 1997, Amadou Diallo in 1999, Patrick Dorismond and

Sean Bell in 2006, among many others. This activism reignited the struggle that had been at the center of decades-long organizing by Black and Latinx activists, many of them former Puerto Rican and Black revolutionaries. A few years later, starting in 2011, the Occupy Wall Street movement originated at the seat of New York's finance center and became a global movement against austerity and the control of politics by business elites. Anti-police and anti-austerity protests bespoke a growing popular fury at public policy run by, and for, the private market, with the proverbial carrot of social spending increasingly replaced by the stick of redoubled policing and imprisonment. Both protest issues were notable for drawing considerable interest and participation from far outside the usual activist milieus, and for naming the dual specters of structural racism and class inequality that had become taboo in mainstream US politics.[24]

Channeling this inchoate left populism, the liberal public advocate Bill de Blasio, Bloomberg's successor, rode the campaign theme of "a tale of two cities" all the way to a landslide victory in 2013.[25] His campaign also emphasized his opposition to the controversial stop-and-frisk policing tactic, which he highlighted in an advertisement starring his Black son, Dante.[26] This new era of New York City politics coincided with the rapid corrosion of popular consent surrounding the Rikers Island penal colony. The city's elites justified their growing power and lavish wealth with their ability to manage society harmoniously, and Rikers Island was a stinging rebuke. It was, as two leading jail boosters would soon remark, "a stain on our great city's reputation."[27]

Today, the enduring human costs of neoliberalism have made the Rikers Island penal colony a national emblem for racial injustice, at a time when liberal antiracism and critiques of mass incarceration have moved into mainstream US politics and into the progressive wing of the ruling class. A steady stream of damning Rikers news has intensified in recent years, including a scathing Department of Justice investigation and high-profile deaths like Browder's. Rikers generates bad public relations for New York City's elites, who have run the city as a laboratory for neoliberal governance since the 1970s. The legitimacy of this order has increasingly come to hinge on cleaning up Rikers.

Moreover, New York City's organized guard workforce has historically provided an essential service in forcefully imposing austerity on working-class New York, a Faustian bargain that involved the corrections and police unions swearing off solidarity with other city unions in exchange for special treatment. But today, with incarceration rates a fraction of the heights they reached in the 1990s, Rikers guards outnumber prisoners. In the eyes of many elites, it seems, the Correction Officers' Benevolent Association is just another city union with too many members and too much power, just waiting to be downsized. These factors, along with the city's renewed interest in responding to demands for racial justice, have combined to spur an organized public-private partnership of foundations, nonprofits, and liberal politicians to turn on Rikers and demand its closure and the construction of new skyscraper jails.

FERGUSON INC.

The Black Lives Matter movement was a key factor in the emergence of the skyscraper jail campaign. As Barbara Ransby has argued, BLM emerged as a response to state violence against Black people, and it "rejected the representative politics" of President Obama, whose historic victory as the first Black US president did not translate to significant material gains for poor and working-class Black Americans.[28] In response, BLM also spurred intensive efforts from organized factions of the American ruling class to engineer the movement away from the street skirmishes that had occasioned its rise and into peaceful, business-friendly, and election-oriented forms shepherded by the progressive nonprofit sector and the Democratic Party. Beyond the undeniably organic militancy in Ferguson and elsewhere that propelled the protests everywhere, however, this was not the simple co-optation of an otherwise autonomous radical movement. Multiple tributaries that converged into the national movement, like the protests around the Garner case in New York, had been initiated and led by seasoned reformists like Rev. Al Sharpton. Prior to Ferguson, the Garner movement was the kind of staid, top-down affair one could expect from this leadership. Ferguson changed that, and in the process, it introduced the present terrain in which the abolition of police and prisons has become a topic of mainstream debate.

Meanwhile, the useful hashtag #BlackLivesMatter quickly spawned claims to ownership of the movement—primarily by activists Patrisse Cullors, Alicia Garza, and Opal Tometi, who claimed to have come up with it. Much to the chagrin of many activists on the ground, this soon extended to claims of leadership over the entire movement, claims which were further exaggerated in the eyes of outsiders who did not understand the diffuse, horizontal methods of organizing popular among this generation of activists. The trio of avowed founders established the BLM Global Network in 2013, and soon a growing nexus of "official" Black Lives Matter chapters announced themselves, marked their territory, and began to raise funds.[29] Thus by the time progressive philanthropy juggernauts like the Ford Foundation began to pump money into the segments of the movement deemed sufficiently reformist and business friendly, and to push the movement to isolate its left wing—just as some of these same organizations had done with the original Black Power movement—the ground had largely been prepared in advance. While the movement in Ferguson had been a confrontational response to the particular working-class Black experience of neoliberalism, the potentially revolutionary implications of this were quickly sidelined in the official BLM organizations.[30]

It is important to consider the social position of the big foundations helping to make this all happen. Anchored today in a footloose finance sector, which hops the globe in search of fresh sources of capital valorization, this class fraction's interests at home include cultivating innovators and leaders from all social groups, creating profitable markets within marginalized communities, removing barriers to capital mobility like racial prejudice, and breaking up local power blocs resistant to change. Beyond cynical public relations efforts, these are the deeper motivations behind so many corporate entities, to the great dismay of American cultural conservatives, "going woke."

It is, of course, quite easy, given their patent absurdity, to roll one's eyes at the perfunctory public relations statements issued by elite institutions denouncing tragedies like the death of George Floyd. Nike, for instance, a notorious purveyor of sweatshop labor in the Global South, was suddenly opposed to "inequality in all its forms, indirect and overt," and gave its consumers some dutifully branded yet ultimately curious advice about racism: "For once, don't do it."[31] Cringe-inducing as this branded content may be, there's good reason to believe that many at the highest echelons of the ruling class, in fact, want to end *overt* interpersonal racism, barriers to advancement for talented individuals, backward local power structures like renegade police departments, and other obstacles to maximizing profitability. Nike, like most transnational corporations, seeks long-term accumulation through stability and public consent, including among marginalized populations—who are, after all, still consumers, in addition to being potential innovators in business and leaders in politics, albeit as isolated individuals. "The more a dominant class is able to absorb the best people from the dominated classes," observed Marx, "the more solid and dangerous is its rule."[32] Big philanthropy also understands this.

The march of big philanthropy into post-Ferguson Black activism was therefore not merely an instance of cynical self-promotion or of guilty white consciences. In particular, an organized progressive bloc of the ruling class, gathered around big foundations, has long advocated for a social order that draws freely on the talents of traditionally marginalized people with exceptional skill, industry, and leadership abilities in order both to manufacture consent within these communities and to maximize the efficiency of market reproduction and expansion. This becomes especially important as capitalism is wracked with crises, symptoms of which include open displays of vulgar racial violence by American police and the wretched conditions of the country's prisons and jails. Foundations are positioned, far better than corporate entities, to adopt an activist stance and help intervene to shape the unfolding struggles around these and other issues central to optimizing stable, long-term capital accumulation.

"Ultimately," argues activist-scholar Keeanga-Yamahtta Taylor, "funders and other philanthropic organizations help to narrow the scope of organizing to changing 'policy' and other measures within the existing system."[33] Through the process of "elite capture," as recently described by philosopher Olúfẹ́mi O. Táíwò, movement values, tactics, and strategies are remade in the class interests of the foundations and the strata of middle-class professionals who call the shots. But philanthropic organizations do not capture movements like Black Lives Matter to simply end them, though for activists primarily interested in street militancy, the effect is the same. There is also a productive function, as movements are put to work for a different set of interests than those that first animated them.[34] From a progressive ruling-class perspective, the creative energy and innovations of movements like BLM, therefore, offer the opportunity to modernize capitalist social relations and resolve crises under the terms most favorable to stable accumulation in the future while recapturing the legitimacy of the ruling class.

Accordingly, amid the Ferguson rebellion and its immediate aftermath, millions of dollars poured into the relatively impoverished city, including six-figure endowments to avowedly radical groups like the Organization for Black Struggle, from George Soros's Open Society Foundations.[35] By November of 2015, decidedly less militant organizations were being courted by the inner sanctum of Democratic Party philanthropy, the Democracy Alliance.[36] In 2016, the Ford Foundation announced $100 million in funding to the Movement for Black Lives, a federation of nonprofits in the orbit of BLM, which had by this point become a distinct entity from the exciting grassroots street activity that also bore its name.[37] By 2020, donations to organizations affiliated with BLM, and to historically Black colleges and universities, ballooned to the *billions*. Journalist Sarah Kendzior dubbed this growing cash nexus "Ferguson Inc."[38]

This is not to suggest that BLM funding was solely elite; when BLM Global Network later issued its first public disclosure of assets, covering the year 2020, in which it raised a staggering $90 million, the average donation was just over $30.[39] Nonetheless, the patronage of mega donors, the tutelage of fiscal sponsors, and the courtship of powerful Democrats evince a coordinated effort among the progressive wing of the ruling class to bind Black revolt within the constraints of lawful, business-friendly civic participation capable of strengthening capitalist social relations in a moment of great social turmoil.[40] Police violence was one obvious target of intervention. And in the post-Ferguson political climate, Rikers Island soon became another.

SHUT DOWN RIKERS NOW

In mid-November 2015—as select groups of BLM protesters were preparing to be feted by the Democracy Alliance—the Board of Correction, the civilian watchdog organization for New York City jails, hosted DOC commissioner Joseph Ponte to discuss the growing scandal of violence on Rikers Island. Formerly the commissioner of the Department of Corrections for the state of Maine, Ponte had been appointed by de Blasio based on his reputation as a prison reformer. Earlier that year, the duo had unveiled a plan to reduce violence at Rikers, albeit one that sought to curtail visitors' contact with prisoners, increase DOC's ability to restrict individuals from visiting, and collect a database of people visiting Rikers, all based on the dubious premise that most weapons come through the visiting area and not through the employee entrance.[41] If Ponte had expected a hospitable reception among this venerable reform body, which traces its roots back to DOC's postwar heyday of progressive penology, he was soon disappointed. Shortly after he began speaking, Ponte was interrupted by several activists unfurling a banner that announced them as the Campaign to Shut Down Rikers. They chanted, "Hell no to the status quo! These prison walls have got to go!" Other activists stood up and displayed photographs of Kalief Browder. Their demand was the immediate closure of Rikers Island, and the evidence they cited was well known to all.[42]

The Campaign to Shut Down Rikers was part of a long-standing nexus of organizing against structural racism in the city's punishment system, which included campaigns against stop-and-frisk policing practices, the War on Drugs, and solitary confinement for juveniles, and activism for the decriminalization of low-level misdemeanors and greater transparency in policing, courts and supervision.[43] The campaign drew direct impetus from at least four distinct sources.

The first was the case of Kalief Browder. Among its principal organizers was Browder's older brother, Akeem, an outspoken abolitionist who campaigned for the closure of Rikers in his brother's name and argued for no new jails to take its place. The second was a long tradition of activism against the inhuman conditions of Rikers incarceration. The third was the activist-led marches and rallies calling on city officials to close the notorious jail complex. In 2013, the February 23 Coalition led a march that featured calls for the closure of Rikers. In 2014, the group Resist Rikers was formed and held several rallies outside the jail complex to demand an end to the use of solitary confinement and youth detention. The first rally was held in solidarity with protests in Ferguson over the police murder of Mike Brown, and protestors held banners that read "Solitary Is Torture" and "Justice for Mike Brown."[44] Another group, the Jails Action Coalition, a grassroots alliance of formerly incarcerated people and their allies, participated in these rallies and continuously called for Rikers to be shut down. The group was also driven by the activist energy and political framework of the nascent Black Lives Matter movement. Key participants hailed from Millions March NYC and NYC Shut It Down, groups that emerged from the large street mobilizations of late 2014.[45]

Finally, there was growing agitation against Rikers within the nonprofit sector and among New York City's progressives. The increasing unpopularity of Rikers, including public exposés of its hellish and deadly conditions, had also led to quiet investigations behind the scenes in city government, evidenced by a 2015 joint report entitled *Alternatives for Rikers Island*, conducted by the Mayor's Office of Criminal Justice, the

Department of Design and Construction, the Department of Correction, and the Office of Management and Budget. The report which considered options to build new facilities to replace Rikers was leaked the following year, and it was yet another year before the mayor would have anything to do with the plan.[46] The *New York Times* had even waded into these waters in July of 2015, publishing an op-ed from Marshall Project founder Neil Barsky making the case to close Rikers down.[47] This was followed in the fall of 2015 by a series in the publication *City Limits* entitled "Closing Rikers," by journalist Ed Morales.[48] In November of that year, New York City comptroller Scott Stringer spoke at a New School panel entitled "Rikers Island: Reform It—or Shut It Down?," where he outlined the rising cost of Rikers incarceration and guard violence alongside declining rates of incarceration. He was joined on stage by former DOC commissioner Martin Horn, a longtime advocate of the borough-based jail plan, along with Glenn Martin, from the recently formed JustLeadershipUSA.[49] Martin's participation heralded a new player on the scene, which would soon displace the vision of Shut Down Rikers altogether. But in these early days, the momentum belonged to them.

Shut Down Rikers was effective in its simplicity: activists called for the immediate closure of Rikers Island. In Rikers's place, they argued, the city should erect no new carceral facilities but should instead allocate resources to underfunded communities most impacted by mass incarceration—an early expression of the divest/invest redistributive schema that would subsequently become famous under the banner of Defund the Police. "Rikers is a potent symbol of a racist criminal justice system that has waged a war on Black, Brown and low-income people," the campaign wrote in a petition addressed to Mayor de Blasio. "Rather than policies that criminalize and incarcerate, we demand funding for community-based social services, mental health care, rehabilitation, and due process protections."[50]

Shut Down Rikers worked diligently into 2016 to publicize the demand to shutter the penal colony, drawing on the activist energy of BLM to stage a number of small vigils and demonstrations. Their optics and tactics bore the mark of a scrappy grassroots campaign, complete with handmade placards and street props. These included a casket they delivered to city hall in the name of Kalief Browder and paper-mache piñatas representing New York City politicians, which they beat to reveal photos of guard abuse contained inside. The campaign organized around seven talking points, which also adorned handmade signs at their rallies.

- Rikers is racist.
- Rikers punishes poor people.
- Rikers breeds physical and sexual violence.
- Rikers abuses children and people with mental illness.
- Rikers acts as a prison, not a jail.
- Rikers is a waste of public spending.
- Rikers is a torture chamber.

Befitting its origins in the street mobilizations the year before, Shut Down Rikers also continued to press an issue central to the Millions March: the removal of Brooklyn district attorney Ken Thompson, who had allowed the cop who murdered Akai Gurley a plea deal that involved no jail time. Above all, however, Shut Down Rikers's messaging revolved around the story of Kalief Browder and came to rely on the leadership of his media-savvy brother Akeem.[51] But the activist momentum the group helped generate would prove difficult to hold on to when big philanthropy threw its hat in the ring.

A STAIN ON OUR GREAT CITY'S REPUTATION

In February of 2016, New York City Council speaker Melissa Mark-Viverito delivered the State of the City address. An affluent Puerto Rican representing parts of East Harlem and the South Bronx, Mark-Viverito rose to political prominence for her vocal support of the Occupy Wall Street movement. On November 17, 2011, following months of unintentional and often violent arrests of Occupy activists across the city, she joined a small group of politicians and union leaders who orchestrated a photo opportunity in which they were deliberately arrested at an Occupy march. Meanwhile, union staffers commanded ordinary occupiers, who had been taking the streets on their own volition for months, to stay out of the way and simply watch from the sidewalk as the city's progressive machine reasserted its power over a movement that had escaped its grasp.[52] By 2016, Mark-Viverito had distinguished herself as a voice for criminal justice reform, and she drew once more on the momentum of activists' hard work in the streets, this time the activism to shut down Rikers.

Evoking the name of Kalief Browder and the DOJ's famous characterization of Rikers Island's "culture of violence," Mark-Viverito announced the formation of the Independent Commission on New York City Criminal Justice and Incarceration Reform, subsequently dubbed the Lippman Commission after its chair, the progressive chief judge of the state's highest court, Jonathan Lippman. The commission was tasked with studying the long-term viability of shutting down the penal colony on Rikers and designing alternative uses for the island. And while much of Mark-Viverito's remarks that night echoed what activists had been saying in the streets, they also included reference to a key feature of the Lippman plan that would distinguish it from the Shut Down Rikers campaign: "borough-based jails."[53]

Shut Down Rikers immediately recognized what was happening; the new plan not only deferred the closure of Rikers to a distant date but also introduced the concept of building up more carceral capacity to replace it. The campaign had a different idea. "Releasing the 85 percent of people on Rikers legally considered innocent [pretrial detainees]," the campaign wrote shortly after Mark-Viverito's address, "is not only the humane and civil course of action but can lower the population enough to make shutting down Rikers an immediate reality. *We reject the plan to build borough-based jails as an alternative to Rikers Island.*"[54]

At a subsequent protest, Shut Down Rikers organizers called attention to Mark-Viverito's plan to hire 1,800 *more* jail guards. This plan to add more staff to the already bloated DOC workforce provided a clear line of demarcation between Mark-Viverito's political vision and that of the abolitionists, who sought to wither away the carceral state without adding any more to it—as much as Mark-Viverito's use of progressive and radical buzzwords attempted to erase this distinction. "Every investment in the police and prison state is a divestment from our communities," remarked organizer Nabil Hassein. "I'm talking about the 1,300 new cops and the 1,800 new correction officers. Those hundreds of millions of dollars should have been spent on social services that actually keep our communities safe: health care, education, jobs, mental health care, rehabilitation."[55] Mark-Viverito had a more limited focus; it was she and Lippman who had promoted the idea that Rikers was a "a stain on our great city's reputation."[56] In short, the legitimacy of capitalist New York was on the line.

By mid-2016, a new campaign to shut down Rikers was gaining steam, one more closely aligned with Mark-Viverito and Lippman's vision than that of Shut Down Rikers and often indistinguishable from the Lippman Commission itself. Despite its outward similarities to Shut Down Rikers, the two campaigns could not be more different. Launched by cash-flush carceral nonprofits from the highest echelons of big philanthropy and city politics, and building on the political momentum of Ferguson Inc., this new campaign was called #CLOSErikers. Glenn Martin's appearance alongside Scott Stringer in November was part of its savvy media strategy.[57] The campaign would soon become synonymous with the demand to shut down the Rikers Island penal colony, crowding out the more grassroots abolitionist initiatives. But in a short time, #CLOSErikers would add a new demand: the creation of skyscraper jails to replace Rikers.

CHAPTER 2

#CLOSERIKERS

The private foundation can act as an instrument of social innovation and control in areas which the government has not yet penetrated, or in areas where direct government intervention would draw criticism.

—Robert L. Allen, 1969

The proposal to replace Rikers Island with borough-based skyscraper jails has relied on a dense and interconnected network of jail boosters, operating inside and outside the city government and especially concentrated in the nonprofit sector. Funding the skyscraper jail campaign was a veritable who's who of liberal foundations. Its principal actors drew funding and resources from philanthropy juggernauts the J.M. Kaplan Fund, the Tow Foundation, the W.K. Kellogg Foundation, the MacArthur Foundation, the Open Society Foundations, Google.org, the New Venture Fund, the Chan Zuckerberg Initiative, and of course the Ford Foundation.[1] These are traditional "social entrepreneurship" investors who had mostly already made forays into Black Lives Matter before getting involved with Rikers.

A far more interesting backer of the new jails, however, is Arnold Ventures LLC, which is not a charitable trust but a limited liability corporation, freeing it both from restrictions on political lobbying and, hypothetically, from prohibitions from making a

profit. Arnold Ventures is an offshoot of the Laura and John Arnold
Foundation, resting on the fortune John Arnold built as a natural
gas trader, including as a star energy trader for the disgraced firm
Enron. Whereas dozens of his colleagues emerged from the firm's
collapse with indictments, Arnold left Enron with good legal standing and an unprecedented $8 million bonus from his performance
in its final year of 2001, in which he brought in roughly $750 mil-
lion speculating on natural gas. Arnold retired from energy trading
in 2012, at age thirty-eight, and together with his wife, Laura, a
former oil executive, began aggressive "philanthropy" that far more
closely resembles political activism. The Arnolds have emerged
as a powerful enemy of public-sector unions, pushing for charter
schools, which siphon off public funds for use in nonunion private
schools, and the aggressive curtailment of public workers' pensions
across the United States. Unsurprisingly, the newly founded Arnold
Ventures backs the neoliberal think tank CUNY Institute for State
and Local Governance (ISLG), headed by skyscraper jail booster
Michael Jacobson, which pushes to apply private-sector-manage-
ment science to rein in public-sector institutions.[2]

The Lippman Commission itself was an interesting and novel
force in the jail campaign. Like most blue-ribbon commissions,
it was appointed by a government body to investigate a particular issue of growing concern, in this case what to do about one
of the nation's largest jail complexes. Commissions are politically
credible in the eyes of local governing elites because they are seen
to be independent of government and to bring together the "best
and brightest" to propose a bipartisan solution to a gnawing social problem. The Lippman Commission's twenty-seven members
reflected the public-private partnership that has been essential to
neoliberal governance in New York City. They included seasoned
punishment system reformers alongside academics, elite lawyers,
and emissaries of New York City real estate.

The commission enjoyed funding from the New York City Council, alongside the Ford Foundation, Open Society, Trinity Church, and J.M. Kaplan. The commission lists its "partners" as the law firm Latham & Watkins (Jonathan Lippman's law firm), ISLG, the criminal justice reform group Center for Justice Innovation (formerly the Center for Court Innovation), the public relations firm Global Strategy Group, and the Vera Institute of Justice. Staffing and support services were provided by JustLeadershipUSA (JLUSA) and the Katal Center for Equity, Health, and Justice (henceforth Katal).[3] These organizations' support of technocratic fixes to slowly decarcerate Rikers and eventually replace it altogether represented exactly the vision of reform that the city elites could embrace in a moment of protracted crisis.[4]

But the most important actor in the skyscraper jail campaign was the activist arm of the jail boosters, organized in the campaign #CLOSErikers. Launched in April of 2016, #CLOSErikers was the brainchild of two nonprofits founded in the wake of the Ferguson rebellion: JLUSA and the Katal Center. Riding the wave of Ferguson Inc., these upstart organizations successfully branded themselves as criminal justice reformers and received considerable funding from multiple foundations in the orbit of the Lippman Commission.[5] JLUSA founder and #CLOSErikers campaign leader Glenn Martin is a former vice-president of the Fortune Society and speaks regularly about his past experiences with incarceration. JLUSA, in particular, regularly showcased its supposed connection to directly impacted people and adopted the mantra "Those closest to the problem are closest to the solution."[6] Given that a new jail plan would surely face activist challenges, especially in the post-Ferguson era, the importance of #CLOSErikers securing the social justice bona fides of the skyscraper jails cannot be understated. With millions of dollars from big philanthropy, the #CLOSErikers campaign fought for reforms that would rescue the legitimacy of the US punishment system, and the ruling class itself, while deploying the vernacular of social justice and even abolition.

ONE NO, MANY YESES

The arrival of #CLOSErikers in April 2016 completely changed the terrain of activism against Rikers Island. "In recent months," warned the Campaign to Shut Down Rikers,

> following years of grassroots organizing and multiple high-profile cases, the topic of shutting down Rikers has breached and found some permanence in mainstream conversation. A variety of liberal political figures began weighing in, rapidly co-opting the work of the grassroots movement that valued, above all else, community inclusion. Specifically, a separate effort to close Rikers formed with at least $900,000 in funding from billion-dollar philanthropic foundations. The conversation of closing Rikers has become increasingly synonymous with building new neighborhood jails, which is entirely incompatible with our campaign's abolitionist perspectives.[7]

While Shut Down Rikers had signed off on the original statement launching #CLOSErikers, it now announced the group's intent "to re-strategize effective next steps in confronting agendas that promote re-incarceration, such as smaller community jails and other re-branded extensions of the racist police state."[8] But no substantive action followed, and key players in the campaign, like NYC Shut It Down, pivoted to more broadly focused advocacy work, like the short-lived Abolition Square programming in City

Hall Park.[9] On the specific questions of closing Rikers Island, the momentum now decisively belonged to #CLOSErikers, and by extension, to JLUSA.

Founded in November 2014, JLUSA became a major player in the carceral nonprofit sector virtually overnight. In a short time, its founder, Glenn Martin, received a considerable platform to discuss criminal justice reform in New York City and beyond.[10] By 2017, the group was flush with cash from Kellogg, MacArthur, Tow, Ford, and other foundations, amounting to over $12 million.[11] Meanwhile, Martin situated JLUSA in the grassroots prisoner rights activism of decades past, including fights around jail and prison conditions, the campaign to "ban the box," meaning the section of a job application that asks about a criminal record, and the movement for "human-centered language" that trades loaded words like "convict" and "felon" for neutral terms like "justice-involved person."

Martin also claimed to be building on the organizing work of the Formerly Incarcerated, Convicted People, and Families Movement (FICPFM), which held its first conference in 2016. Interestingly enough, Martin also cited approvingly one of their points of unity: "We demand the end of mass incarceration and commit ourselves to fighting the notion and the practice of building new prisons, juvenile detention facilities, and immigration detention centers."[12] As we will see, Martin seemingly saw no contradiction between this principle and supporting the building of the skyscraper jails.

The Katal Center, founded in early 2015 by Lorenzo Jones, Melody Lee, and Gabriel Sayegh, is a smaller criminal justice reform organization sharing donors with JLUSA, including Ford.[13] The group is named after the scientific term *katal*, a unit of measurement for quantifying the ability of a catalyst to make change. This is a direct reference to "evidence-based solutions," a popular model for nonprofit management, and it tells us much about the #CLOSErikers campaign.[14] Based on a 2011 Ford Foundation–funded study at the University of Southern California, this model proceeds from the reality that "the philanthropic sector, upon whose support movement-building organizations largely rely, is increasingly asking for the 'evidence' that their investments are making a difference along the social change spectrum, from social services to advocacy, from organizing to movement building."[15]

While it may seem like common sense that any organization should quantify the efficacy of its actions and tailor its future strategies accordingly, in the managerial world of big philanthropy, this has a particular meaning: organizations that wish to remain financially viable must demonstrate a consistent pattern of success at meeting stated goals, so-called deliverables. If an organization like Katal should publicly announce an objective like securing a city council vote to close the Rikers Island penal colony, for instance, then checking this box becomes an all-encompassing objective, no matter what collateral damage this might entail.

JLUSA functioned as the engine of the #CLOSErikers campaign, fueled by its paid staff, multimillion-dollar war chest, political connections via big philanthropy, and a growing number of volunteers and "formerly incarcerated leaders" attracted to the idea of closing Rikers. The comparatively smaller Katal also brokered funding and provided labor. The #CLOSErikers campaign also shared funders, support staff, and several key personnel with both the immediate orbit of the Lippman Commission and the commission itself, including JLUSA president Glenn Martin, who served as a commissioner. The same names recur time and again throughout the skyscraper jails booster network, both of individual reformers and the philanthropic organizations backing them—and #CLOSErikers is no exception.[16]

Strategically, the official #CLOSErikers campaign divided its objectives into three distinct phases. Phase One, beginning in late 2015, called for building support for the demand to close Rikers, not reform it, and to organize this demand around Martin, who would be the campaign's public face. A high-water mark came at the aforementioned November panel, when Martin appeared on stage at the New School with progressive New York City comptroller Scott Stringer and Martin Horn, a longtime advocate of borough-based jails. This event corresponded with an increasing number of op-eds and other public statements in support of closing Rikers, by Martin and others, and a social media campaign around the #closeRIKERS hashtag, subsequently modified to #CLOSErikers.

In early 2016, the group met with Michael Jacobson, executive director of ISLG, former president of the Vera Institute of Justice, and a former commissioner of both the New York City Departments of Probation and Correction, under mayors David Dinkins and Rudolph Giuliani, respectively. Jacobson tacitly supported the plan to close Rikers and teased out its viability. All the while, the group worked behind the scenes to build an impressive coalition of New York City nonprofits, progressive politicians, and other social justice actors to sign on to the demand to close Rikers. #CLOSErikers received a tremendous boost with Melissa Mark-Viverito's 2016 announcement in support of shuttering the penal colony, albeit in the distant future. Enlivened by the formation of the Lippman Commission, which included its own Glenn Martin, the campaign made its public debut at an April 2016 rally, kicking off Phase Two.[17]

Phase Two of #CLOSErikers demonstrated the novelty of this unique campaign, as over two hundred activists gathered on the steps of city hall. This would not be mistaken for a rally of Shut Down Rikers: their signs were high quality and mass produced, including professional graphic design and the campaign's careful branding, prominently featuring pink, white, and black, the colors of JLUSA's distinctive brand. But despite this polished veneer, the speakers were largely people who had been locked up on Rikers or who had family there. The campaign's real connection to the suffering on Rikers Island was palpable. Accompanying the rally was a statement signed by over sixty organizations endorsing #CLOSErikers. It was a classic activist "big tent" coalition bringing together progressive criminal justice practitioners and faith leaders, with a veritable who's who among the New York City activist left, including the official chapter of Black Lives Matter, the Jail Action Coalition, and even the Campaign to Shut Down Rikers.[18]

As this broad base of support demonstrates, the #CLOSErikers campaign benefited immensely from obscuring what exactly it was up to in the long term. Many of these actors, as time would tell, would hesitate to be involved in a campaign that immediately demanded new jails. Within the campaign, this strategy was called "one no, many yeses."[19] The reader might recognize this pithy phrase as a guiding principle of the Zapatistas, likely held over from Katal organizer Gabriel Sayegh's far more honorable days as an alter-globalization-era anarchist.[20] What this meant to Sayegh by 2017, however, was a far cry from the direct democracy of Chiapas. Katal reflects,

> Campaign leaders organized to strengthen and expand the consensus on closing Rikers, and left questions about "What comes next?" for open discussion in the future. This also served the campaign strategy; no one had to answer that question, because the first and second phases were to build the campaign and then focus, like a laser, on getting the mayor (primary target) and influencer

organizations/people (secondary targets) to agree to close
the facility. Questions about the future would be more
urgent during Phase Three.[21]

Phase Three was going to be new jails.[22] But the campaign
shrewdly kept its future plans as vague as possible, maximizing its
capitalization on the good will of New York City progressives and
radicals, before the thorny issue of what would take the place of
Rikers was allowed to arise.

Keeping control of the turbulent shift to Phase Three
within the campaign itself would, however, be relatively easy.
#CLOSErikers was, Katal later reflected, "a campaign, not a coa-
lition." Organizations that supported the campaign did not have
any say in its functioning; they simply signed on to a project run
by a very small group of people employed by JLUSA and Katal.
"Thus, there was no formal process for other groups to weigh in on
strategy or direction," Katal wrote, "the campaign did not adopt a
coalition structure, which often includes more consensus-oriented
decision-making processes."[23] This would prove decisive in Phase
Three, when the campaign's leaders began to push for skyscraper
jails, and anybody who had a problem with this could simply
leave, to whatever extent they were ever actually a part of it. For
the time being, however, #CLOSErikers enjoyed the support of
many people who would not have supported a jail-construction
plot, including the authors.

Similarly, the campaign claimed that the formerly incarcerated volunteers were its "leaders," but this, too, concealed the fact
that the entire operation was run by a handful of insiders from the
carceral nonprofit sector. In one 2016 meeting of "formerly incarcerated leaders," Jarrod sat as paid staffers solicited strategy advice
based on the prompt "Where does power come from?" Various
answers were written on butcher paper. As the collected "leaders"

brainstormed the different ways of building power, Jarrod's eyes wandered to the meeting agenda of the woman sitting next to him, a paid #CLOSErikers staffer. Whereas Jarrod's agenda simply had the question, the agenda printed for staffers had the answer: power comes from lobbying politicians. Unsurprisingly, this is what the meeting concluded, once the staffer running it had synthesized all their suggestions. Jarrod soon deduced that very little was decided by his fellow "leaders," or by virtually anyone at all, besides a handful of people at the top.[24]

Drawing on activist themes and aesthetics, #CLOSErikers led protest marches and rallies building support for the campaign throughout 2016 and 2017. In September, a large crowd numbering upward of a thousand marched through Astoria, Queens, to the Rikers Island Bridge, in a clear echo of the Black Lives Matter movement. Behind the scenes, #CLOSErikers waged an impressive public relations campaign and aggressively lobbied Mayor de Blasio to support its agenda, as he continued to drag his feet in getting behind a plan supported by virtually every other progressive Democrat in the city. The campaign's use of traditional activist networks, tactics, and optics, coupled with aggressive realpolitik, resulted in de Blasio announcing support for closing Rikers in March of 2017, just hours before the release of the Lippman Commission's plan calling for the closure of the penal colony— and its replacement with new jails. Soon enough, #CLOSErikers would be united behind this agenda, whether its previous supporters liked it or not.[25]

This context is important. While #CLOSErikers was building public support during Phase Two, the Lippman Commission had been crafting a detailed report in support of closing Rikers and replacing it with new jails. Much of the report, entitled *A More Just New York City*, revolved around a number of technocratic fixes to the city's punishment system, constituting "off ramps" for leading arrested people away from incarceration. Some of these reforms, like speedy trials and the elimination of cash bail for most misdemeanors and nonviolent felonies, augured well for the poor people stuck at Rikers because of their inability to pay. Other reforms, like enhanced supervision and other "alternatives to incarceration," simply extended the surveillance and control of the jail into the neighborhoods most enveloped in its shadow.[26] The report's numerous suggestions for getting the jail population low enough to close Rikers were left up for debate. However, the necessity to build new jails to take the place of Rikers Island, which the commission accepted as an article of faith, was not.

"The new jails should be integrated into their surrounding neighborhoods," the report argued, "both in terms of design and uses. Benefits to communities such as new community meeting spaces and services or retail space for local business should be incorporated into each facility." Sitting atop this retail and meeting space, the report concluded, the city must anticipate building a total of five thousand human cages. Many of the off-ramps discussed in the plan revolved around how to get down to that number.[27] A subsequent publication called *Justice in Design*, examined in detail in the following chapter, demonstrated the Lippman Commission's dedication to progressive human caging.

In June of 2017, de Blasio released his own report, entitled *Smaller, Safer, Fairer*. The mayor's office agreed with the number of jail beds to be constructed, five thousand, and shared some of the proposed off-ramps to get there, but not all.[28] The commission had recommended a few modest reforms to street-level policing, namely that civil charges, comparable to traffic tickets, take the place of arrest for "offenses" such as sex work, possession of small amounts of marijuana (still illegal at the time), and possession of so-called gravity knives.[29] *Smaller, Safer, Fairer* did not adopt these reforms, indicating that the commission's cautious encroachment on the power of street-level policing was still a bridge too far for de Blasio. Befitting the tortured locution of its title, *Smaller, Safer, Fairer* engaged in political contortionism that sought to please both the would-be downsizers of the city jails and the cops and courts happily keeping them filled. Rather than embrace any potentially controversial changes, city hall diplomatically asserted that decarceration trends, such as that of reducing the incarcerated population of Rikers to five thousand, were largely already inmotion.[30]

The mayor's report was similarly coy about a timeline for closing Rikers. While supporting the construction of new jails, de Blasio was firm that Rikers would not be closed until the city jail population dipped below five thousand. "Once the jail population reaches 5,000," he said in the report's introduction, "the City will be in a position to close Rikers Island for good." And the responsibility for executing this plan—along with the blame for its failure—was not to rest on de Blasio. "Doing so will depend on the desires of neighborhoods and their elected officials, as even a jail population of 5,000—significantly smaller than the jail population today—will still require identifying and developing appropriate sites for new jails as well as renovating existing facilities in the boroughs." Nonetheless, the mayor was clear, saying, "We have made it the official policy of the City of New York to close the jails on Rikers Island."[31]

This is the setting in which #CLOSErikers unfolded. Far from the grassroots efforts of abolitionists and BLM activists fighting in their spare time for a world without jails, #CLOSErikers and the well-heeled, well-connected funders, politicians, and social entrepreneurs in its orbit represented a highly professional, and remarkably effective, multipolar coordination of big philanthropy, the carceral nonprofit sector, real estate interests, progressive Democrats, and punishment system reformers. Despite the formal distinction between these different organizations and actors, the line demarcating the Lippman Commission—never mind its satellite organizations and individuals, and the vision outlined in these reports—from the #CLOSErikers campaign was never clear. The skyscraper jail campaign was, as the foundation-coordinating body Philanthropy New York subsequently observed, a "complex, multi-front, intergovernmental reform playing out here in our own community."[32]

PRESSURE FROM ALL SIDES

On December 14, 2017, Philanthropy New York organized a daylong event entitled Funders Summit on Justice Reform: The Nation's Eyes on Rikers. Summit organizers and funders included dozens of big-name foundations, including key supporters of the Lippman Commission like Ford, Tow, and the New York Women's Foundation. Speakers included representatives from the mayor's and governor's offices, Vera president Nick Turner, ISLG's Michael Jacobson, JLUSA's Glenn Martin, Brooklyn district attorney Eric Gonzalez, and the Honorable Jonathan Lippman himself, alongside representatives from Ford, Tow, the Fortune Society, the Brooklyn Org (formerly the Brooklyn Community Foundation), and Philanthropy New York. "Throughout the day," organizers subsequently reflected, "we heard from three sets of major stakeholders actively working to close Rikers: government, the advocacy community, and philanthropy. All of the speakers reflected on their collective efforts and how they fit into the larger reform movement."[33] A fourth set of stakeholders, real estate capitalists, were not mentioned, but one is safe to assume that their interests were well represented in the room that day.

The purpose of the summit was to reflect on the unfolding movement to close Rikers, which by late 2017 included the avowed imperative to build new jails. The organizers emphasized key priorities that main funders believed should continue to underscore both this campaign and future reforms to the punishment system modeled after it. Some of these insights followed the trail blazed by Ferguson Inc. several years earlier, such as "centering conversations on race" and applying "an intersectional analysis to better understand and address the criminalization that immigrants, women, LGBTQ individuals, and communities of color increasingly experience." More to the point, the summit emphasized how "emboldened by local consensus on Rikers' closure, New York has a particularly powerful opportunity to reimagine one of America's largest and most expensive jails."[34]

Moving forward, the organizers argued, it was imperative to "recognize that efforts from both 'outside' and 'inside' the formal power system produced consensus for closure" and the construction of new jails, which pointed to the success of "pressure from all sides." The strategic lessons were clear: "Summit participants noted that Mayor de Blasio's commitment to jail closure in April 2017 followed the efforts of two complementary forces. The #CLOSErikers advocates further amplified the voices of grassroots organizers pushing for closure and provided a platform for the formerly incarcerated. The Lippman Commission—with its leadership and diverse membership—lent additional credibility to the cause and moved the inside game forward." And crucially, if not obviously, "philanthropy played a major role in supporting both of these efforts."[35]

While Katal, and other organizers, seemed to consider it merely serendipitous that the Lippman Commission dovetailed with its own organizing—musing that "this couldn't have been better if the campaign staff had scripted it"—the Funders Summit represented a room full of people who had more or less done just that.[36] There probably wasn't direct, top-down coordination in setting up #CLOSErikers, Lippman, and all the rest to occur at roughly the same time. And if there was, unmasking a secret conspiracy is not nearly as interesting as considering the likelier story that long-standing political and economic cooperation, unity of class interests, and improvisational symbiosis among big philanthropy, the progressive nonprofit sector, and the Democratic Party had resulted in an ad hoc coalition acting with considerable coordination to shape the unfolding of the crisis around Rikers Island and resolve it in terms favorable to city elites. And while some organizations were said to have played distinct roles, such as #CLOSErikers representing an activist orientation to the jail booster effort, disparate functions—fundraising, political maneuvering, public relations, and technocratic planning—also blurred together significantly as the campaign unfolded.

With attention to this rough division of labor, the funders identified key objectives for realizing the closure of Rikers under the heading "New Targets for Inside-Outside Game." These included proceeding, at the state level, with bail reform measures necessary to lower the jail population to five thousand. Locally, however, the major tasks moving forward revealed the strategic challenges facing Phase Three: "encourage City administration & City Council to identify jail sites, expedite ULURP [Uniform Land Use Review Procedure], and engage community in decision-making"; "address NIMBY ["not in my backyard" opposition] backlash through op-eds and community education & engagement"; and "focus press/media coverage to keep pressure on Mayor and Governor and sustain momentum."[37]

Of particular importance to this strategy is ULURP, the process through which a large development project must pass in New York City before ground can be broken. Its protocol mandates public hearings and consultation with local community boards, borough presidents, the city planning commission, and the city council.[38] Land use and environmental review processes are necessary steps for carceral construction in many places, and these hearings have often served as key choke points for jail opponents of all stripes.[39] Accordingly, the propaganda and policy writing of the skyscraper jail boosters had long identified this as the most treacherous step in the process.

This strategy was particularly informed by Martin Horn's experiences trying to build a new jail to replace Rikers in the aughts. References to Horn's plan, and the opposition the plan inspired, recur in the jail booster literature—such as a large stylized pull quote in a Katal document in which Horn, deploying a tactic #CLOSErikers would rely on in the months and years ahead, dismisses the abolitionist opposition to his new jails as selfish NIMBYism.[40] With Horn in mind, the boosters were keenly aware that a previous plan similar to the skyscraper jails had been defeated by community opposition, including from abolitionists, and that they needed to get ahead of this at all costs—including by preemptively adopting the rhetoric one can anticipate from anti-jail activists. And just as predicted, ULURP soon became the primary obstacle facing an increasingly cohesive network of jail boosters, for whom closing Rikers would soon take a back seat to the imperative to build skyscraper jails.

NON-REFORMIST JAILS

As the boosters plotted Phase Three, the new jail plan was taking shape. In early 2018, in collaboration with the global architecture and design firm Perkins Eastman, the city hurried to select four sites.[41] The finalists were all owned by the city: the present site of the old Brooklyn House of Detention in Brooklyn; a parking lot adjacent to a courthouse in Kew Gardens, Queens; a municipal building at 80 Centre Street in Manhattan; and an

NYPD impound lot sitting on the former site of Lincoln Hospital in the South Bronx. The Bronx facility would be zoned for upward of 27 stories; Queens, 31 stories; and Brooklyn and Manhattan, 43 stories. Despite their varying heights, each facility would have 1,510 beds, constituting a total of 6,040 beds, meant to house a maximum of 5,000 prisoners. Each facility would have 250 beds for women.[42]

These new facilities were sold as "borough-based jails," offering locally sourced incarceration across the city. The skyscraper jails were also given the euphemism of "justice hubs," as part of a bizarre carceral humanist rebranding examined in detail in the following chapter. Staten Island would not have a jail, or even a justice hub, despite Lippman's recommendation that it host one, same as all the other boroughs.[43] Later, it would be announced that Staten Island prisoners would instead go to Brooklyn.[44] While Staten Island's share of the jail population would be roughly two hundred in the city's plan for reaching five thousand, it is difficult to ignore that this move left the city's whitest borough, and the borough with the highest concentration of NYPD cops per capita, continuing to bear no responsibility for the jailing of New York's predominantly Black and Latinx citizens.[45]

The announcement of each site summoned fierce local resistance from residents in the neighborhoods slated for jail construction. Residents organized into groups like Queens Residents United, Neighbors United Below Canal in Chinatown, and an organization of residents in the Diego Beekman Houses in the Bronx. Jail opponents included a number of abolitionists and progressives who supported the closure of Rikers but did not believe it should be replaced with anything at all.[46]

The opposition in Chinatown, which had temporarily stopped a borough-based jail with intensive community activism in the early 1980s, was particularly fierce.[47] Eventually, organizers forced the city to abandon plans to build on the controversial location of 80 Centre Street, where it would replace the Louis J. Lefkowitz Building, the nine-story historical landmark that is home to the famous Marriage Bureau wedding facility, and would cast a shadow over nearby Columbus Park. But despite this victory, the construction would proceed in Chinatown, taking place instead on the present site of the Manhattan Detention Complex, commonly known as the Tombs and adjacent to Chung Pak low-income senior residence.[48]

Adding insult to injury in the eyes of these residents, the city was *moving as quickly as possible*, in de Blasio's own words. City hall announced jail locations shortly before beginning the legally mandated process of crafting an environmental impact statement (EIS) prior to breaking ground. The jails, slated for four very different sites, were bundled into a single mammoth review process and would accordingly be fast-tracked through ULURP. All the while, the city was not required to provide substantive images of what the jails would actually look like. Since the project followed the practices of "design-build" in which design and construction are unified under a single plan with the same developers working at a breakneck pace, the clearing and breaking of ground would proceed while the final blueprints for the jails were still being drafted!

Many citizens expressed considerable anger that the city's pushing of a design-build project through ULURP meant the project would be approved before the plans were even finalized. In response, city hall admitted that they weren't quite sure what the jails would even look like, and to make matters worse, they were actually telling the truth.[49] It's also worth noting that while jail boosters, like the forces organized by Philanthropy New York, celebrated the novelty of the design-build process, this method was a key component of the carceral buildup that covered the surface of Rikers Island with so many miserable jails so quickly in the early 1990s, as the War on Drugs packed the city's jails with low-level drug users from Black and Latinx communities slated for gentrification.[50]

As the skyscraper jails sailed over one bureaucratic hurdle after another, dozens of community groups and hundreds of residents flooded the city with complaints about this expedited process. The jail boosters were quick to write complainants off as selfish NIMBY, or "not in my backyard," interests. Some surely objected to the jails in thinly veiled racism toward incarcerated people and their families. But many valid criticisms emerged as well, only to be tarred with the brush of NIMBYism. "These accusers," China-town activist Jan Lee told journalist Eva Fedderly, "mainly from these big foundations, are operating under this suffocating blanket of morality."[51] In contrast to the one-dimensional view of Lee and countless other anti-jail activists offered by #CLOSErikers, re-spondents offering public comments consistently emphasized the rushed nature of the project, the city's lack of substantive transparency or consultation with locals prior to the site announcements, and its packaging of four jails slated for four very different places into one uniform environmental and land-use process. Frustrated residents also pointed to the plan's stark binary: either New York City could build all four jails or it would take no action at all to redress the humanitarian disaster of Rikers.

Residents also pointed to the staggering size and density of the jails and their potential impact on the community; the skyscraper jails would tower over their surrounding neighborhoods and leave little in the way of open space on their designated lots. Many residents wondered if de Blasio would support a jail near his home, in the affluent Brooklyn neighborhood of Park Slope.

Beyond these fairly predictable complaints, however, citizen critics also pointed to glaring holes in the plan: What would the city do if its jail population failed to decrease below five thousand? What sense did it make to build a Bronx facility miles away from the courthouse, and no Staten Island facility at all, if the point was proximity to local courts? How could jails this tall be evacuated in case of an emergency? Would someone from one borough arrested in another be jailed near the court where they faced trial, or near their home? Why didn't the flat, uniform population caps for each jail reflect actual incarceration rates in that borough? Since the $11 billion price tag referred only to the *projected* cost of construction, not to the ultimate amount the city would pay the financiers who floated the bonds necessary to fund the project, what would the plan actually cost? How could a uniform plan even be made for four neighborhoods as different from one another as New York neighborhoods could be? And most importantly, what about the new jails would change the way DOC guards act toward prisoners, including at the already-existing borough-based jails?[52]

While it could be argued that these questions were the bad faith of NIMBY interests willing to say anything to stall the process, the city's lack of substantive answers did not exactly inspire confidence. Moreover, these grievances revealed that, contrary to the pretense to public participation performed by the Lippman Commission, the city had failed to honor even its own meager commitments to public hearings leading up to the site announcement. State senator Brian Kavanagh and US congressperson Nydia M. Velázquez noted, "The city's public engagement on this proposal has begun in earnest only after virtually all of the major decisions have been made about the location, number, and scale of the facility."[53] And while the jail boosters responded by painting opponents to the plan with the broad brush of NIMBY, many opponents followed in the footsteps of the Campaign to Shut Down Rikers and advocated for a prison-abolitionist approach to closing Rikers.[54]

For his part, Glenn Martin saw no contradiction between abolitionism and the construction of the skyscraper jails. In 2017, to silence critics on the left, Martin described the plan as "on the road to abolition."[55] Befitting the public tenor of #CLOSErikers, Martin even took it a step further, arguing that he was in fact the *realest* abolitionist. "If you are a staunch abolitionist and your suggestion is that we can go from having 2.2 million people locked up to having no one locked up," he argued, "that's extremely elitist and very academic and doesn't match the reality of what it takes to reform the system." This tactic—baiting jail opponents as out-of-touch elitists in contrast with the veritable salt of the earth who supposedly supported the skyscraper jails—would recur throughout the jail debate. As a coup de grâce, Martin even appeared to argue that the replacement of Rikers with new jails was a "non-reformist reform," which, in abolitionist terms, means a reform that does not enhance the capacity of the carceral state. At the risk of stating the obvious, this criterion is not used to describe the *construction of new facilities*—or, at least, it hadn't been until #CLOSErikers came along.[56]

PHASE THREE

As the Funders Summit had predicted, the EIS and ULURP processes were the juncture at which the #CLOSErikers campaign became hotly contested. Following the release of the Lippman report and the mayor's subsequent plan, the campaign switched gears from the simple "no" of closing Rikers into a dramatic "yes": the passage of the new jails through ULURP. These hearings, held throughout April of 2019, were tumultuous affairs. The #CLOSErikers campaign, and JLUSA in particular, mobilized aggressively, distributing T-shirts and placards and encouraging staffers, campaign members, and allies to speak out in favor of the new jails.

The campaign had hit an embarrassing snag in late 2017 with the sudden departure of Glenn Martin amid the disclosure of sexual harassment complaints, which included hush money paid within the organization. But with the city poised to adopt a plan it had advocated and incubated for years, the organization and its banner campaign had found their stride. Their jail boosterism was not unopposed, of course. In attendance at these hearings was a predictable smattering of locals opposed to jail construction in their neighborhood. And a louder and more organized contingent came from the abolitionist coalition No New Jails NYC (NNJ).[57]

The NNJ network built on the foundation laid by the Campaign to Shut Down Rikers, which had not survived the co-optation of its demand by jail boosters. It included a number of veteran abolitionists from organizations like Jail Action Coalition, Critical Resistance, and NYC Shut It Down. Launched in September 2018, as the plans for the new jails moved through environmental review toward ULURP, NNJ waged an impressive intervention in the discourse around the skyscraper jails, especially given its relatively small size, with just a few dozen core members and a nonexistent budget, especially compared with the deep pockets of the jail boosters. NNJ organized public events and demonstrations and crafted accessible propaganda to discredit the skyscraper jails. This included an alternative investment plan, which, following a central theme of Shut Down Rikers, explained how the city could close Rikers without new jails and could subsequently invest the money designated for the new jails into the communities most impacted by mass incarceration.[58]

The skyscraper jails plan and subsequent entry of NNJ into the fray polarized an activist community that had come together around the demand to close Rikers and that now grappled with how to respond to the demand for new jails. The Bronx Defenders, a progressive organization of public defenders who had initially signaled support not just for #CLOSErikers but also for the new jails, reversed its position in September 2019. "The ULURP process requires us to ask what is the right location, size, and capacity for new jails," the organization wrote. "As public defenders, our role is not to answer these questions; our role is to prevent our clients from being caged and minimize the harm caused by the carceral state." Without naming NNJ, the group outlined an alternative vision of eliminating Rikers with no new infrastructure taking its place.[59]

The same day, the nonprofit Voices of Community Activists and Leaders (VOCAL), a decades-old progressive advocacy organization and early supporter of #CLOSErikers, released a statement disavowing the plan. While not as stridently anti-jail as the Bronx Defenders, VOCAL outlined some hard facts. The plan had been originally packaged as new jails *alongside* intensive community investment, they recounted, and VOCAL had supported it for that reason. But amid Phase Three, community investment had been forgotten as the plan simply had become carceral construction with little other benefit. There wasn't much of a point supporting the jails anymore, even in the name of cynical realpolitik.[60]

Further dissent within the progressive community was evinced by a petition signed by hundreds of New York City law workers, many of whom were affiliated with the nonprofit public defender organization the Legal Aid Society, denouncing the new jails and supporting NNJ.[61] Legal Aid itself subsequently decried the way that reformers and politicians created a "false binary" between keeping the old jails or building new ones. "By creating this false choice, modest reforms have deeply fragmented communities of impacted people," they wrote. "For that, the City should be ashamed."[62] NNJ was also supported by the National Lawyers

Guild and celebrity politician Alexandria Ocasio-Cortez.[63] The public relations success enjoyed by such a small group, in such a short time, was testament not only to the skills of its organizers, but more profoundly, bespoke a public appetite for alternatives to the carceral status quo. But victories in public relations are not to be confused with actually winning.

FARCE

The growing popularity of NNJ shook the #CLOSErikers campaign. #CLOSErikers organizers had always worked to place rhetorical distance between themselves and city hall and preserve the appearance of a grassroots activist campaign. This posture became more difficult as they pivoted to supporting, and even helping to design, a massive jail-construction project that would operate under the auspices of the New York City Department of Correction. And while there were surely disagreements behind the scenes, #CLOSErikers remained firm in its support for the new skyscraper jails.[64] Meanwhile, their campaign had been designed to weather controversy. Phase Three did not rely on unanimous popularity, especially among the activist left who had been deployed as foot soldiers in Phase Two. By their own estimation, all the jail boosters needed was enough support to push their plan through city government. But victory was not assured, and the boosters still felt the need to continually assail the abolitionists. The most effective attacks came not from the political right but from those who spoke the language of social justice, and even abolitionism itself.

Case in point was putative abolitionist Soffiyah Elijah. At the time of the skyscraper jail debate, the former criminal justice attorney and veteran activist was executive director of the Alliance of Families for Justice, which she helped to launch in September 2016, on the anniversary of the Attica rebellion. This group received funding from the New York Women's Foundation, a key foundation supporting the Lippman Commission, whose president, Ana L. Oliveira, was a commission member.[65] Elijah had also joined the Working Group on Culture Change established by the Mayor's Office of Criminal Justice to oversee the administration of the new jails.[66] Taking to the pages of the tabloid *Daily News* in defense of the skyscraper jails, Elijah attempted to outflank NNJ from the left and right simultaneously, arguing that the campaign did not go far enough in its demands for abolition but, simultaneously, was not sufficiently versed in city politics to understand that the choice simply boiled down to new jails or the old ones. This was the "false binary" Legal Aid would soon bemoan. More alarmingly, Elijah argued for the skyscraper jails on the grounds of carceral humanism. She wrote,

> "No new jails" would mean no new mental health services, no new safe, humane and sanitary living conditions, no new accommodations for pregnant women and LGBT people, no reduction in New York City jail capacity. It would mean clients and attorneys will continue to have strained relationships caused by the inability to spend meaningful time together preparing a defense strategy.[67]

Such was the political imagination of the jail boosters, that the provision of necessary services for vulnerable people required them being in jail in the first place, and the construction of new carceral infrastructure to boot.

In fact, it was an encounter just like this that led James Kilgore to first theorize the concept of carceral humanism a decade prior. Kilgore is part of a protracted campaign against jail construction in Champaign, Illinois. The first round of that campaign deployed progressive and abolitionist arguments to build local opposition against the jail, and succeeded when the plan was shelved by the county board in 2014. In response, the jail boosters adopted a new lexicon; the sheriff leading the campaign found a new architectural firm and began promoting the jail as a mental health service provider. Simultaneously, the sheriff argued that the opponents of the new jail *supported* the abysmal conditions in the existing facilities. "He completely changed the message," reflects Kilgore, "and cast us as being the villains who wanted to keep these poor folks in horrible jail cells, rather than give them a nice, soft bed to sleep on, and a big gymnasium to play basketball."[68] Elijah's deployment of these same tropes in New York City is an important reminder that carceral humanism is being deployed nationally and internationally, albeit with key regional differences; Kilgore's nemesis, for instance, was a conservative local sheriff, not a supposed abolitionist with deep ties to New York City's activist milieu.

When Elijah's strange argument was widely critiqued by younger abolitionists, she let the new generation know exactly how she thought about social movement politics, tweeting, "To the mud slingers, haters & folks who are upset that I told the truth about the Rikers situation & think they're capable of challenging me—forget about it. I only debate my peers, all others . . . I TEACH! Later."[69] While Katal had wisely (and quietly) quit its formal role in the #CLOSErikers campaign at the conclusion of Phase Two, its cofounder Gabriel Sayegh joined the fray, arguing that "conditions of confinement" should be at the center of the debate, not the question of whether to build new jails—because, after all, the city was always going to need lots and lots of jail space. Sayegh nonetheless argued that the skyscraper jail construction could be counted as a form of "decarceration."[70]

This perspective was also tirelessly advanced by a particularly unlikely partisan of the new jails: Dana Kaplan. Before taking a job as the deputy director of the Mayor's Office of Criminal

Justice, Kaplan was known as a seasoned anticarceral activist, working with the Juvenile Justice Project of Louisiana and the Center for Constitutional Rights. In the latter capacity, Kaplan was responsible for compiling the Californians United for a Responsible Budget (CURB) organizing dossier *How to Stop a Jail in Your Town*.[71] In the wake of Black Lives Matter, de Blasio's office recognized the importance of a left-talking emissary to represent its punitive policies; Kaplan was responsible for "community engagement," using the language of social justice and abolitionism to cast the skyscraper jails as "a decarceration plan."[72]

Abolitionists quickly took note of the city's sleight of hand. "In a moment where abolitionist movements are gaining popularity and mainstream credibility," wrote Rachel Foran, Mariame Kaba, and Katy Naples-Mitchell, in explicit reference to Kaplan, "there is a growing tendency to describe reformist fights as abolitionist, when in fact those fights only further entrench the power of the prison industrial complex."[73] When Kaplan appeared at a Manhattan public hearing to face down a room full of activists trying to stop a jail in their town, NNJ supporter Bryan Welton prefaced his remarks with an acute observation: "My, my, Dana Kaplan, what a strange journey you've had."[74]

Despite the best efforts of boosters like Elijah, Sayegh, and Kaplan, the new jails met significant opposition at the local level. The mandated public hearings around the new jail construction gave vent to extreme public anger, and the process also demonstrated an alternative vision for how New York City could use the crisis around Rikers to effect real decarceration, which we explore in detail in chapter 4. As a result of this pushback, Queens borough president Melinda Katz and Bronx borough president Ruben Diaz Jr. opposed the jails, while Gale Brewer in Manhattan and future mayor Eric Adams in Brooklyn supported them. Community boards in *all four* boroughs slated for skyscraper jails voted them down: CB1 in Manhattan, CB1 in the Bronx, CB2 in Brooklyn, CB9 in Queens. Unfortunately, these votes were simply advisory in nature, meaning the city planning board had the authority to overrule the local boards.[75] And it did.

City hall's further effort to streamline the jails, and effectively railroad the process through, earned the rebuke of a chorus of community organizations and local politicians.[76] These were mostly not dedicated anti-jail activists. A rebuff typical from this group came from the Municipal Art Society of New York, an established urban planning nonprofit otherwise friendly to the skyscraper jails plan, which objected on the grounds that too much of the plan's particulars were ill defined and that some details, like the sheer height of the facilities, were troubling and begged for more clarification.[77] Other skeptics included planning boards, borough presidents, and neighborhood groups, especially the Neighbors United Below Canal in Chinatown, a coalition of small business associations, building associations, nonprofits, and local notables. The city's overruling of the community boards only further enraged this opposition movement, and supporting the jails became politically dangerous for politicians near a proposed site.[78]

Facing this pressure, in October 2019, with just two days before the final city council vote, the jail boosters within city hall blinked. The final plan was dramatically amended to limit the Brooklyn and Manhattan facilities to twenty-nine stories, and the Bronx and Queens facilities to nineteen, with a combined total capacity of 3,300, down from the original 5,000 called for by Lippman.[79] It was perhaps great serendipity that *just the previous day*, the Mayor's Office of Criminal Justice had abruptly announced this exact figure, 3,300, as the projected jail population for 2026, the year slated for the Rikers closure.[80]

There was one major problem with this compromise. Kaplan, as sympathetic reporter Maurice Chammah observed at the time, faced "a policy puzzle": "Each proposal to reduce the height of the jails entailed changes—such as moving certain cells away from direct sunlight or housing more inmates in each area—that seemed likely to cut against the goal of making the facilities more humane and rehabilitative."[81] Each compromise moved the jails further away from anything resembling the plan that progressive jail boosters had been selling. For instance, while moving the site from 80 Centre Street to the Tombs may have been a victory for Chinatown activists, the Tombs had been the city's original choice, but the location had been abandoned because the "land area of the facility . . . did not have adequate space for our programming goals."[82]

This crunch also resulted in the designation of the Queens facility as the sole site for incarcerated women, replacing the original plan for each facility to hold 250 women. Moving them all to a central site cut against much of the justification of locally accessible "borough-based" jails in the first place and offered New York's incarcerated women yet another remote location in Queens that they would share with men.[83] Meanwhile, the robust community reinvestment that had framed Lippman's original plan had been winnowed down to a paltry offering of piecemeal investments into local programming and infrastructure, much of which would have likely occurred anyway and all of which was explicitly framed by jail advocates in the city council as the compromises necessary to gain community support for the jails. This investment package was far from a serious effort to reverse the socioeconomic causes of mass incarceration, and its authors did not even pretend to have a vision for how this larger goal could occur.[84]

The jail boosters, however, were undeterred by the obvious failure of their plan to build anything besides the same old jails, and the glaring fact—apparent to many people even at this early date—that the skyscraper jails would likely not even result in the closure of Rikers. Instead, the boosters fused a unique blend of fanatical belief in the righteousness of their plan with technocratic gaslighting, arguing that critics simply did not understand how legislative sausage is made. Soon enough, public hearings devolved into JLUSA supporters shouting that abolitionists wanted to keep people on Rikers forever. At a community board meeting in the Bronx that the authors attended, Councilmember Diana Ayala argued that building a 245-foot-high jail in the Mott Haven neighborhood was necessary, as there was no other place to put it, and it was "the only way to close Rikers Island."[85] Meanwhile, when Kaplan was asked why, given the accumulating obstacles to realizing the lofty design goals for the skyscraper jails, she did not advocate instead for a diffusion of smaller jails more in keeping with the principles of the justice hubs, her response drew not from penology but from public relations. Four jails were bad enough to build public support for, Kaplan replied. Eight would be exponentially more difficult.[86]

The jail boosters who acted in good faith to reform the system, it seemed, had looked around the proverbial poker table, and not recognizing a mark, believed it to be a fair game. But, in fact, the mark sat in their chair. By the end of the process, the plan had been shorn of most of its progressive veneer, and called instead for a quartet of more or less ordinary jails, coupled with little in the way of community investment or benefit of any kind, to be *added* to the city's carceral system, with no guarantee that Rikers would be taken out. One noteworthy politician even raised the fear that the construction of the skyscraper jails would not necessarily entail the *demolition* of Rikers facilities, ensuring they would not be used again. His name? Brooklyn borough president Eric Adams.[87] When the jail boosters were asked about this possibility, or what the city would do if the projection for a lower jail population did not come to pass, they had no answer.

While they consistently postured as the adults in the room, the naïveté of jail boosters could be astounding. During the EIS process in 2018, a "senior community organizer" with JLUSA, meaning a high-ranking paid staffer, wrote to the city on behalf of the #CLOSErikers campaign, distressed at having made the discovery that the skyscraper *jails* would, upon their opening, *be administered by the New York City Department of Correction.* The organizer cited "ongoing reports on the treatment of people in the custody of the Department of Corrections [indicating] a lack of respect for human life and dignity, and ultimately, a degradation of the 'community resources' that those people are and can be." As JLUSA kicked its campaign for skyscraper jails into high gear, this senior organizer argued that "the Department of Corrections [*sic*] has made no indications of its ability to operate as anything other than a vehicle for punishment. It does not serve and is not capable of serving any corrective or rehabilitative function." Citing the city's commitment "to create 'rehabilitative facilities designed to improve health, educational, and social outcomes,'" the organizer asked, "What evidence is there that the Department of Corrections can or will do that?"[88] It was a question abolitionists had raised, only to be shouted down as NIMBY protestors or out-of-touch academics. This strange message was sent in mid-2018. But if the #CLOSErikers ranks continued to hold such doubts, they were kept quiet.

Outside of #CLOSErikers, however, there was a sense among some reformers who had supported the original Lippman report that the final plan represented, in the words of Brooklyn state representative Jo Anne Simon, "recommendations from the Lippman report . . . cherry picked to suit the City's political concerns."[89] Nonetheless, the Lippman Commission itself issued a special addendum to *A More Just New York City* amounting to a plea for the measure to pass. In the preface, Lippman himself argued that "rejecting this plan will mean Rikers, the jail barge in the Bronx, and the existing borough jails will continue to exist for genera- tions to come." And in a clear rebuke of NNJ, he added, "There is no viable path to closing Rikers that does not include rebuilt borough facilities." Interestingly, Lippman did note that the plan can "be improved upon," namely, by filtering mentally and phys- ically ill people out of the jail system altogether and undertaking community investment—two issues central to the original Lip- pman plan that had largely fallen by the wayside—in addition to planning the hasty demolition of Rikers jails to prevent their reopening later.

This last item was a hint that Lippman was all too aware of how tenuous the city's commitment to closing Rikers actually was, despite the jail boosters' public dismissal of those who pre- dicted the new plan would lead to Rikers *plus* new jails. But Lip- pman remained true to the cause that bore his name. Dropping all pretenses to objectivity and adopting the verbiage of a political rally, Lippman concluded his message by saying, "Let's seize the moment, and pass this plan to close the Rikers jails on October 17."[90] Of course, as Lippman knew, the resolution guaranteed no such thing.

And so the plan arrived at the city council, where some coun- cil members, like Daniel Dromm of Queens, had long supported it and welcomed its appearance in city hall.[91] Even as the move- ment against the jails heated up, the sustained, yearslong activism and advocacy of the jail booster network, and the compromises the boosters had been willing to make around jail design to get the plan through, set up the city council vote as a blowout vic- tory. Yet, as an important signal of the boosters' priorities in this period, even as crunch time approached, no binding commitment to close Rikers was ever included in the resolution that the city council entertained; the only commitment made was to build the new jails. This was all the boosters cared about accomplishing at this time. This was Phase Three.

TRAGEDY

As the vote approached, NNJ activists continued to play an impressive media game, sufficient to even force a key member of the philanthropy community to enter the fray. In an open letter published in late September 2019, Ford Foundation president Darren Walker, a Lippman commissioner, rebuked the skyscraper jails' critics as not comprehending "nuance," and letting "perfect be the enemy of progress."[92] In response, hundreds of Ford fellows, organizers mentored by the organization, signed a letter of protest, and a coalition of groups in the orbit of NNJ picketed the Ford Foundation offices in Manhattan.[93] These events are remarkable, not just for Walker wading into the political fray so publicly, but for the dramatic rebuke of Ford by some of the very people it has striven for decades to cultivate as business-friendly leaders in marginalized communities. These dynamics, as they exist in the broader nonprofit sector, should be watched closely in the future.[94]

By mid-October, however, the city council vote in favor of the new jails seemed a fait accompli. The most NNJ could do was disrupt the vote as it cleared the way for the skyscraper jails. The sophisticated network of boosters would have their jails, in addition to 250 beds' worth of jail wards to be added to existing city hospitals, under the euphemism "outposted therapeutic housing units." But there was still no telling what was going to happen to Rikers Island; the new plan contained no guarantee to close it down.[95]

Ultimately, the city council approved the $8.1 billion skyscraper jails plan. This massive public-spending project would not be financed out of the city's expenses but from its capital budget.

To procure these funds, the city floats debt on the private market, most often in the form of bonds, which offer tax-free interest
payments on top of the principal. These investments are coveted
by finance capitalists because of their tax-exempt status, steady
yield, and backing by the state.[96] This means that $8.1 billion re-
lates to the actual price of the new jails the same way that the cost
of four years of college tuition translates into how much a person ultimately owes on their student loans. Naturally, this massive windfall for the private sector comes out of taxpayer money.
"Debt draws from the future to arrange the present," cautions
Ruth Wilson Gilmore.[97]

Why were the city bureaucrats and carceral nonprofits willing
to be so shortsighted in their commitment to such a rotten plan?
Part of the answer comes from the funding structure of nonprofits
themselves. Funders do not invest in open-ended concepts. They
expect clear, quantifiable outcomes, the meeting of goals set and
met with proficiency and measured by the *katals* of management
science. The same goes for city politics: politicians live from election to election and must demonstrate that promises have been
kept in the short term, even if they will fall apart in the long term.
Similarly, employment in high-level city governance and nonprofit management—to the extent they can even be disentangled
anymore—has a high rate of turnover, with ladder climbers always looking to pad their resume for a bigger and better job. The
nominal victory of a campaign like #CLOSErikers can load up
a resume with success stories, and then it's on to the next paid
organizer or administrator position, with no need to look back.
Whatever compromises were necessary will not impact organizers'
ability to say their campaign met its objectives.

Of course, many jail boosters also may have sincerely believed that they were working for decarceration, racial justice, and
a more just world. For example, even recently, Elizabeth Glazer,

the former director of the Mayor's Office of Criminal Justice and a supporter of the skyscraper jails, claimed that "at its core, the borough-based jails plan is a decarceration plan."[98] But the outcome was just the same as it would have been if Glazer believed in nothing at all.

"We recognize that local jail reform activists have a vision beyond the closure of Rikers, and see this as a step forward in their greater plan of bail reform, decriminalization of their communities, and ending mass incarceration," wrote the Incarcerated Workers Organizing Committee in response to the plan,

> However, setting aside the likelihood of the Lippman Commission's plan for the closure actually even being fully executed, this move from the establishment is part of an ideological, political, and development strategy. It is just the most recent example of the state successfully shifting public opinion without creating actual systemic change. . . . It recuperates the political stability and palatability of incarceration while leaving intact all of its violence, injustice, and tragedy.[99]

Tragedy is right. JLUSA has always claimed to believe "those closest to the problem are closest to the solution." But their empowerment of bourgeois politicians, greedy developers, progressive cage builders, and even lingering remnants of the Koch and Giuliani administrations like Herbert Sturz and Michael Jacobson, ensured that those closest to *causing* the problem would be closest to *preventing* the solution.

Over the course of the campaign for skyscraper jails, radical challenges shook the project, but time and again the jail boosters responded by absorbing as much of the opposition as they could and by coding the new jails in ever more social justice dressing.

"The people of New York City . . . and the world have experienced enormous, ongoing upheaval since 2019," the New York City Department of Design and Construction wrote in the "principles and guidelines" documents for each of the four jails. Evoking the racialized class violence of the COVID-19 pandemic and the righteous uprising carried out in the name of George Floyd, the city situated the new jails as a response to the pressing social issues of the current moment:

> The City is facing both an unprecedented health crisis and an economic crisis. Both crises have sharpened the focus on the deep racial inequities in our country, a condition that the death of George Floyd in May 2020 further highlighted. Since 2014, the City has been working to meet and overcome the challenges of racial equity that these three intersecting issues distilled, and that are embedded in the criminal justice system. Our approach is centered on answering the following questions: "What does a fair and equitable criminal justice system look like" and "How do we deploy resources, beyond the criminal justice system, to keep all New Yorkers safe?"[100]

It had long been noted that little of the original plan extending "beyond the criminal justice system" had survived, most notably the community investment that the Lippman Commission suggested as the proverbial carrot alongside the stick of the new jails. And by 2023, under Eric Adams, city hall's answer to what *keeps all New Yorkers safe* would be a familiar refrain: law and order.

Beyond the professional carceral nonprofit milieu, the city council vote would not have been possible without the activism and militancy of countless people fighting racism, capitalism, and incarceration. It was produced by a moment characterized by the refusal of subjugation and a great awakening among an American population long written off by many on the left as apolitical, or even reactionary. Arriving in a moment of renewed courage, strength, and hope, the #CLOSErikers campaign, as Katal later acknowledged, "benefited extensively from a strong existing reform movement in New York City. From activists on the street to service providers and public defenders, from advocates to community organizers to impacted people in neighborhoods across the city demanding change—there was (and is) a robust reform ecosystem to work with."[101]

To this we must add, the #CLOSErikers campaign harnessed and reshaped this vibrant activism against the racist violence of mass incarceration toward the creation of skyscraper jails. In the process, these organizers outmaneuvered and foreclosed a more radical politics seeking to redress the problems of structural racism through the redistribution of wealth and power. Purporting to speak on behalf of some of the city's most powerless people, this cash-flush and politically connected campaign was money well spent for the funders in its orbit. The city government and financial elites who represent its unelected governors received a possible reprieve from a damaging legitimacy crisis and enjoyed, however temporarily, the posture of forward-thinking criminal justice reformers. Non-profiteers racked up their katals, adding lines to their resumes and accomplishments to their yearly statements to donors. Designers padded their portfolios. Academics added to their CVs. Construction firms got contracts. Financiers floated public loans. Developers reaped profits. Innovative neoliberals on the hazy borderlands between the public and private sectors built their power and influence. And everyone else got a continuation of the neoliberal status quo, plus skyscraper jails.

CHAPTER 3

"JUSTICE HUBS" BUILDING CARCERAL UTOPIANISM

And they said, Go to, let us build us a city and a tower, whose top may reach unto heaven; and let us make us a name, lest we be scattered abroad upon the face of the whole earth.

—**Genesis 11:4**

Jail booster Stanley Richards, deputy CEO of the Fortune Society, has publicly scolded opponents of the skyscraper jails to stop talking about their foreboding facades or their imposing heights as if these are somehow the jails' defining features. "Like so much in life," Richards writes, "it's really what's on the inside that matters."[1]

The most striking feature of the skyscraper jails' design is the degree to which these buildings have been represented by their boosters as anything but facilities for large-scale human caging. We are invited to consider them as good neighbors, sites of life opportunity, anchors for commerce, and centers of "civic unity." Even the word "jail" itself has been purged from much of the already scant references to skyscraper jails to be found in the jail booster literature. In a particularly impressive dodge, following their quiet exit from #CLOSErikers as it pivoted to supporting new jails, Katal outlined Phase Three of the campaign—"transformation of the entire system, with reforms necessary at the neighborhood, city, and state levels"—without naming the obvious *neighborhood transformation* of skyscraper jails.[2]

In the most systematic extrapolation of the new jails' design and guiding principles, a visual collaboration of the progressive architecture nonprofit Van Alen Institute and the Lippman Commission entitled *Justice in Design*, the jails are pictured as "justice hubs," multifaceted assets to any community lucky enough to receive one. The version of society offered by this brightly colored literature is akin to *The Busy World of Richard Scarry*, where a whimsical cast of characters negotiates daily life in an idyllic simulacrum of urban society as seen through the eyes of a child. Its representation of the skyscraper jails is worth examining in detail, as is the body of design scholarship that constitutes its troubling horizon. This chapter, therefore, takes a close look at these so-called justice hubs, as the jail boosters represent them.

We encourage the reader to pay particular attention to three recurrent and interrelated themes that have assisted us in making sense of the disorienting spectacle of skyscraper jails erected in the name of social justice. The first theme is *carceral humanism*, which, as abolitionist scholar James Kilgore warns us, "recasts the jailers as caring social service providers."[3] Recent scholarship has examined the pervasiveness of this trend.[4] Scholar Judah Schept has analyzed the carceral humanism of a prospective jail complex in Bloomington, Indiana, rebranded as a "justice campus" following a "hybrid welfare-carceral" model.[5] Carceral humanism is never far from the literature surrounding the skyscraper jails, as the justice hubs are depicted as "new community resources, woven into the fabric of neighborhoods to provide much-needed services and community facilities" to both the people locked inside them and the community outside.[6] Carceral facilities are thereby represented as dispensaries of needed services for communities in desperate need of state investment.

A second, and related, theme is *carceral citizenship*. Distinct from the citizenship status afforded to formally free people, argue scholars Reuben Jonathan Miller and Forrest Stuart, "carceral citizenship begins at the moment of a criminal conviction and is distinguished from other forms of citizenship by the restrictions, duties, and benefits uniquely accorded to carceral citizens, or to people with criminal records."[7] The result is a unique type of subjectivity in the eyes of the state, meant to inhabit a web of interconnected systems of surveillance and control. As we will see, the jail boosters have crafted a complex visualization of the overlapping social uses surrounding the justice hub. This demonstrates the exclusionary nature of carceral citizenship better than any theorization can.

The third, and most prominent, theme is what we call *carceral utopianism*. While this perspective might make obligatory gestures to state and civil institutions not functioning optimally—largely because of the vestigial racism held over from a less-enlightened epoch—carceral utopianism holds that these institutions can be corrected and made to work according to their stated intent of managing and reproducing an equitable democratic order for the benefit of all. Carceral utopians need not dispute a single sentence of *The New Jim Crow*; in fact, such critiques have now become an important part of how punishment is reconfigured in the name of social justice. At the same time, carceral utopianism casts social institutions like police, courts, and carceral facilities as politically neutral, simply a set of tools among many that a society uses to improve itself. Echoing a pet theme of the Vera Institute, #CLOSErikers called for the "reimagining" of the city's punishment system, as if the task at hand was a question of architectural innovation versus entrenched political forces keeping things the way they are.[8]

At its worst, such reimagining is simply rebranding. At best, carceral utopianism refuses to consider the inherent class interests guiding policing and punitive policy, and is equally silent on the powerful political blocs these institutions have created, such as police and guard unions. Insisting that these institutions are broken, carceral utopians never consider that they just might be functioning exactly as they're supposed to. Instead, they argue that the legitimacy of carceral institutions must be restored, and with it the legitimacy of the society in which they play such an essential part.

JUSTICE IN DESIGN?

The most concrete representation of the justice hubs, the Lippman Commission's rebranded jails, comes from the report that gave them their memorable appellation, *Justice in Design*, a collaboration with the progressive architecture nonprofit the Van Alen Institute. The project's process involved focus groups and tours of local jails, capped off by a contest for the best jail design, which solicited images of the new jails for which the project is now famous. The very public-private nature of *Justice in Design*, argues design scholar Katie Wilson, is mirrored by its vision for urban transformation, bridging as it does the ideology of public-sector progressivism with the real estate marketing imperatives that dominate New York City politics in the twenty-first century. After all, ground floor space for retail is a prominent component of the plan, neoliberal politicians and developers lurk in the wings of any discussion of the new jails, and much of the campaign for skyscraper jails was itself an extended commercial advertisement.[9] In this context, Wilson continues, "it's not surprising that traditionally undesirable spaces of administrative necessity, like the jail, would be next in line to tumble through the spin-cycle of urban commodification."[10]

Setting aside the obvious material interests—a real estate bonanza for the designers and developers of billion-dollar skyscraper jails and increased funding for the carceral nonprofits and other profiteers clinging like barnacles to this massive public investment—what are the proponents of these new jails actually imagining they will get for this great investment?

"A complex set of problems with overlapping histories and difficulties has produced a crisis in jails," write the authors of *Justice in Design*. "In order to move forward, there will need to be significant efforts in several areas: political, public, programmatic, and economic. In each of these areas, we must continue to foreground the overarching idea that jails are at their foundation civic institutions that define who we are as a society."[11] The authors of this remarkable text are keenly aware of both the crisis around Rikers and the broader crisis of legitimacy engulfing the punishment system in the United States, and, hence, its very social order. Their response is to fight for the legitimacy of the jail in American society and to actually expand its centrality in the social fabric.

Justice in Design, therefore, represents a radical penal philosophy, which argues for the justice hubs to assume a cohesive role in communal life. Its design team defines these facilities, determined to leave no buzzword behind:

Justice Hubs are facilities that create healthy, normative environments and support rehabilitation for incarcerated or detained individuals, while simultaneously providing neighborhoods with new public amenities. These facilities take into account the context of surrounding communities. The guidelines offer **resources for all neighborhood residents**, reducing the fear and stigma surrounding jails while providing **shared amenities**, such as community gardens, art studios, exercise facilities, medical clinics, and social services. Calling for **on-site programs** such as job training centers, community courts, a police department, and probation offices, the guidelines position Justice Hubs as public **sites of civic unity** with integrated routes for detainees to return to life in the city, restoring dignity to people who are incarcerated while making the criminal justice system more **visible, accountable, and responsive.**[12]

Later in the text, the authors insist that the jails must be "perceived as part of the culture and integral to the community."[13] As prudent scholars, we hesitate to call this plan "fascist," but nonetheless note that it seeks to craft a strong and cohesive civic identity through the reconciliation of private capital with a unified public interest, anchored in towering monuments to the might and benevolence of the security state.

The sentiment that jails ought to be central institutions of social reproduction in New York City neighborhoods recurs throughout the jail booster literature and is one of the defining features of the skyscraper jail campaign. The original Lippman report suggests that the jails should house "community meetings or public services like a library, a job training center, classrooms, as well as commercial and retail businesses."[14] The Department of Design and Construction design and planning guidelines for the new jails proclaims, "No longer isolated and out of sight, these new jails must be understood as significant civic institutions, as much a part of the city's life as libraries, fire houses, and schools."[15] A slideshow later circulated by city hall to promote the skyscraper jails attempts to leverage this ideology against public outcry over their prospective height, imagining the public to consider the new jails as a "civic presence on the skyline."[16] And *Justice in Design* argues that their proposed justice hub "cultivates positive civic identity and understanding."[17] Wilson dubs this argument "carceral intimacy," a refutation of the idea that jails are bad neighbors to residents and businesses, packaged with the civic ideology that affirms the rightful place of jails at the center of communities.[18]

Despite these social justice trappings, there is of course nothing radical or even progressive about the idea that communities ought to revolve around incarceration. This has long been the de facto state policy in working-class communities, especially communities of color, in the United States. It is a trend that was significantly amplified in New York City and across the United States in the last five decades. Carceral utopianism grants all this, of course, but counters that these institutions have not been functioning properly, and to make them do so would be to realize social justice.

COURT INNOVATION

A central part of the justice hub is its location in close proximity to a criminal court. The jail boosters' design hinges significantly on a utopian conception of the role of courts in New York City social life. Frank Greene, a veteran "justice [carceral] architect" of the firm Ricci Greene Associates, an experienced prison and jail design firm presently working on the skyscraper jails, has expressed his belief that America is in a promising new moment of realizing the humanist potential of its courts.

> Many things that weren't considered concerns of the justice system, now are. Many urban courts feel that the majority of people who walk through their doors every morning have great needs. And the courts' posture now—and old buildings make it really difficult to achieve this—is, "How can we meet your needs?" It's really

customer-oriented from the judges all the way down to the clerk staff and the social service agencies and community partners that are employed to help serve those needs. Many things that weren't considered concerns of the justice system, now are.

This hellish conflation of customer service jargon with carceral humanism represents a further degree of subsumption of public infrastructure into the private sector than perhaps even James Kilgore could foresee when he coined the term *carceral humanism.*

Echoing more familiar themes, Greene continues by characterizing courts as "a social safety net" that "have realized that if they can catch [!] people in a compassionate, humane, helpful way, then these people can go on and have productive and rewarding lives." Greene's partner, Kenneth Ricci, for his part even looks back fondly on the "local courthouses" of New York's past, especially the Jefferson Market Prison in Greenwich Village. These courthouses, Ricci imagines, "brought justice closer to the citizens, both physically and psychically."[19]

This is a nice thought. In real-life New York City, however, the Jefferson Market Prison was a barbaric institution, where poor women were held in squalid, dungeon-like conditions. The jail was known for housing sex workers at the bottom tier of that labor market, "$2-a-trick girls" in the indelicate words of one journalist, alongside women accused of petty theft.[20] A 1921 report from the New York Probation and Protective Association found that justice was brought *physically and psychically* to women as young as fourteen via "dark unsanitary cells" that were regularly overfilled, as prisoners suffering from widespread communicable illnesses received nothing in the way of privacy, sanitation, or even flushing toilets. The court itself was a parasite on working-class New York, criminalizing the survival mechanisms women adopted in the harsh tenement environments where they lived. Its proceedings degraded and brutalized women for engaging in sex work while offering no serious remedies for the myriad social problems quarantined in its jail. All these women got was further exploitation in the form of fines, or else more incarceration in one or another putrid facility guaranteed to simply make their lives worse.[21]

The Jefferson Market Prison is not an isolated case; there's plenty of more recent evidence that structuring the social life of a community around a jail would in fact be terrible for many people in it. Four decades ago, legal scholar Malcolm Feeley set out to study the specific role and function of lower criminal courts and shed broader light on the nature of the punishment system itself. "Next to the police," he wrote, "the lower criminal courts play the most important role in forming citizen impressions of the American system of criminal justice."[22] Observing a lower criminal court in New Haven, Connecticut, Feeley found that defendants are subjected to a variety of humiliating and perplexing rituals amid proceedings that drag out interminably, wasting the accused's time during hours when they are likely supposed to be at school or work. The result is nothing but punishment, which comes less from the case's outcome than from the process itself; Feeley titled his study *The Process Is the Punishment*.[23] Not much has changed since Feeley's study, which applies neatly to New York City, then and now. But the crisis of legitimacy that envelops courts from time to time has prompted important reform efforts to restore the public's faith in the system, including the decentralization of criminal courts and the advent of the community court model.

The community court movement began when the first such court opened in 1993 near the Times Square area on the West Side of Manhattan. Today about thirty community courts exist throughout the United States.[24] The Midtown Community

Court (MCC) was established in 1993, a collaboration between the New York State Unified Court System and its private research and development arm, the Center for Court Innovation. Befitting the carceral humanist imperative to repackage criminal justice institutions, MCC was renamed Midtown Community Justice Center (MCJC) in 2023. The court was built as a solution to the widespread discontent among business and real estate leaders with petty crimes in the Times Square area. As the NYPD began to crack down on these so-called offenses, the Manhattan Criminal Court proved incapable of dealing with such a high volume of cases. MCJC helped the police keep the arrests coming, while integrating so-called social service providers into proceedings, encouraging punitive sanctions that are enveloped in a rhetoric of care and help. Most importantly, community courts operate within the logic of broken windows policing, which advocates for dealing effectively with minor-level crime to deter more substantial criminal activity and build legitimacy for the criminal justice system.[25] According to Greg Berman, founder and director of the Center for Justice Innovation, the community court model, with its individualized approach to cases, represents an alternative to the run-down and flawed existing criminal courts, and supposedly inspires public confidence in the criminal justice system, especially in poor Black and Latinx neighborhoods.[26]

Unlike a centralized criminal courtroom, community courts intervene more effectively into the life of a defendant, relying on the collaboration of criminal justice actors and social service providers, usually nonprofits, to ensure that defendants follow their court mandate, usually in the form of community service or unpaid work to various city agencies. Critical scholars call this process "net widening," whereby innovations like community courts and alternatives to incarceration expand the carceral net by bringing more people into the criminal justice system.[27]

While the community court model is heralded as an innovative step in reform circles, little is said about the ways it has helped to redevelop Times Square by essentially criminalizing and arresting panhandlers, people without housing, sex workers, and others seen as undesirable by retail companies and real estate moguls that make up the business improvement districts. The MCJC has closely cooperated with the Times Square Alliance and has helped to gentrify the area into a dizzying, corporate Disneyland. It is not unusual to see mostly Black and Latinx men in uniform picking up trash the tourists leave behind, an integral part of their "community service." The community court model has solidified the necessity of public-private partnerships like the Center for Justice Innovation, which worked behind the scenes to staff the Lippman Commission, producing laudatory reports and giving it further legitimacy in city reform circles.[28]

But community courts are just one expression of the ways in which the crisis of legitimacy is making itself evident, spurring a whole slew of reforms to the organization of courts around the country. For example, the death of Michael Brown and the protests that erupted in Ferguson and across America revealed that Ferguson residents were hemmed in at all sides by the city's municipal court. A DOJ investigation into Ferguson's municipal court found not only "substantive evidence of racial bias among police and court staff" but also that 23 percent of the city's revenue was coming from the fines and fees imposed by the courts.[29] As the city's main cash cow, the municipal court made its revenues by targeting and criminalizing Black residents.

In response, legal scholars have sought to *reimagine* the future of municipal courts. For example, scholar Alexandra Natapoff argues that municipal courts "are central to the larger criminal justice governance project" because of their "regulatory" nature that oversees a large portion of criminal case dockets.[30] While its localism and informality can be a recipe for disaster, as it was in Ferguson, Natapoff argues that municipal courts can nonetheless be reformed into institutions of "local accountability."[31] In a critique of Natapoff, lawyer and scholar Brendan Roediger argues that municipal courts were an outcome of Progressive Era reforms that sought to manage poverty more effectively, and today, they are a way to expand police power by punishing those who violate city ordinances. Municipal courts, Roediger argues, ultimately exist to maintain the racial and class order of our society and should be abolished, not reformed.[32] Unfortunately, Natapoff's views remain the dominant ideology. Today, the facade of "community" and "local accountability" fuels the design of new coercive institutions to take the place of the old, discredited ones. This is precisely what the *Justice in Design* project did—even as its proposal reads an awful lot like it came straight from the drafting boards of Ricci Greene, and all community input amounted to little more than window dressing.

PARTICIPATORY ACTION

According to the jail boosters, the ideology guiding the skyscraper jails, and their attendant design, did not simply emanate from above. To this end, the *Justice in Design* project, justice hubs and all, was purportedly crafted in community-based workshops, where a diverse swath of everyday New Yorkers—"formerly detained and incarcerated people, families, correction officers, staff, and interested members of the community"—were invited to brainstorm "how the experience of jail could be better."[33] In the appendix of the report, the authors reveal that this amounted to a total of ninety-three people stretched across three workshops. Participants appear to have been largely mobilized by a handful of carceral nonprofits in the orbit of the jail boosters, including social service providers like the Osborne Association and the Fortune Society, and, of course, JustLeadershipUSA. This background likely made the participants ideologically predisposed to supporting the borough-based jails and recognizing the legitimacy of the jail boosters, which, as we will see, was a precondition for taking part in the project.[34]

On the off chance that any participating community members or designers were not already supportive of the skyscraper jail project, or of the broader mission of carceral utopianism, the entire *Justice in Design* project was framed around the following questions:

1. How can we create jail designs that are more healthy, rehabilitative, and respectful?
2. What impact does jail have on the community, and how can a decentralized jail system improve these negative effects?
3. What social services and programming can be included to help people reenter communities?
4. What site elements are important to include in the design of community-based jails?
5. What types of neighborhood services can be offered to complement a community?[35]

According to these parameters, it is not up for debate whether jail design can be improved to make facilities "healthy, rehabilitative, and respectful." The answer is yes. More to the point, the open-ended question of *what impact does jail have on the community*, which itself would be a worthwhile topic to explore in depth among this supposed representative cross section of New Yorkers, is foreclosed, no sooner than it is raised, by the assertion that the borough-based jails will be a solution to these problems. These parameters additionally force participants to take for granted that a jail can be a complementary presence in a community, making it better than before. The only serious question left is how to build them.

Tellingly, the report notes that a persistent theme raised by formerly incarcerated participants—that "oppressive and racially discriminatory policing in their neighborhood" resulted in their arrest and jail incarceration in the first place—was *omitted from discussion of the new jails* and relegated to a perfunctory footnote, since it fell outside the project's scope.[36]

Justice in Design does not stand alone. Design scholar Shana Agid points out the remarkable similarity between *Justice in Design* and another recent project in carceral utopianism, the Polis Station project, designed by the architectural firm Studio Gang to replace the existing police station in Chicago's Tenth District, on the city's west side.[37] Like the justice hubs, Polis Station was formulated in response to the crisis of legitimacy surrounding US police, courts, and incarceration in the post-Ferguson era. It was proposed to be built a little more than a mile away from Homan Square, a converted Sears warehouse that drew national attention in 2015 when a journalist published a series of articles uncovering its use as as a secret detention center, or "black site," where Chicago cops interrogated and detained thousands of Black Chicagoans without the knowledge of their lawyers, their families, or the general public.[38] A year later, Black Lives Matter protesters occupied its parking lot, renamed it Freedom Square, and demanded the site be shut down and the money reinvested in surrounding communities.[39]

Meanwhile, the 2015 Polis Station project had attempted to whitewash the brutal violence of everyday policing that surrounds Chicago's Black and Latinx neighborhoods by inviting residents to reimagine their community, with a sprawling new police station running through the center of it. As in *Justice in Design*, Studio Gang interfaced with purported "community leaders" and organized meetings of locals in a community hit particularly hard by mass incarceration, North Lawndale. Participants were provided with similarly narrow questions to frame their input: "What would a police station look like as a mixed-use facility?"; "If the community designed a police station, what would it look like?"; and "How does the station contribute to police and community relationships?"[40]

Departing from premises similar to those of *Justice in Design*, Studio Gang arrived at similar conclusions. In the plan for Polis Station, presented at the 2015 Chicago Architecture Biennial, the firm proposed "police stations be reoriented toward their communities and become sites of social connection where officers and neighborhood residents can find many opportunities to interact," including the extension of police station space to surrounding public space like schools, parks, and sports fields, and for their use for social purposes like day care, event promotion, and the provision of free internet access. Police stations can thereby become "full-service community centers that improve public safety, enhance social cohesion, and strengthen the economy of the surrounding neighborhood."[41] Carceral humanism and carceral utopianism appear on full display, embodied in the project's very name "Polis," a reference to the Greek city-state. Again, we see the police-state notion that "civic unity," as *Justice in Design* put it, comes to communities through carceral infrastructure.

While both projects purported to neutrally reflect the wishes of community members, there was, of course, clear political framing in advance, delineating what was possible and what was not. Both projects proceeded from the premise that cops and jails, respectively, *ought* to be central to social life and were effectively public goods that at present are being misused, or worse yet, misunderstood by the public. The Polis Station project originated in protests against systemic racism and human disposability at the hands of US police. But rather than pursue the line of thought that the US police deserve their hard-won illegitimacy in the eyes of the communities they brutalize and degrade, Studio Gang instead followed an unfortunate number of police reformers (and cops) by turning the formulation on its head and arguing that the problems with policing in the United States stem from their lack of legitimacy in the eyes of the public.

"The Justice Hub proposal builds specifically on this idea," writes Agid. "The Commission proposes that 'forging stronger bonds' between enforcement agencies like courts, police, prosecutors, and probation, and 'local residents,' has been a cornerstone of 'criminal justice reform,'" laying responsibility for fixing the evils of Rikers at the feet of people who are rightfully distrustful of the system.[42] In this view, communities' lack of faith in the police is seen as more socially corrosive than the actions that precipitated it, and this is the problem that ultimately must be solved. As a result, Agid concludes, in both instances, "increased discourse in public-interest design about the violence of policing and incarceration and the structures of the carceral state has led to design proposals for enhanced spaces to both police and cage people."[43] This is not a flaw of projects like *Justice in Design* and Polis Station. It is their *central* feature.

"INTERIOR SPACES FOR LIVING AND WORKING"

But what of the actual plan for the justice hubs? While the designers make a great show of participatory research with directly impacted stakeholders, what they came up with was largely in keeping with the current trends in carceral architecture, coupled with the exigencies of building a skyscraper jail.[44] Some of the designers' insights have been represented as unique and profound by prison architects for centuries, such as, "all interior spaces will benefit from greater access to natural light, air, and outdoor spaces for activities and views."[45] Others give us a glimpse into the chic theories of optimal human caging that animate contemporary discussions of prison reform.

Unsurprisingly the plan favors a "direct supervision" layout in self-contained, two-story mini-jails stacked on top of each other. "Direct supervision" has been a pet model of progressive jail architects since the 1970s.[46] It calls for "a residential plan that stations a correction officer within the living area, with cells arranged around a dayroom with clear sight lines, to visually observe and maintain personal, one-on-one relationships with people being detained."[47] "You're trying to create normal behaviors," explains skyscraper jail architect Frank Greene. "The officer is able to monitor who's saying what to whom and what's going on. If you take that officer and you put them in a glass bubble, or even worse, if they're just looking through a little window and they can't fully hear what's going on, they can't see everything, then among the detainees it becomes a pyramid of who's strongest, toughest, meanest, most connected."[48]

Greene's belief is that inserting the guards into the social life of the dormitory will engineer the opposite effect. However, as the Program, a violent collaboration between guards and ruling prisoners, has revealed, NYC guards already play a vital role in the social lives of prisoners, promoting "a pyramid of who's strongest, toughest, meanest, most connected," with themselves at the top.[49] Moreover, direct supervision is also not new to the Department of Correction; it has been in effect for decades at the Tombs in Manhattan, where violence often rivals that at Rikers Island.[50]

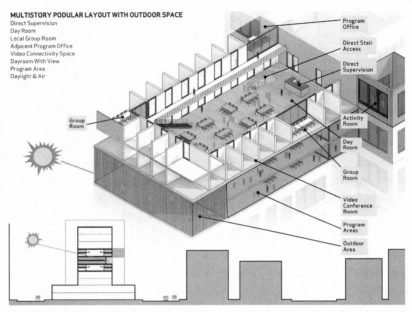

This rendering of a skyscraper jail, the only honest assessment of the facilities' height to be found in *Justice in Design*, sheds some (improbable) light, alongside much shadow. (Dan Gallagher et al., *Justice in Design: Toward a Healthier and More Just New York City Jail System* [New York: Van Alen Institute and the Independent Commission for New York City Criminal Justice and Incarceration Reform, 2017], 21.)

Jail boosters are quick to point out that the skyscraper jails will ultimately consist of a series of miniature jails, two stories each, stacked on top of each other. The designers celebrate this centralized exercise in "minimizing the need for complicated circulation between residential, outdoor, and exercise areas within the larger facility," which ultimately means prisoners will spend most of their time in the same minuscule indoor space. While the boosters attempt to dress this tight foreclosure of prisoner mobility in penological niceties, *Justice in Design* ultimately concedes that it is a necessity of building vertically: "Given the verticality of New York buildings, interconnecting adjacent floors will create useful connections between living and program spaces. By creating sectional adjacencies with access via stairs it reduces the need for time-consuming elevator travel."[51]

The seemingly trivial point of elevator use cannot be understated in facilities with the need for elaborate daily transportation of a population deemed a security risk. This issue becomes particularly urgent when we consider coordinating the use of the comparatively minuscule space on the buildings' roofs, which will presumably be the prisoners' only place to go outside at all. Board of Correction member Robert Cohen anticipated that the jails would need to rely on elevators that would "fail chronically."[52] A civilian veteran of the jail system, Cohen is likely aware of the many logistical problems facing vertical jails far shorter than the proposed skyscraper facilities. When the Women's House of Detention in Greenwich Village was engulfed in scandal in the 1960s due to widespread squalor, overcrowding, and prisoner abuse by the staff, the Department of Correction blamed much of the building's woes on the building's height. DOC commissioner Anna Kross called the building a "vertical monstrosity" and welcomed the opening of the Rikers Island Bridge as an opportunity to "eliminate the skyscraper type jail design that we inherited" from previous administrations and to construct "horizontal" facilities more amenable to intra-facility prisoner mobility and programming to fill the day.[53] Of course, the problems of the vertical facilities soon recurred on the horizontal ones—and here we go again.

The *Justice in Design* project is also forced to grapple with the stubborn existence of the skyscraper jails that already exist in New York City, especially the Brooklyn House of Detention. "The marble facade hides what the building really is," observes one community participant. "Jail is hidden by street-level architecture," remarks another, "it serves the desire of the community for the jail to be hidden." These comments are presented by *Justice in Design* as if they do not double as a strong rebuke of the boutique retail presence touted in the new jail design.

Curiously, the report also claims that the absence of direct lines of sight into present jails, available to civilians on the outside, are responsible for enabling brutal conditions inside. This raises a host of privacy issues for prisoners, especially: Are they to live in fishbowls casually accessible to outside voyeurs? But this is not a serious claim. It is instead a flippant dismissal of the real political challenges of holding DOC guards accountable for violence, invoking instead the unrealistic prospect that civilian witnesses will somehow be able to document and redress abuses glimpsed through skyscraper jail windows. In short, the boosters have tried to use the jails' biggest political weakness—their presence in the coveted New York City skyline—to improbably argue that eliminating "the sharp boundary between the jail and the community," by building skyscraper jails in crowded downtown areas, will help solve the violence of incarceration.[54]

But the most inexcusable instance of the bad faith at the heart of *Justice in Design* is not buried in a convoluted logical word game, but blatantly splashed across dozens of pages in the report's visualization of the skyscraper jails themselves. Time and again, the justice hub is depicted as four or five unimposing stories tall (concealing within them doubled floors, only discernible to the careful eye, amounting to around ten stories total). Only in one instance is the hub visualized as a proper skyscraper at all. And even then, the skyscraper jail appears as a small colorless rendering in the bottom corner of a much larger and more colorful design. It stands only twenty stories tall, significantly shorter than the proposed jails. It is also depicted in harmony with a surrounding landscape that conveniently boasts large open spaces all around the hub, to facilitate improbable sunshine on the lower floors.

To support the report's claims of open space, ample programming areas, abundant resources for staff, and the ubiquitous invocations of sunlight, roughly thirty-five cells are pictured in the two stories of the jail depicted. The result is a warm and spacious interior that looks a whole lot like the chic open-concept offices where people draft these kinds of reports. The designers' guiding ideology is given a prominent boost by this visual, designed to be viewed by people who will likely not read the fine print. But in the real world, in order to accommodate the 1,500-prisoner population specified by the Lippman Commission within the cellblocks of this layout, the city would need around eighty-five stories for prisoner housing alone, plus dozens more for programming space, without even factoring in the plans for retail space on the ground floor—making this modest community hub roughly the height of the Empire State Building.[55]

The designers of the justice hubs also practice deft Orwellian gymnastics in defining their own relationship to the ethics guiding their field. In an appendix to *Justice in Design* entitled "Values," the authors outline the humanistic underpinnings of their jail design philosophy—inclusivity, health and well-being, reduced violence, care, respectfulness, and so forth—which, they argue, places the project in full alignment with the NYC Department of Design and Construction's "Design and Construction Excellence 2.0 Principles" of "equity, sustainability, resilience, and design for healthy living." They even situate their work as fulfilling a proposed amendment for the ethics code guiding membership in the American Institute of Architects: "Members shall not design spaces intended for execution or for torture or other cruel, inhuman, or degrading treatment or punishment, including prolonged solitary confinement."[56] Of course the skyscraper jails, if built, will

almost certainly prove, like all New York City carceral spaces before them, to in fact be sites of cruel and unusual punishment
tantamount to torture. It is sadly predictable that, echoing these
same principles, the jail boosters of tomorrow will simply respond
with the demand for newer, better facilities to take their place.
Regardless, we can only hope that tomorrow's cage builders have a
far more difficult time finding anyone to listen to them.

A DAY IN THE LIFE OF A CARCERAL UTOPIA

The most striking feature of *Justice in Design* is its presentation; it
is a document attuned to the highly visual nature of contemporary information consumption. While few New Yorkers will ever
sit down and read the report itself, much less the more text-heavy
documents coming out of the Lippman Commission, these colorful visuals were destined to make the rounds in the local press and
constitute the only publicly available images of what kind of figure
the skyscraper jails would cut in city life.

"From its contents and scope," writes design scholar Leah
Meisterlin, "*Justice in Design* appears to serve a singular purpose:
translating the Lippman recommendations for a wider public
through the schematic illustration of a county jail within a 'pro-
totypical urban context.' Without question, this purpose was an
interesting exercise in architectural illustration and visual communication." Meisterlin argues that the findings of the Lippman
report, and its underlying politics, would not be abundantly clear
to a lay reader, who might experience "frustration trying to connect one chapter to another." Therefore, Meisterlin concludes,
Justice in Design represents an important intervention in "commu-
nicating those findings to a broad audience of potentially affected
communities" and, we would add, in arguing for their correctness,
using largely visual language.[57]

In these two recurring representations, the "justice hubs" appear quite unimposing. (Gallagher et al., *Justice in Design*, 28–29).

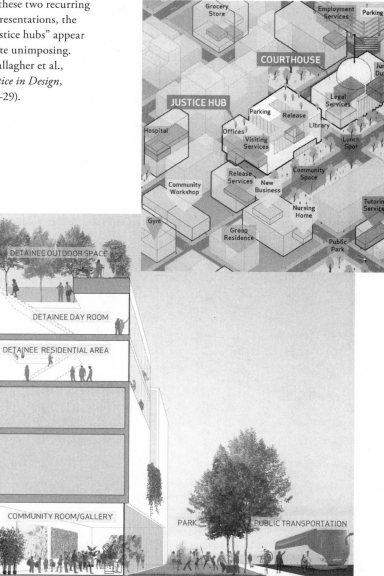

The central ideological work of the project's design comes in a graphic spread taking up eleven of its sixty-one pages and accounting for much of its generous helping of colored ink. It depicts the intersecting uses that people in different social positions can make of the urban terrain anchored by the justice hub. The first visualization depicts the justice hub as the central location of a landscape stratified with civic, commercial, residential, and, of course, punitive facilities, easily accessible by public transit and otherwise enviably walkable. These include a grocery store, a hospital, a nursing home, a gym, an employment center, a day care center, a small correction academy, and ample green space. It is a vision of social life with the justice hub and courthouse at the center, appearing quite unimposing in their stature as they hold the community together.

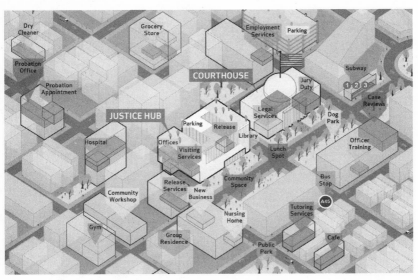

The justice hub at the center of this image, we are told, is a site of civic and commercial unity. It is surrounded by labels like "grocery store," "lunch spot," and "gym." (Gallagher et al., *Justice in Design*, 29.)

The second visualization, entitled "City People/Diverse Narratives," depicts a "diversity of people" inhabiting this terrain, rendered in a flourish of pixelated eight-bit nostalgia. Some of the characters are familiar to the carceral landscape: a lawyer enjoys an easy commute; a guard invites colleagues to a nearby deli; a newly released detainee celebrates being able to "get things moving in a good direction"; the family of a detainee plans a "good day for us and our loved ones"; and a current detainee appreciates how their detention "is going to help [them] stay connected and get [them] ready for [their] next steps." Meanwhile, a teacher, a student, and a community member enjoy "so many opportunities" afforded by this urban space. So many figures of "civic unity." But what are these opportunities, and whom are they for?

This question is partially answered as a business owner benefits from increased foot traffic; a "local artist" (read: gentrifier) takes advantage of "working space in a happening neighborhood"; an architect spouts the familiar developer jargon of "growing communities, new buildings, new ideas;" a "community advocate" dressed suspiciously like a high-end real estate agent gushes, "Being part of a diverse place is the reason why I live in New York City"; and an odd figure simply labeled "friend" (read: gentrifier) announces, "Psyched to be able to check out the new neighborhood, what do you think?" Meanwhile, a child simply wants a "FroYo," slang for a frozen yogurt.

These figures, interspersed with the civic ideology of the previous set, clearly signal the opportunities for capital accumulation and gentrification promised by the skyscraper jails.[58] Echoing a popular sentiment during the environmental review period, Olivia Ahn of Brooklyn, a volunteer provider of doula and yoga services at the Rose M. Singer Center on Rikers Island, called the new jail plan "gentrified incarceration at large."[59]

CITY PEOPLE / DIVERSE NARRATIVES

Communities are defined by a diversity of people utilizing an array of places and programs in the City. The location, programming and services provided at a Justice Hub will benefit detainees, their families, jail staff and the broader community.

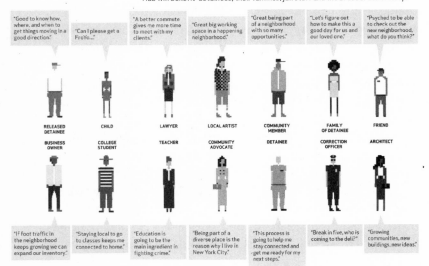

The Busy World of Jonathan Lippman. (Gallagher et al., *Justice in Design*, 30.)

"Can I please get a FroYo...."

CHILD

This child simply wants a frozen yogurt. Does this require a skyscraper jail? (Gallagher et al., *Justice in Design*, 30.)

The most elaborate exposition of the justice hubs' urban imagination comes through customized maps that follow key figures in their "diversity" of interactions with this carceral landscape. Entitled *A Day in the Life*, this series colorfully illustrates the intertwined daily routines of detainee, guard, community member, family of detainee, lawyer, and, of course, business owner, in the thriving community anchored by the justice hub.

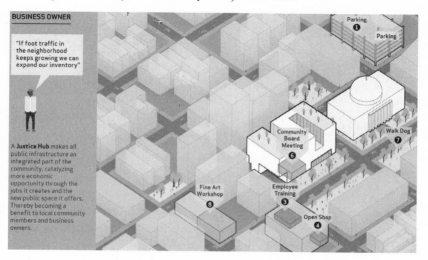

Does "open shop" mean what we think it does? (Gallagher et al., *Justice in Design*, 35.)

Predictably enough, the incarcerated detainee, a carceral citizen with few options, doesn't get very far. Their full spectrum of motion is limited to the justice hub and adjacent court. Their visiting family, carceral citizens by association, can arrive on the subway, enjoy library services within the jail along with their visit, and patronize day care, legal services, and youth and family services facilities, on top of a little shopping and some dinner at the end of their day in the shadow of the justice hub. Meanwhile, the guard overseeing their loved one's captivity is able to enjoy their lunch in a nearby park, catch up on some training in a nearby academy, and either grab some dinner or grocery shop on the way home.

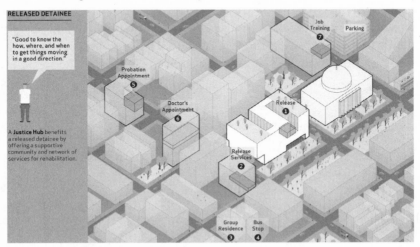

A harsh reality. (Gallagher et al., *Justice in Design*, 37.)

The so-called community member is able to attend a community meeting in the jail, and in addition can access civilian health services, employment and business opportunities, day care, and mail services, all of which are somehow contingent on the erection of a jail in the center of their locality. Interestingly enough, the community member, depicted with light brown skin, does not shop or dine anywhere. This could be an innocent omission. But given how the buzzword "community" has become synonymous with the pregentrification inhabitants of New York's neighborhoods of color, this could be an accidental admission that the spaces of consumption opened up around the justice hub will simply be outside of the means of the average citizen of Chinatown or the South Bronx. By contrast, the darker-skinned business owner benefits from day care, a fine arts workshop, dog walking, and a parking garage—strongly indicating they live elsewhere.

The most interesting character in this story is the "released detainee," a carceral citizen turned loose into the free world. Technically, at least, this is a free person. For the released detainee, however, the terrain surrounding the justice hub is harsh and restrictive. Release services, a probation office, job training, a group home, and a single bus stop (distinct from the subway the other characters ride) characterize the released detainee's sole horizon. No shopping, no dinner, no arts, no enjoyment of public space, only the austere life of a second-class citizen. It is difficult not to conclude that this is meant to appeal to the would-be business owners in the area, arguing that the ostensibly rehabilitated former denizens of the justice hub will not be showcasing their newly honed civic graces in local establishments. On the section's final page, which visualizes the crisscrossing trajectories of justice hub consumers throughout the city, the released detainee is the only character missing altogether. Don't worry, this omission seems to assure the reader, they won't cross your path.[60]

This is, of course, a terribly reductive treatment of social life surrounding four jails slated for construction in four extremely different areas of the city. Surely its designers will claim that we are reading far too much into their little mock-ups. But this simplicity is actually the problem. As design critic Leah Meisterlin argues, "The complexity of an urbanism replete with diverse experiences is annulled by a compressed, frame-by-frame [*Day in the Life*] narrative that negates known differences, conflicts, and competitions between individuals and communities through their equivalent, atemporal, and separated representations."[61] It would be easier to believe that this was all an innocent mistake if these omissions did not significantly bolster the jail boosters' cause.

It is also interesting that the *Day in the Life* series doesn't even bother making overtures to the "community member," who is depicted as living an austere life removed from this new reality, as the buzzards of gentrification circle. More attention is paid to marketing the jails to the local petty bourgeoisie. "By reconnecting jails to the urban context," *Justice in Design* argues in impeccable corporate-speak, "existing businesses can be leveraged to serve a broader group of people."[62] This balance of social justice rhetoric and appeals to property values and boutique urbanism represents the plan's attempt, in the words of design critic Katie Wilson, "to appeal to both a class of urban neoliberals and to the masses who identified and rallied against the crises in New York's criminal justice system."[63]

The stridency of activism in one neighborhood in particular, Chinatown, did produce an effort to placate the locals. It demonstrates at once the city's concern with anti-jail activism and its condescension to the idea that the community ought to have any input at all. A key Department of Design and Construction document implored that the Chinatown jail architects "consider ways to complement the neighborhood cultural traditions in design."[64] Today, we may glimpse one version of what this means in a city-commissioned mock-up of the Chinatown jail. In it, the prospective skyscraper is depicted as an ordinary facility, indistinguishable from the surrounding municipal buildings except for one detail: the jail is adorned with a large red sculpture of a dragon, red awnings, and red banners painted with the stylized characters 文化. This inscription recurs in plain text scrawled atop the jail's entrance, alongside its English translation: "CULTURE." Curiously, none of the other borough plans include the consideration that their destination neighborhood has a cultural tradition. And, of course, this rendering of the Chinatown jail is strategically cut off at the point where it would clearly become a skyscraper.[65]

The 文化 industry. (New York City Office of the Mayor, *Beyond Rikers, Towards a Borough-Based System [Confidential]*, 2018, 35.)

One final aspect of the *Justice in Design* document speaks to the jail boosters' increasingly simplistic viewpoint, as their plan progressed through the sausage factory of municipal bureaucracy and many of its social justice components—like community reinvestment and decriminalization—were trimmed away to clear the way for more or less orthodox jails that may or may not replace Rikers. *Justice in Design*, Meisterlin argues, grossly simplifies the spatial problems posed by the Rikers Island penal colony. The report sets aside "the tangled and varied criminal justice system involving policing, arrest discrepancies, bail practices, detention, legal representation, incarceration, and probation that choke our courts and our communities in daily routines and annual cycles"—which the Lippman report, to its credit, did not shy away from—and presents instead a simple image of the "Rikers Knot."[66]

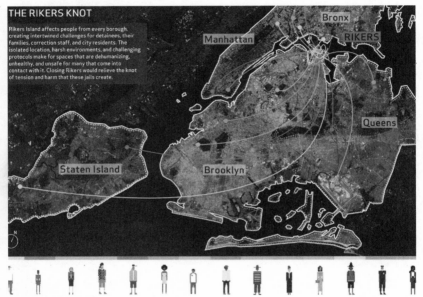

"The Rikers Knot" awaits its Alexander. (Gallagher et al., *Justice in Design*, 11.)

In the Rikers Knot, the city is rendered as a monochrome satellite image, with Rikers as the remote terminus of prisoners sent from central locations in each borough. This supply chain is depicted as multicolored lines converging in a frantic tangle. Alongside the image, the authors write, "The isolated location, harsh environments, and challenging protocols make for spaces that are dehumanizing, unhealthy, and unsafe for many that come into contact with it [*sic*]. Closing Rikers would relieve the knot of tension and harm that these jails create."[67] In a second rendering, Meisterlin writes, the justice hubs save the day, as "the knot of confusion, chaos, and constrained collection is rendered effortlessly resolved, a drawing that vaguely points to neighborhoods where new jail facilities are suggested within a flat, undifferentiated, neutral city."[68]

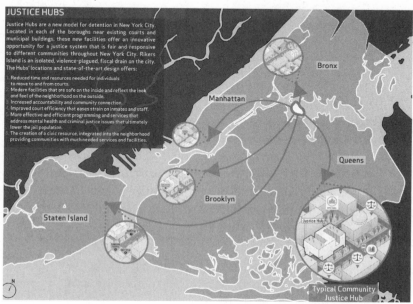

Voilà! (Gallagher et al., *Justice in Design*, 27.)

This neat and decisive untangling of the Rikers Knot calls to mind the words of the immortal Bard:

Turn him to any cause of policy,
The Gordian knot of it he will unloose,
Familiar as his garter.[69]

We are further reminded of an early version of the legend of the Gordian Knot, recounted by the Greek historian Arrian of Nicomedia (86–ca. 160 CE): "Alexander could find out no way to loosen the cord and yet was unwilling to allow it to remain unloosened, lest it should exercise some disturbing influence upon the multitude, he struck the cord with his sword and cut it through, saying that it had been untied by him." Masking his desperate flailing as the finery of sagacious statecraft, Alexander thus rescued his legitimacy and went on to become Alexander the Great.[70] And with similar solemnity do today's jail boosters pretend, with their vulgar hacking, to have solved the Rikers Knot, *unwilling to allow it to remain unloosened, lest it should exercise some disturbing influence upon the multitude.* In the place of serious engagement with the spatial problems attendant to structural racism in the punishment system, bold and simple lines emanate outward from Rikers, all in the signature pink of JLUSA and #CLOSErikers. But just as mass incarceration has not resolved capital's inability to reproduce itself on a global scale but simply has deferred the reckoning of perennial crisis to another day, neither will this false unraveling of the Rikers Knot solve anything, outside of empty boasts on glossy colored paper.

Meisterlin, who is highly sympathetic to the Lippman proposals, ultimately believes that *Justice in Design* falls short of representing the jail proposal honestly and usefully to the communities that must be won over to the plan. "The drawings do not function analytically," she writes, "nor describe the geography of corrections practices, its concomitant logistics, uneven spatial burdens, and diversity of impacts."[71] Even from this friendly perspective, *Justice in Design* was not a serious, good-faith exercise in conveying information to the public. Much like the jails themselves, the project largely existed for those taking part in it: for the designers who added glossy new images to their portfolios; the academics who added lines to their CVs; the foundation sponsors, who enjoyed an advanced experiment in public-private social engineering; and the jail boosters, who checked a box toward marketing the jails as both crowdsourced and cutely shorn of the ugly realities of large-scale human caging. In Meisterlin's words, "the drawings did not illustrate an implementable project; they were an implemented project."[72]

Put otherwise, a spokesperson of the New York City Correction Officers' Benevolent Association (COBA) compared *Justice in Design* to "kids starting a startup company."[73] We derive no satisfaction from this almost singular point of agreement with any representative of COBA.

EXPERTS AGREE

It is worth emphasizing how self-styled experts who focus narrowly on their own pet interests, at the expense of a broader social or political analysis, can provide dangerous ideological cover for carceral construction projects like the skyscraper jails. For instance, Rebecca Bratspies, a CUNY Law professor and the director of the Center for Urban Environmental Reform, has celebrated Lippman's plan as the opportunity to realize "environmental justice" in New York City. Bratspies rightly cites the long-standing environmental racism surrounding New York's power grid, which deposits pollution in the communities of color that use the least electricity. She advances the laudable goal of reversing this trend by moving peak-load facilities, which accommodate the grid at its highest capacity, from these neighborhoods to a vacated Rikers, alongside wind/solar and wastewater infrastructure. This move, Bratspies argues, can at once free up green space in the neighborhoods presently home to polluting power plants, create new jobs for the people most impacted by mass incarceration, and even reroute "the school-to-prison pipeline into a school-to-green-jobs pipeline."[74] These are noble causes. But why do they require skyscraper jails?

Bratspies's argument also makes numerous questionable assumptions about a repurposed Rikers: that the waterfront space vacated by power plants will be public green space and not high-rise condos, that jobs in the new facilities will be distributed based on the principles of social justice and not on the same structural racism and prejudicial hiring governing the rest of the labor market, and that Rikers will even close for carceral purposes at all. Beneath all this lurks the most dangerous assumption: a naive embrace of the skyscraper jails plan as a social good. After perfunctory pages spent dissecting the structurally racist history of Rikers and the untold harm it has caused, Bratspies uncritically reiterates the verbiage of Jonathan Lippman and Bill de Blasio, concluding with de Blasio's cursed words: "The era of mass incarceration is OVER in New York City."[75] We are reminded not only of a banner that once proclaimed "Mission Accomplished," but also of the potential environmental harm of the skyscraper jails, discussed in the next chapter, that is apparently not on Bratspies's radar.

Similarly, environmental psychologist Todd Levon Brown, who participated in the *Justice in Design* competition, recently published a fascinating entry in the *Palgrave Handbook of Prison Design* discussing the skyscraper jails from a design perspective. Brown argues that the jails will be "beacons of social consciousness," important steps toward "creating new psychosocially sustainable carceral spaces" guided by progressive design. Like Bratspies, Brown elides the political debates around the jails altogether, conflating Shut Down Rikers and #CLOSErikers, and neglecting to mention that the jails have any opposition. Brown's subsequent intervention hinges on the question of how to make *more* carceral facilities that resemble New York City's skyscraper jails. It apparently does not bother Brown that the jails have yet to be built and that their actual plans do not yet exist.[76]

Like many skyscraper jail boosters, Brown evokes the case of Kalief Browder to support his claim. Brown lingers especially long on Browder's heartbreaking testimonials of life in solitary confinement, rehashing this ordeal in excruciating detail. Brown emphasizes the hostile and dehumanizing environmental factors that contribute to poor mental health in these facilities and that ultimately led to Browder's suicide.[77] This requires an urgent intervention, the importance of which cannot be understated. What is to be done?

It is here Brown argues that tragedies like Browder's death are best studied by trained experts in carceral architecture such as himself, "to identify problematic spaces within correctional environments that contribute to and facilitate negative experiences." For solitary confinement in particular, many of the most onerous features of the cell "can be easily identified, and, in most cases, readily remediated via innovative design interventions that seek to optimize the spatial and experiential quality while not compromising safety." Brown cites approvingly an article in the obscure WordPress site *Correctional News* that advocates "more doors and windows" in solitary confinement cells like Browder's, facilitating "privacy, tranquility, vision, and daylight control." Its author, whom Brown does not cite, is Jean-François Couturier, the president and CEO of Unicel Architectural, a high-end glass company specializing in the same products the article advocates.[78]

In short, a discussion that began with the horrors of Kalief Browder's suicide concludes with the facile invocation of sunnier solitary confinement, complete with an advertisement for designer prison glass. Nowhere is the practice of solitary confinement, even for teenagers like Browder, called into question as anything more than a practical matter for jail designers to solve with the latest design fads. Such are the *beacons of social consciousness* to be found among today's progressive jail designers.

CULTURE CLUB

This leaves us with the most abstract figure of a plan haunted by many phantoms. In his response to critics of the skyscraper jails, Stanley Richards argues for the necessity of new jail architecture to abet "culture change," to make sure the abolitionist prediction—that the new jails will soon resemble the old ones—does not come true. The jails of Rikers, Richards argues, "help breed the culture of violence and danger" for which the complex is known. In response, Richards argues, the new jails can facilitate "culture change" through their design: "naturally lit, open, communal spaces that lend themselves to programming, direct service, and therapeutic priorities for those detained, while supporting correction officers with better work facilities," like gyms and common spaces. "By investing in an environment built to promote safety and overall health," Richards continues, "a critical foundation is laid on which a new culture can be built."[79]

Throughout the jail booster literature, reference is frequently made to the idiom "culture of violence" famously deployed by the Department of Justice in its notorious 2014 report. The solution, whether in *A More Just New York City*, *Justice in Design*, or the mayor's plan, *Smaller, Safer, Fairer*, goes by the name of *culture change*. De Blasio even announced a "Culture Change Working Group" of its Justice Implementation Task Force, as part of the original plan to transition from Rikers to skyscraper jails.[80] *Justice in Design* argues that "living and working spaces can be enormously improved by changing the entrenched and embedded cultures through training and ongoing discussions with individuals living and working in jails."[81] In the Lippman Commission's October 2019 plea to the city council to approve the skyscraper jails, it argued that "redesigning jails will not be sufficient, on its own, to create a better environment. Equally, if not more, important, is changing the operational principles and culture at the Department of Correction"—changes that "cannot wait for the closure of Rikers. The process of culture change has to start today."[82]

For his part, Richards emphasizes that the necessary culture change "is not an issue of brick and mortar" alone, arguing that "the physical environment either supports or hinders culture change goals." Without qualifying what this culture is or where it comes from—besides, that is, the architecture of the bad old jails begging replacement—Richards concludes with the stunning contention, "If the interior space designs are corrupted and allowed to re-create even a small measure of the institutional bleakness and inhumane isolation of Rikers, we will truly and simply be trading one set of buildings for another."[83] Osborne Association CEO Elizabeth Gaynes similarly argued that absent culture change, the skyscraper jails would just be "four little Rikers Islands."[84] This sentiment is further echoed by Michael Jacobson, who concedes that the failure to effect "culture change" in the new jails would simply "create little Rikers around the city."[85] This important admission, made by a number of jail boosters, echoes the words of anti-jail activist Liz Blum: "A building is just a building."[86]

Culture change, then, appears to be the linchpin of the entire skyscraper jails plan. Much like "community," however, the term "culture" is commonly wielded as if it possesses a clear definition, yet is sufficiently malleable to mean just about anything—and hence, most often, signifies not much at all. We could even go as far as to say, as Don Mitchell provocatively argued, "there is no such thing as culture," at least as distinct from the admixture of historical, political, and economic forces that make up the

cultural expressions of social activity.[87] But the jail boosters all
speak of the culture of the city jail system as if the meaning of
this term is not only readily apparent but sufficiently robust to
explain virtually all of the problems that cannot be fixed by new
jail construction alone. So what exactly *is* the jail culture that
every reformer agrees is so toxic, where does it come from, and
how can it be changed?

In a lengthy article entitled "Beyond the Island: Changing
the Culture of New York City's Jails," Jacobson and colleagues at
the neoliberal think tank the CUNY Institute for State and Local
Governance (ISLG) provide the most sophisticated treatment to
date of what exactly "culture change" means in the context of a
jail system, and how it can be affected in the skyscraper jails. "Organizational culture," the authors write, "consists of the beliefs,
assumptions, and values that guide an organization's operations
and affect how its members think and act. Culture involves the
unspoken ways that an organization solves its problems, and the
assumptions and habits that members, including new members,
share and adopt."[88]

So where does this culture come from? Jacobson and his coauthors are never quite clear, besides to formulate an almost bacterial
theory of bad jails, which posits that cultures of violence grow
absent the antiseptic of sound management, in the unsterilized
climate of aging infrastructure, and are, thereafter, transmitted
congenitally from one generation to the next. In this context, "beliefs, assumptions, and values" germinate ex nihilo among correctional officers working in poorly sanitized settings, with no
discernible connection to the outside world, whether in politics,
popular culture, or the broader social order in which the jail culture exists.

In practical terms, the authors' plan for "culture change" is
much of the same police and prison reform panacea, repeated ad

infinitum for the past decade: training, more training, and failing that, *retraining*. Their entire vision revolves around populating the skyscraper jails with guards who are professionally trained and managed, and therefore do not reproduce the violence and dehumanization of the present system. This plan is also alarmingly similar to the ideology underlying an earlier episode of progressive jail boosterism, the construction of many Rikers facilities in the 1950s and 1960s under DOC commissioner Anna Kross. Like the jail boosters of today, Kross imagined that connecting Rikers to the shore with a permanent bridge and erecting a growing network of rehabilitative jail facilities could be accomplished alongside a professionalization of DOC to produce model institutions. Changing the department's culture, Kross argued, would make Rikers Island a worldwide model of progressive penology under the control of civilian experts like Jacobson and his cohort. Kross, who had far more political clout—and significantly less opposition—than any jail reformer today, designed considerable carceral infrastructure with the goal of culture change in mind. When the culture did not change, however, the infrastructure remained. And here we are.[89]

Most impressively, the authors make it through their entire account of DOC's "culture" without once mentioning the power wielded by the Correction Officers' Benevolent Association, the union representing the rank-and-file guards in the New York City system.[90] COBA is one of the most powerful unions in the city and was a key backer of Mayor Eric Adams.[91] Through a history of workplace militancy that has episodically exploded into spectacular violence against prisoners and even civilian monitors of the jails, the union has spent the better part of the last century fighting for the rights of guards to disrespect and abuse prisoners as much as they see fit, free from civilian oversight. As incidents like the 1990 staff riot at Rikers Island have demonstrated,

COBA—and its highly energized rank and file—views the right to wield unchecked violence against prisoners as nothing short of a barometer of its power within DOC and the city at large.[92]

While COBA is likely what Jacobson and his coauthors have in mind when they obliquely reference "subcultures" standing in the way of reform in "correctional organizations," by all appearances, COBA *is* the correctional organization at Rikers, and DOC effectively works to accommodate it.[93] Any serious effort at "culture change" in DOC would involve mortal combat with this organization, which has striven so assiduously over the years to throw down roadblocks to nearly any check on guards' power or any guarantee of prisoners' basic constitutional rights. Jacobson, in particular, who worked as DOC commissioner in the 1990s, knows this. And Jacobson and his cohort must surely anticipate a potentially explosive encounter with COBA on the horizon, since plans to reduce the city's jail population are also plans to cut its number of guards. The Lippman Commission explicitly recommended reducing DOC guards *by a third* as part of the new jail plan, a proposal brilliantly euphemized by the Vera Institute as the "rightsizing" of the jail system.[94] This recommendation provoked immediate and enduring public opposition to the skyscraper jails from COBA, which can be counted on to fight the reform effort every step of the way.[95]

Rather than confront the most explicitly organized "culture" at DOC, and the foremost obstacle to the new jails emerging as anything but "little Rikers around the city," Jacobson and his coauthors default instead to the clichés of twenty-first-century managerialism. On the one hand, they opine, "strong performance measurement facilitates greater accountability," while on the other, they begrudgingly acknowledge that such numbers can simply be made up, as they often are at Rikers.[96] In this tug-of-war between paper solutions and real-life problems, the former wins out. The authors advocate that DOC adopt the "Achieving Performance Excellence Initiative (APEX)" system: "(1) plan and assess; (2) define the goal; (3) organize for results; (4) plan the implementation strategy; (5) implement the change management plan; and (6) sustain the change effort."[97] Eliminating the culture of violence at Rikers Island, then, sounds a lot like managing an Applebee's.

"At the deepest level of an organization's culture," Jacobson et al. argue, "lies shared underlying assumptions about the workplace—theories about 'the way things are' that are not debatable within the context of the organization or the field."[98] Here, at *the deepest level* of the matter at hand, we encounter the true cause of all our woes: bad ideas. This is not so much analysis but a placeholder indicating a stubborn refusal to have an analysis at all. Safely removed from the political and economic realities of contemporary New York City, the authors attribute the problems plaguing *all* city jails everywhere to faulty systems of management, which can be replaced with new practices rooted in the neoliberal imperative to make the public sector resemble the private.[99] Thus these emissaries of ISLG, which proudly boasts high atop its literature that it does not rely on "abstract theories," end up doing exactly that.[100]

At the deepest level, as the authors might say, the "culture of violence" on Rikers is a microcosm of the racialized class violence that structures New York City and American society as a whole. Jacobson and his coauthors are unable or unwilling to face this, since doing so would by necessity shift their domain away from technocratic tinkering in the facilities where the worst of this violence is concentrated, and toward its root in the system of class domination that they faithfully serve. In the process, their numbing filibuster of managerial minutia calls to mind the words of philosopher Raoul Vaneigem: "Everyone is asked their opinion about every detail in order to prevent them from forming one about the totality."[101]

CHAPTER 4

ANOTHER WORLD IS POSSIBLE

Abolition requires that we change one thing: everything.
—Ruth Wilson Gilmore, 2024

The conservative NIMBY ("not in my backyard") jail opponents so vilified by the jail boosters were doubtless a real presence in the opposition to the skyscraper jails. Some of these voices argued to simply keep Rikers open. During the period of public comments for the skyscraper jails' environmental review, an argument typical of this position ran "I am all for jail reform, but the time and money should be spent fixing Rikers' issues. It is a perfect location with plenty of space to rebuild." Another respondent even tried to create a meme of their own demand: "Renovate Rikers!" Others were more blunt. "Its location on an island is appropriate to keep those guilty of criminal activities away from the rest of society," argued one. "Rikers is the appropriate location to punish criminals," insisted another.[1]

Other arguments characteristic of a particularly nasty NIMBYism included "Kew Gardens doesn't want to live near violent criminals"; "It is clear that the mayor values the convenience of convicted felons [sic] above the welfare of the citizens of Kew Gardens"; "I believe keeping prisoners and their friends [meaning *visitors* to the jail] in isolation is the best way to protect our communities"; "The value of all our homes will be significantly diminished and our lives damaged!!!!! How dare you??"; "These are the worst of the worst inmates and they do not belong in such a beautiful community"; "I will have murderers, rapists, and pedofiles [*sic*] looking in my window"; "Drug addict [*sic*] and criminals' place is the jail, far away from the city"; "Brooklyn should not be the sanctuary location to house dangerous criminals with inmates' 'families' [???] visiting the Brooklyn prison"; "We are tired of the ridiculous Liberals wanting to remove the Christopher Columbus Statue, yet have no problem welcoming hardened criminals/thieves/rapists/sexual predators into our neighborhood"; "Fix up Rikers if you must, but keep the criminal away from families with children"; "We don't need to walk by a prison every day to see the ills of the prison system."[2]

Additionally, many residents of Kew Gardens complained that the jail was simply the latest affront, on top of a Comfort Inn recently converted into a homeless shelter by the city, that had flooded their neighborhood with supposed undesirables.[3]

These perspectives were surely real, but as the skyscraper jails debate heated up, the jail boosters did their best to impute this reactionary and sometimes racially coded venom to *all opponents* of the new jail construction. This was not fair, for several reasons. On the most basic level, most of the complaints that we could potentially call NIMBYism contained valid concerns about such a series of ill-defined, yet utterly massive, public construction projects shrouded in opacity at key moments in the planning process. Thousands of residents vocalized understandable hesitation around the erection of towers, far exceeding present zoning restrictions, that would soon dominate their neighborhoods. Many were concerned about the impact of the jails on local green spaces, and in particular, about the shadow they'd cast on surrounding residences, streets, and parks. Others pointed to traffic, parking, and congestion, especially given cops' and guards' propensity to ignore parking rules, with impunity, surrounding police stations and jails. Many cited the obstruction of views and the further disruption of the historical character of neighborhoods. A number of complainants raised concerns about the potential pollution from the demolition and construction processes.[4]

Some of this feedback was quite poetic. "You build a 40-story tower that's going to take away sunlight," remarked Chinatown resident Diana Tse, "not just physical sunlight, but sunlight from young memories."[5] Many of these voices insisted that they believed Rikers ought to be closed and that the city's punishment system should be dramatically overhauled but felt, for a variety of reasons, that the skyscraper jails were not the way to do it. Residents in Chinatown and the Bronx, in particular, related the choice of sites in their neighborhood to their own long histories of racist divestment and the disproportionate siting of unwanted hazardous facilities in their backyards.[6] The Diego Beekman Mutual Housing Association in the Bronx, representing many neighbors of the prospective jail site, made clear its members were not opposed to construction on principle when the association proposed its own project, a large affordable housing development with retail space along with manufacturing shops and space for community organizations, on the same lot.[7] This was, as scholar Amanda M. Philip argued, only the latest episode in a decades-long struggle to reverse that neighborhood's abandonment by the city.[8]

But the most thoughtful critics of the new jails, including many neighborhoods of prospective jail sites, could not be considered NIMBY at all. Their responses to the skyscraper jails demonstrated sophisticated analyses of the political-economic and structurally racist components of new jail construction. In place of the new jails, many of these respondents imagined how the city could organize itself in a radically different way.

We turn now to extracting, from the deafening cacophony of the jail debate, the remarkable social vision expressed by everyday New Yorkers who demanded the closure of Rikers but believed that it could be replaced with another way of organizing society.[9] We will focus especially on the substantive remarks received during the city's public comment period for the jails' environmental review, and also examine the most sophisticated expression of this vision, crafted by the network No New Jails NYC (NNJ). As the jail boosters argued that the only two options for moving forward were new jails or no action at all, these voices revealed a stark alternative to this binary, and pointed to a world beyond the violence of Rikers and all human cages in New York City.

Of course, the public comment process for massive construction projects like the skyscraper jails is almost entirely perfunctory, with city officials seldom pretending otherwise. This was doubly true in the case of the skyscraper jails, as not just the city but an organized network of well-funded boosters viewed the review process as an obstacle to be overcome, not as an opportunity to develop the project in cooperation with the community. Befitting their neoliberal political orientation, the jails boosters even did their own privately funded community outreach in meager offerings like *Justice in Design*, and by the time of the public comment period, acted as if they had nothing to learn from anyone. This is particularly unfortunate, because much of the public input evinced a thoughtful consideration of the problem and the desire for policy pointing far beyond the gray technocracy of the skyscraper jail boosters.

NOT IN ANYONE'S BACKYARD

Like many residents of Kew Gardens, urban planner Lucia Cappuccio was dismayed to discover a new jail was slated for that community.

But it was not simply because the jail would be in Cappuccio's back-yard. "I do not oppose this project out of NIMBYism," Cappuccio wrote in a letter to DOC design director Howard Fiedler as part of the city's environmental review process. "I would feel the same way if it was being built in Flushing or another Queens neighborhood. I oppose this project out of an ethical commitment to racial justice and an end to mass incarceration. Rikers is an abomination and must be closed, but the solution to ending mass incarceration is not building shiny new community jails."

Sadly, Cappuccio added, "I know enough about planning to know that these public comments will be pushed to the side and ignored. This proposal will go through anyway, despite tremen-dous community opposition, and the administration will pretend it is a moral victory and a community benefit. But this isn't a new bike lane—this is a new jail that will cage humans."[10]

While Cappuccio was ultimately correct about the futility of speaking truth to power during the environmental review pro-cess, an alternative perspective to NIMBYism and the jail boost-ers' worldview nonetheless characterized a noteworthy plurality of voices raised during the environmental review. "Jails and prisons are infrastructural nightmares," wrote Zoe Alexander. "Jails and their surrounding areas put community members in proximity to violent and [abusive] police and corrections officers, and trans-form neighborhood character by incorporating dehumanizing and austere 'security' like razor wire, police barricades, and austere, imposing buildings designed to separate us from our community members locked inside."[11] "It is simply revolting to think of retail on the ground floor with incarcerated people in cubicles above," wrote Enid Braun, likening the jails' proposed ground-floor retail to "lipstick on a pig."[12] "We cannot solve old jails with new ones," argued Sivan Amar of Queens. "It will only be a matter of time until the new jails become another Rikers."[13]

Some used the logic of the jail boosters against the skyscraper jails plan. Gaurav Jashnani of Brooklyn, a member of NNJ, wrote, "With the most basic reforms like pretrial detention, cash bail, speedy trial laws and so on that have been proposed by the Lippman Commission, verbally supported by our garbage governor, and/or advocated by the JustLeadership campaign that has been fighting for these jails, we can reduce the detainee population so that we don't need Rikers OR any new jails. If we end pretrial detention, we can close Rikers tomorrow!"[14] "Ultimately," argued Queens resident Katie Winkelstein-Duveneck, "what has been demonstrated to be effective in restoring and maintaining healthy communities and raising healthy children is preventing and reducing incarceration, not changing its form."[15]

Notable responses identified the key flaw of the plan: it did not ensure the closure of Rikers but threatened *the addition of* jails to a city system that includes Rikers. "The new jails will be built before Rikers is closed," wrote Sharon Hughes of Brooklyn, "with no guarantee that the city will actually close Rikers. This could leave NYC with the capacity to jail over 16,000 people per day."[16] "I agree that we must close Rikers forever," argued M. J. Williams of Brooklyn, a member of NNJ, "but New York City does not. The city admits it is powerless to close Rikers alone. In its plan, closing Rikers is only a goal, not a commitment. In the meantime, the city is RUSHING to build new jails." Williams predicted, "The city's plan will fail. NYC will end up with four new jails AND Rikers. The police will continue to fill jails with New Yorkers targeted by unnecessary, predatory arrests—even as crime drops—unless the Mayor and City Council commit to changing the nature and breadth of policing in this city." Which, of course, there was no plan to do.[17]

Some respondents also demonstrated historical knowledge superior to anything produced by the Lippman milieu. Linda Banta of Queens reminded the city that "the jail complexes on Rikers Island were created as jail reform. The atrocities perpetrated there clearly show new jails to replace old ones never solve the root of the problem." Instead, new jails will continue to "criminalize and warehouse Black and Latino people in facilities that are hazardous to their health."[18] "Just like we look back on Rikers Island seventy-five years later with shock and dismay that we could ever have thought it was a 'modern, humane' jail," wrote Zoe Alexander, "so too will we look back at these detention complexes in horror. Close Rikers now without opening new jails."[19] A widely shared 2017 article by Jarrod and scholar Jack Norton entitled "A Jail to End All Jails" outlined this history of failed reforms, which became a common theme in public remarks.[20]

Some respondents pointed to the blackmail of carceral humanism and the fool's errand of addressing social problems by building more carceral facilities. "The proposed action provides for mental health services, health care, job training, education, and other social services within the new Brooklyn structure," wrote Scott H. Jacobs of Brooklyn. "These are all needed services, but wouldn't it make better sense for some of this programming, particularly the preventative programs, to be located within the very communities at risk versus at the [Brooklyn Detention Complex]?"[21] "Spending billions of dollars to build new prisons dedicates huge amounts of money and time to the most inflexible and destructive aspect of criminal justice—imprisonment," wrote Brian Kelly of Manhattan. "It supposes that we can solve difficult social problems by spending money without addressing their sources."[22] Carolyn Yao of Queens argued that the plan "means the city intends to put more people in cages out of convenience," ensuring that "children [will be] born with jail cells ready for them" and "communities [will] become overpoliced, and in the most damning and tragic case, people die."[23]

"There are plenty of experts who can present the data on the viability of eliminating bail and the social and economic benefits of divesting from policing [and] prisons in favor of investing in communities," wrote Allison Brown of Brooklyn. "Why is the Mayor's Office not listening to them? Moreover, why is the Mayor's Office not listening to actual New Yorkers who are telling the mayor that policing and prisons are causing profound harm and that what their communities need is more affordable housing, education, and employment opportunities, and better access to health care and other facilities for the community's well-being?"[24] "New cages cannot reform old ones," wrote Frank Braio of the Bronx, "you must know that. The city needs to address the issues of over-policing and criminalization of poverty in communities of color and look at true proven reform such as ending cash bail and pretrial detention."[25]

Other respondents demonstrated an acute awareness [of] a problem that the jail reformers were either unwilling or unable to address in their plan: the cops, who are largely responsible for filling the jails in the first place. Tristan Beach of Brooklyn argued, "We need to focus on the source of the problem: policing. The impact on public policy of the new jail plan will be to lock us into policing and incarceration into the future. Criminalizing poverty, homelessness, mental health, substance use, sex work, immigration, and being a person of color gives the NYPD outsized and unwarranted power to surveil our most vulnerable community members, with disastrous results."[26]

"Building more jails will not eliminate the actual issues that Rikers presents: inhumane violence, sexual assault, lack of mental health support, ripping families away from their children and children away from their families," argued Queens resident Jessica Ngok. Instead of the new jails, Ngok argued, serious solutions could come from "reforming our current bail system/ending cash bail, creating alternatives to incarceration programs (especially for people facing mental health and substance use issues), ending the school-to-prison pipeline by providing viable opportunities for low-income students of color, ending broken windows policing, and more."[27]

Many respondents focused on the city's overreliance on police and prisons to the serious detriment of other social spending. In the most thorough of these arguments, scholar Nadja Eisenberg-Guyot, of NNJ, broke it down numerically: "The DOC budget for 2017 was $1.4 billion," they argued.

> NYC additionally spent $5.2 billion on policing and approximately $950 million on criminal courts. That's over $7 billion that the city could be spending on affordable housing, schools, health care, and parks; on repairing New York City Housing Authority housing; and on investing in transformative justice processes that actually heal communities. For comparison, the Housing Authority budget for 2017 was $3.3 billion (of which $1.7 billion was raised through rents); the Department of Health budget was $1.6 billion; the Department of Homeless Services budget was $1.8 billion; the Department of Parks and Recreation budget was $500 million; and the Department of Education budget was $24.4 billion ($12 billion of that is city funds), or $14,500 per student. The borough-based jails plan will cost the city approximately $10 billion. Meanwhile, until Rikers is closed, the city will continue to incarcerate people on Rikers for an average yearly cost of over $200,000 per person.[28]

Respondents like Eisenberg-Guyot, who focused on the staggering figures of the city's expenditure on law-and-order policies, considered the new jails not a departure from this trend but a continuation of it. The solution, then, was to reverse this course.

DEFUND DOC

Several years before the divest/invest strategy of "defunding the police" became a national policy debate, many New Yorkers were ready to defund DOC, and the NYPD too. "Ten billion dollars should be invested in building a more capacious system of supports," wrote Bryan Welton of Brooklyn, "that secure the basic needs of New Yorkers, toward preventing, mitigating, and undoing harm and establishing conditions where healthy communities flourish."[29] "Shouldn't those funds be used for something that could benefit ALL residents?" argued Fabio Sborea. "Namely, improvements to the city's outdated and crumbling transit system? Or could those funds be put toward more community-oriented endeavors in order to keep NYC residents out of the prison system? Or could they be used toward endeavors that actually reform the justice/prison system as opposed to merely putting 'band-aids' on the issue?"[30] "It's time that the city stops investing millions of dollars in the over-policing and incrimination of our communities," argued Jorky Badillo of the Bronx. "We want an investment toward more restorative and transformative practices that address the help our communities need."[31]

Sivan Amar proposed the city spend "[$]10.6 billion on community resources like public schools, childcare services, health care, drug counseling, and food programs."[32] Linda Banta of Queens argued, "We need to instead invest in the community resources that truly keep all New Yorkers safe, healthy, and in our neighborhoods and communities. Decriminalizing poverty, eliminating pretrial detention, and investing in transformative justice could close Rikers within the proposed ten years without opening new jails."[33] "The city must close Rikers without spending public money and time on creating new buildings to incarcerate people," wrote Tanya Nguyen of Manhattan. "We must invest those resources into better education and housing instead. I do not want any jail construction, which will only imprison more people in my community and contribute to the cycle of violence and poverty."[34]

The irony that the jails could be considered a massive public development plan meant to house poor people, decades after the city stopped building affordable public housing, did not escape many respondents. "The city should devote public land to the public good rather than jailing and punishing people," argued Elaine Cao of Manhattan. "For example, NYC has an affordable housing and homelessness crisis—there are currently 62,000 homeless people in the city, including 15,000 families with 20,000 children. Private land development continues to push working-class people out of their communities, neighborhoods, and homes. Gentrification, lack of affordable housing, and the criminalization of poverty go hand in hand. The city should prioritize using land to solve the housing crisis. We want these civic assets without cages in our neighborhoods."[35]

"We will not accept more spending on infrastructure that coerces and controls when our neighborhood is in desperate need of community-driven development," wrote Jose Rodriguez of the Bronx. "Our community demands: community centers, the creation of green spaces, living-wage jobs, truly affordable housing, and other investments in positive things that would alleviate the conditions that push so many into the criminal justice system."[36] "I can never endorse any plan to expand the number of jails in this city," wrote Rowena Chodkowski of Queens, "when it should invest the [$]10 billion in resources that better serve what OUR communities need. Countless New Yorkers struggle to pay for housing, food, and medical care. The subways are antiquated and our transit hubs rot. . . . Do we need another embarrassing eyesore?"[37]

The jails debate also generated a number of concrete proposals from community residents. "A supportive housing complex on

275 Atlantic Avenue, as one potential alternative, could permanently house low-income people at a lower cost than jailing them,
and reduce jail recidivism," argued Sylvia Morse of Brooklyn.[38]
"How about a Welcome Home Plan of $10 billion," argued Dr.
Jim Fairbanks,

> that helps everyone leaving Rikers to rejoin the commu-
> nity with full citizenship, housing, jobs, expanded social
> services, counseling, youth centers, and so on.
>
> How about a Reparations Plan for the South Bronx:
> Does the City understand the incredible and systemic
> damage done by targeting everyone in the entire South
> Bronx for stop-and-frisk, mass incarceration, upstate jail
> for years for tens of thousands? Let alone talk about our
> history of landlords burning down tens of thousands of
> apartment buildings, where hundreds of residents died in
> the fires, in an arson-for-profit scheme that reaped billions
> for landlords. . . .
>
> How about a Restorative Justice System Plan: Restor-
> ative Justice does away with punishment. It seeks to re-
> store relationships and community. It starts a new justice
> system of bringing together the victim, the accused, fami-
> ly, extended family, community, police, district attorneys,
> churches, youth and community organizations, etc. It has
> practices of repentance, forgiveness, mediation, counsel-
> ing, getting lives together on new paths.[39]

In an impressive argument worthy of quoting at length,
Eisenberg-Guyot imagined an alternative use for each jail site.

> Instead of a jail, Chinatown needs more affordable hous-
> ing. After more than 200 years of community struggle

against xenophobia and anti-Asian racism made China-town the neighborhood safe space it is today, gentrifica-tion is threatening its historic and cultural position in our city and for Asian communities.

Instead of a jail, Brooklyn needs affordable housing. When completed, the Barclays Center redevelopment will add 6,000 apartments to the area, but only 2,250 "afford-able" units. Meanwhile, rising rents across Brooklyn are displacing working and middle class families of color. Displacing families of color from Brooklyn harms his-toric and cultural resources by treating the communities who created those resources as disposable and unwanted.

Instead of a jail, Mott Haven needs a hospital and displacement prevention. The proposed site of the Bronx jail was once the only hospital in the area that accepted people of color as patients. As the South Bronx is target-ed for "redevelopment," the city needs to invest now in resources that will prevent displacement and preserve the historic character of the neighborhood.

Instead of a jail, Kew Gardens needs affordable hous-ing, services for elders, and a guarantee of true sanctuary for immigrants. Queens is one of the most diverse areas in the US; yet, gentrification, rising rents, and xenophobic immigration enforcement are threatening the multiracial, intergenerational, and multi-class character of the bor-ough. The city needs to invest in housing for working-class families, rent stabilization and subsidy programs and home health care that allow our elders to stay in their homes and communities, and increased access to legal services for un-documented people facing ICE harassment. No city is a sanctuary when its residents fear police brutality, incarcer-ation, and deportation every day.[40]

The vision offered by Eisenberg-Guyot in this passage bridged the real concerns of many local residents who were written off as NIMBY by the jail boosters with the broader social justice thrust of the abolitionists campaigning to close Rikers and build no new jails to replace it. The most comprehensive and sustained vision for accomplishing this came from a group in which Eisenberg-Guyot was a vocal member: No New Jails NYC.

$11 BILLION FOR WHAT?!

As the city debated the future of Rikers and the broader punishment system, the abolitionist network No New Jails NYC organized tirelessly to promote a radical departure from the jail boosters' vision. While the boosters made it clear they had nothing to learn from the public outcry around the skyscraper jails—having already checked the perfunctory box of "community input" as part of compiling their glossy materials—many in NNJ used this period to educate themselves and others about the pitfalls of the skyscraper jails plan and potential alternatives. As the city council vote approached, NNJ released an impressive document called *Close Rikers Now, We Keep Us Safe*. Later, NNJ organizers followed up with "$11 Billion for What?!"—echoing the student-led "$10 Mil for Real?" campaign against police in Atlanta public schools.[41] Both NNJ texts underscore many insights voiced by everyday New Yorkers in the public comment period around the skyscraper jails and were compiled in cooperation with dozens of people incarcerated in New York City. Taken together, they represent, at once, a critique of the skyscraper jails plan and an alternative vision for how society could be organized. The guiding principles of both studies proceed from the tradition of abolitionism.

"Abolition is not an arbitrary concept that has multiple ambiguous meanings," NNJ writes. "Abolition is less about the absence of prisons and jails, and much more about the presence of everything we need in order to thrive and build a society that does not rely on our imprisonment and premature death."[42] The authors situate their organizing as "part of a broader movement of abolition, that began in the fight to end slavery and now lives in the commitment to create a society where safety is not the job of police and cages but the responsibility of well-resourced organized communities."[43] These organizers emphasize how incarceration harms some of the most powerless people in society. In addition to the well-documented disparities along the lines of race and class, the people most harmed by incarceration include trans and gender-nonconforming people. As NNJ argues, these groups experience victimization at the hands of police for supposed offenses like sex work and self-defense, and their victimization is compounded by the violence of carceral facilities that often place trans women in male facilities, in particular, further amplifying the predation they experience at the hands of guards and other prisoners alike.[44]

NNJ's objections to incarceration are not derived from some ethereal moralism; this argument is imminently practical. "When someone is harmed, they receive little to no support," the authors write, especially in the case of domestic violence or sexual assault, while the person who has caused harm is put through a process that seems designed to break them or make them more violent. That is the punishment system we have today, which begins an unending cycle of violence, despite the fact that many people who have survived violence and other harm do not advocate incarceration in response. Put bluntly, even after decades of research, there is still no evidence that incarceration works to decrease harm or violence, or make communities safe.[45]

It is a point worth making often: if investment in police and prison capacity produced public safety, the United States would be among the most orderly societies in the world.

Of course, antisocial behavior is rampant in many parts of the United States—and academics who insist crime is simply a figment of the right-wing imagination need to spend more time off campus. But unlike nearly any other public agency, police and carceral institutions consistently point to their persistent failure as evidence that they need more money and more power. Carceral construction has failed to stem antisocial behavior, which is the conservative argument, and it is a farce to claim, which the liberal boosters of the new jails do, that constructing *additional* carceral capacity can reverse mass incarceration itself.

"Mass incarceration cannot be solved through the construction of new jails," NNJ organizers argue, "because mass incarceration as a phenomenon has been perpetrated through the widespread construction of new jails and prisons throughout the United States since the 1970s."[46] So what is the alternative?

NNJ uses the staggering initial price tag for the skyscraper jails as the opportunity to discuss what else the city could do with $11 billion to realize a New York City without jails.[47] Echoing many voices from the community feedback the project received, NNJ begins with the need for intensive public housing construction in New York City and for reversing present trends of turning public units over to the private real estate market. The authors emphasize how interpersonal violence, including domestic violence, can be lessened by the supply of dignified and comfortable housing. Jails, they argue, serve as an expensive means of housing poor people, whose incarceration could likely have been prevented by public investment in housing in the first place. "Access to housing and social services should not be routed through policing and jailing," the authors write. "Access to housing should be provided as a basic right to all New Yorkers."[48]

NNJ also points to the dire situation facing the city's unhoused, who are disproportionately represented throughout the city jail system. The shelter system, unfortunately, is in a similar state of disrepair and functions as an extension of the city's carceral landscape, with a focus on surveillance and discipline.[49] The authors argue that in place of new jails, the city could repair and renovate existing houselessness infrastructure while simultaneously investing in underfunded housing-first programming, which places people in subsidized homes as they first enter the system, not after months or years of navigating bureaucratic red tape. The city not only could better fund this program but also could actively construct new housing for people facing housing insecurity, creating new places to live that could absorb people from both the shelter system and the low-quality housing many are presently forced to accept as their only alternative to houselessness.[50]

NNJ makes similar arguments about the inadequacy of mental health care and substance abuse resources (for those who wish to quit), a large burden of which the city has de facto shifted to the jail system in recent decades. These populations combine (and overlap) to represent a majority of prisoners in the city system, emblematic of the city simply giving up on solving their problems any other way.[51] For NNJ, these interrelated issues are part of a broader vision. Ultimately, NNJ argues for increased public assistance, combined with free public transit, improved public schools, and free education at the City University of New York, to be enacted alongside the dismantling of policing, courts, and jail infrastructure.[52] It is a bold, left-Keynesian program for the significant redistribution of wealth and power.

"How would I spend $11 billion to shut down Rikers, instead of on building new jails?" wrote Hakim Trent-El, an incarcerated member of NNJ.

> The first thing I would focus my spending on would be the poverty within the communities. This means providing

job training and job opportunities within New York for those who live in poverty. I would create programs that would give the masses the chance to learn how to cultivate the land and grow natural resources. I would create community gardens so that people can grow their own food in harmony and this would bring a give-and-receive system to the masses. I would create food banks and homeless shelters for those living in poverty. I believe that if money could be spent on trapping or enslaving the masses, then money could be resurrected to give shelter, food, and clothing for the masses.

The next agenda I would focus on would be education; and when I say education, I mean beneficial education. This form of education is a resource that will help the masses overcome the obstacles, trials, and tribulations that are in front of them. In other words, this education is survival, a means that justifies the end. I would spend money toward medical resources. When I say this, I'm relating to building more hospitals, clinics, traveling clinics, health educational resources [and programs promoting] natural medicine. I would spend money [on] the discovery of cures to illness [and] disease.

Ultimately, I would spend money on the proper programs that would aim toward prevention of negative action. Programs that cut to the core of the problem. To me, the problem revolves around improper communication, lack of social skills; lack of parenting or guidance; non-active role models, mental health issues, etc. We as a community must address these things head on so that the absence of prisons and jails can be looked upon as an option that will bring success.[53]

This is a laudable vision, and one that has moved from the margins of the US political discourse to its center in the years since this report appeared, thanks in part to the tireless activism of abolitionists like NNJ. But how can it be achieved?

LIMITS AND LESSONS

NNJ was a high-water mark for abolitionist organizing in New York City in recent memory. The campaign generated useful political analysis and conducted agitation that resonated far beyond its ranks of a few dozen core activists. Its considerable collective intelligence was augmented by its assiduous solicitation of the voices of everyday New Yorkers, especially those who were incarcerated. In the process, NNJ demonstrated the audience for abolitionist ideas to be much broader than the rarefied academic settings that critics insist are the only habitats in which these ideas can survive. But NNJ, from its inception to its dissolution in the aftermath of the city council vote, was simply inadequate to the task of stopping the skyscraper jails.

This is, of course, a testament to the strength of its adversaries; the jail boosters had a sophisticated, cash-flush network bridging some of our society's richest people with the most powerful politicians in New York City. It would have been truly remarkable if a ragtag group of volunteers organizing on an ad hoc basis had succeeded in stopping this runaway train. But there are lessons to be learned from the failure of this campaign, beyond the old cliché that one can't fight city hall. While NNJ's inability to stop the jails reflected the power of its opponent, it also evinced the profound demobilization and disorientation of abolitionist, activist, and other radical milieus in the city, underscoring the need for clarity on matters of strategy, tactics, and organization. We therefore reflect on the limits NNJ encountered not to point fingers but to help elucidate a path forward.

We realize that hindsight is 20/20, but it should have come as no surprise, especially after the release of the Lippman report, that #CLOSErikers publicly pivoted toward advocacy for new jails. Nonetheless, #CLOSErikers had operated without significant countermobilization until the founding of NNJ nearly *eighteen* action-packed months later. In the interim, as #CLOSErikers had absorbed the momentum of the defunct Campaign to Shut Down Rikers, it was able to count putative abolitionists (including the authors) among its supporters, however lukewarm, during months that could have been better spent preparing for an inevitable show-down. Nobody can seriously argue the new jail proposal coming out of #CLOSErikers was a big shock; at least one member of Shut Down Rikers had warned of the coming borough-based jails plan as early as February 2016, and the group itself predicted what was coming in a statement that May.[54]

Nonetheless, #CLOSErikers received the benefit of the doubt from many activists—or at least enjoyed the benefits of experi-enced abolitionists keeping their doubts private. This even ex-tended to the #CLOSErikers campaign enjoying the endorsement of Shut Down Rikers itself. At a time when abolitionists, including the authors, should have been drawing hard lines of demarcation, #CLOSErikers was able to use the abolitionist milieu as a step-ping stone toward the realization of its skyscraper jail campaign. We only hope that this book can help others not make the same mistake in the future. Most abolitionists advocate some kind of "big tent" approach to campaigns like stopping new jail construc-tion, a strategy that emphasizes working with as many people as possible regardless of political differences. American abolitionism is heavily indebted to the old Third International strategy of the popular front, which advocates that communists build campaigns alongside liberals and progressive elements of the ruling class. The #CLOSErikers experience should serve as a cautionary tale moving forward, emphasizing why a more sophisticated strategic orientation is necessary. Just as many abolitionists insist on the necessity of building power for the long haul, we must take seriously that actors antithetical to human liberation are doing the same, and leftists' participation in popular fronts can assist these enemies in consolidating their forces.

By the time NNJ launched in September 2018, the new jail plan was already quite far along. It is not exactly fair to say that a project ought to have existed sooner, but this reflects a profound lack of organization and coordination in the broader political milieus that produced NNJ. Many such activist milieus in the United States are hampered by petty sectarianism or interpersonal conflicts and are divided less along practical or ideological lines than by the chance meetings of otherwise isolated activists or else by the fallout from clashes between individual charismatic leaders. This inhibits groups' decisions on strategies and tactics, sometimes leading to group members having little in common among themselves when the time comes for practical unity. In these moments it becomes clear that small groups of friends, or ad hoc networks of activists, academics, and staffers at small nonprofits, do not add up to an effective political organization.

Meanwhile, anti-organizational politics has made a virtue of a necessity, celebrating the profound demobilization of the US left as if this is a great strategic insight rather than a symptom of defeat. This all comes at the expense of farsighted political organizations capable of mobilizing in moments of relative lull toward those moments of decisive confrontation, the likes of which we saw around the skyscraper jail construction.

NNJ's response to the skyscraper jail campaign was, therefore, belated, and it never really carved out a coherent practical orientation distinct from that of the jail boosters. Some of NNJ's most prominent actions simply replicated those of #CLOSErikers, including demonstrations in the same exact location—the steps of city hall—albeit with fewer people involved. The major political tasks of NNJ devolved into lobbying, staging public demonstrations, and attempting to garner sympathy in the press. This strategy was not much different from that of the campaign's adversaries, except, of course, for the lack of resources to carry it out effectively. At the same time, there was general timidity about publicly expressing the communist and anarchist politics held by many members of the campaign, and in the place of incisive anti-system politics, NNJ relied on many of the same vacant platitudes about "community" that the jail boosters were already deploying.

When a large crowd of New York City activists turned out for the group's September 2018 launch event at the People's Forum in Manhattan, there were some excellent perspectives on offer, including those from activists who had stopped Martin Horn's plan in the South Bronx a decade prior, including Lisa Ortega. But much of the event's time was taken up by speakers who demonstrated no knowledge of the skyscraper jail campaign or plans for opposition to it, and who simply recounted their own life stories, as if they were addressing a room of potential funders, not comrades seeking a path forward against the skyscraper jails. When one frustrated audience member spoke about the lack of strategy on display, a panelist from NNJ instructed her that social change begins within oneself.

Such questions of individual activists' authenticity became a particularly pernicious stumbling block. Universities and the nonprofit sector covet a small set of supposedly authentic voices capable of representing oppressed and marginalized people in the interest of elite institutions. Given the scarcity of resources in these institutions, the activists who emerge from them tend to view other people as potential rivals, rather than as comrades. This is amplified by the general sense of cutthroat competition that characterizes the US labor force and housing market, especially in New York City, on top of the predictable effects of unchecked egos. Allowing the cruel competitiveness of capitalist life to manifest itself in political spaces under the guise of debating individual activists' authenticity severely hampers the ability to engage in principled political debate, which requires good-faith disagreement about tactics and strategies.

Leftist spaces are not immune to the racist, sexist, and class-stratified world we all live in. Many social movements in the US have historically privileged the voices of white people, cis men in particular, and especially so when it comes to questions of theory and the direction of movements. The guiding spirit of so-called identity politics is therefore righteous, and these politics emerged to challenge the old color-blind socialist perspective that put the specific demands of marginalized people on the back burner in the name of some abstract idea of "unity."[55] In recent decades there have been concerted efforts in organizing spaces, and rightly so, to deliberately center marginalized people in movement strategies and tactics. But what emerged as a radical intervention of Black feminists in left movement spaces can often become an appeal to apolitical practices of empty representation, easily recuperated by police, politicians, and the broader ruling class.[56] As pioneering Black feminist Barbara Smith recently remarked, "It's like they've taken the identity and left the politics on the floor."[57]

Leftist spaces have not really found a way to balance righteous imperatives like anti-racism and feminism with the equally important need for open and honest debate, in which all participants say what they are really thinking and are free to disagree. Many projects have succumbed instead to what Olúfẹ́mi O. Táíwò calls "deference politics," the practice of conceding, without substantive debate, to whomever can claim to be most marginalized or impacted by the issue at hand. This comes from a good place, but in practice it isn't much of a politics at all. We say this because it forfeits the responsibility communities have to solve problems together, as well as the ethical duty of every organizer, no matter their background, to speak up when they disagree—and the equally important responsibility of their comrades to hear them out in good faith.[58]

And so it is common today to find putatively radical political milieus where the space that should be allocated for precious discussions of tactics and strategy devolves instead into contests over who is the most authentic voice in the room—at the expense of asking whose ideas are the best. NNJ was no exception, and this was a persistent internal obstacle to the group developing sharper tactics and strategies. This fetishization of authenticity became particularly disastrous as #CLOSErikers successfully activated a number of charismatic formerly incarcerated people of color who represented themselves as the most authentic voices in the debate. NNJ presented no alternative to this framework, having accepted the unfortunate premise that a person's positionality matters more than their politics.

There is, of course, no easy formula for the messy work of redressing the systemic white supremacy and patriarchy that pervade US society and, hence, many of its movement spaces, while simultaneously holding a clear political program aloft. And the fact remains that many white people, and people without the direct experience of issues like incarceration, do in fact need to sit down, shut up, and listen far more than is common practice. We, therefore, do not suggest a vulgar binary of "race versus class" as a lens of analysis, nor do we dismiss identity-based politics as an idealist distraction from some imagined version of the *real* struggle. Instead, we encourage struggling together in good faith to build politics adequate for taking identity-based considerations seriously, while simultaneously foregrounding the importance of informed debate, rigorous investigation, and shared commitments to theory and practice across the very real lines that divide us.[59]

Simultaneously, NNJ failed to properly conceptualize its relationship to its broader community, however this term is defined. Following the model of nonprofits in search of funders, NNJ typically represented itself as *the* authentic voice of New York City's communities of color. So too, of course, did #CLOSErikers. And so does just about every political actor, including Eric Adams. And if abolitionism were as popular among this community as NNJ claimed, Adams would never have become mayor on a law-and-order platform. In reality, communities of color do not think one way or another about political issues sufficiently enough for anyone to speak for them. They are not monolithic but are instead complex assemblages of individuals and institutions with a variety of perspectives. And in many places, including New York City, a plurality of these perspectives is favorable to a law-and-order approach to social crisis.

We believe that abolitionists do not have to falsely deny the real support for police and incarceration in many communities of color. As James Forman Jr. has argued compellingly, saturation policing and mass incarceration were not simply imposed from outside onto these communities. They have always enjoyed crucial support, not necessarily out of any ideological dedication to law and order, but because no other solutions to the real problems of interpersonal violence and drug addiction seem possible.[60] Matters become even more complex when we consider that Eric Adams is a much different sort of politician than the first wave of law-and-order hawks of the 1970s and 1980s. A distinct product of advanced public relations campaigns among US police departments pioneered by the LAPD and modeled on counterinsurgent strategies in imperialist wars, Adams represents a kind of fusion of civil rights leader and benevolent patrolman the likes of which Ruth Wilson Gilmore and Craig Gilmore document as unique to the legitimacy crisis of contemporary American policing.[61]

In the face of this complex reality, it is the abolitionists' job to make their own political vision seem possible. This does not begin from the premise that one already speaks for the people, but starts with the notion that one must speak *to* the people. It was always clear to us that NNJ only represented a tiny minority, even within communities of color, but was nonetheless capable of potentially swaying the masses. NNJ, however, should have begun with the fact that it had not yet accomplished this task.[62]

The campaign's mistaken assessment of its embeddedness in New York City communities of color was reflected in a slogan that became its clarion call: "We keep us safe." The phrase is derived from the work of organizers involved in transformative justice, which focuses on providing alternative approaches to how the state and its institutions respond to violence, harm, and abuse. Transformative justice activists argue that interpersonal harm in marginalized communities reflects wider systems of power and oppression, including the state and its institutions of social control and punishment. To resolve issues related to interpersonal harm, transformative justice activists look to practices that already exist in marginalized communities that, because of their social position in society, have been forced to come up with alternative ways to "stay alive and create safety and healing outside of state systems."[63] Instead of relying on police and other state institutions to address harm, transformative justice activists have attempted to craft community-based responses to harm and violence. The responses range from supporting survivors to facilitating accountability for those who have committed sexual assault.

While necessary and laudable, many of these projects of building community safety and accountability are difficult to implement and sustain in the long run. Marginalized communities have experienced decades of state disinvestment, and there exist today no resources that could remotely come close to addressing the material conditions that are the root causes of harm and violence. A key part of neoliberalism has been the effective dismantling of communities through forced dislocation, harshening of living conditions, and disruption of radical alternatives by state agents like the cops. As a result, the idea that "we," however understood, are today in any position to ensure communal safety is symptomatic of a strategic orientation that vastly underestimates the degree of social change necessary to build a society premised on the righteous values of organizations like NNJ. Important work is being done in the here and now by restorative and transformative justice practitioners, but it is a strategic disaster to assume that the means to scale these projects up to the whole of society, or even up to the small activist subcultures within it, already exist. While it is hardly a feel-good sentiment, we believe it would be more productive to begin with the premise that we *can't* keep us safe—and that's the problem.

Ultimately, while NNJ sometimes spoke the language of anticapitalism and crafted a number of fine critiques grounded in radical theory, these elements were never refined into a distinctly antisystem praxis. Instead, the group functioned as a traditional advocacy organization among thousands like it in New York City, albeit with radical slogans and aesthetics—and fewer resources and less political clout than most. This is not a cause for defeatism but a sober call to consider what the campaign got right, and what it got wrong, to prepare for the fights ahead. We will return to this discussion in the final chapter, where we connect the abolitionist struggle in New York City to others like it unfolding in spurts across the country.

CHINATOWN VERSUS THE SKYSCRAPER JAIL

NNJ was, of course, not the only game in town, and it is worth reflecting on prior forms of community organization that came alive to fight the skyscraper jails. While the jail expansion plan was met with righteous opposition across the city, the proposed skyscraper jail in Chinatown particularly invigorated neighborhood activism and connected the new planned carceral construction to the ongoing battle against gentrification and policies of state abandonment.

Chinatown's skyscraper jail is slated to replace the brutalist fifteen-floor Manhattan Detention Center, also known as the Tombs, which closed down in late 2020. Chinatown activists called attention to the fact that the proposed new jail will be built higher than the four other jails, an estimated 500 feet, which is an increase from the originally proposed 400-foot plan. This, despite an October 2019 New York City Council vote that reduced the maximum height for all new jail construction from 450 feet to 295 feet.[64] A memo from the mayor's office, however, recently left such trimming up to the jail designers, and recognized that the new jail in Chinatown may exceed this cap.[65]

Chinatown remains one of the last strongholds against gentrification in Manhattan. But many of the tenants' and workers' rights groups, like Youth Against Displacement and the Chinese Staff and Workers' Association, part of the larger Coalition to Protect Chinatown and LES, have argued that the new skyscraper jail will lead to greater displacement of working-class residents, a process that has intensified over the past decade. Situated in a prime real estate market and within walking distance of the Financial

District, Tribeca, and SoHo, Chinatown has become a prime target for developers seeking to expand their portfolios. In recent years, developers have overcome various restrictions and built luxury hotels and condos that threaten to price out many residents and displace one of the last remaining working-class immigrant neighborhoods in Lower Manhattan.[66]

On March 20, 2022, Neighbors United Below Canal (NUBC), a coalition of residents, activists, and small businesses south of Canal Street, organized a march to protest the city's plans to build a mega jail in the heart of Chinatown. About two thousand people marched from Chinatown to Columbus Park to urge Mayor Adams to reconsider the plan. Jan Lee, head of NUBC, told news outlets, "We're looking at the fourth iteration of the city using this neighborhood as a dumping ground for failed policies of incarceration, building bigger and bigger jails, and disrupting this neighborhood every 40 years."[67]

Lee was referencing an earlier controversy around skyscraper jail construction in Chinatown. In November 1982, about twelve thousand Chinatown residents marched to city hall to protest the building of a new five-hundred-cell borough-based jail next to the newly remodeled Tombs. They took the streets, blocking traffic to the Brooklyn Bridge and calling for "day care centers, schools, housing, jobs" instead of new jails.[68] As the Koch administration pursued its law-and-order crackdown that filled the city's jails to capacity, necessitating more and more human cages, Chinatown residents argued that there were already enough carceral facilities there, including two federal prisons and city detention centers. Koch dismissed Chinatown residents, some of them undocumented immigrants, by saying, "If you don't vote, you don't count."[69] While the new tower was ultimately built, expanding the capacity of the Tombs, the city struggled to overcome the community opposition, and the memory of this powerful movement is very much alive in Chinatown today.

City officials have tried various tactics, including promises of investment in Chinatown, to appease the growing chorus of opponents. For example, in 2019, Mayor de Blasio promised $35 million to fund the performance space of the Museum of Chinese in America, next to which the new mega-jail in Chinatown would be built. In response, the Chinatown Art Brigade, a group of Asian American artists and organizers, penned an open letter to the museum board and executive leadership to reject the mayor's "community buy-back" and to "publicly oppose the construction of a new thirty-five-story high-rise jail in New York's Chinatown."[70] On April 13, 2022, ten protestors were arrested for attempting to form a human blockade to disrupt the construction trucks headed to break ground in Chinatown's proposed jail site.[71]

More recently, pushed by opposition to the new jails coming from various directions, the city council moved to establish a commission on "community reinvestment," chaired by the commissioner of the New York City Department of Social Services and including representatives of other designated city agencies. The commission, which will operate until 2027, is responsible for making a list of recommendations for how city agencies can reinvest in social services that support communities of color most affected by mass incarceration. In its most recent report, the commission identified sixteen communities throughout the five boroughs that are most affected by mass incarceration and made recommendations, including the creation of job training centers.[72] However, without any substantial political willpower or financial commitment, the commission remains yet another toothless bureaucratic tool.

Working-class New Yorkers, however, do not need to read a report to recognize the material deprivation they live with on a day-to-day basis. As elites propose to spend billions of dollars on skyscraper jails, the city's mass transit infrastructure is falling apart, public schools remain underfunded, and working-class New Yorkers of color are locked into low-wage part-time service work while forced to fork over the better part of their income to landlords. Amid such madness, the fight against the new jails politicized many ordinary New Yorkers to confront the ways the city elites' austerity politics continue to prioritize the criminalization of poverty over basic necessities like housing and health care. The fight against building skyscraper jails in New York City signals an important shift in the local politics of mass incarceration and is an example of a potential flashpoint for the kinds of anti-austerity struggles we can expect to continue in the future.

CHAPTER 5

WHAT'S AT STAKE?

Each generation must, out of relative obscurity, discover its mission, fulfill it, or betray it.

—**Frantz Fanon**

"It's an amazing story," former director of the Mayor's Office for Criminal Justice Elizabeth Glazer boasted to journalist Eva Fedderly, celebrating the victory of the skyscraper jail campaign. "I think it's an extraordinary, world historic story, actually, because it's certainly about the buildings, but it's about so much more than that."[1] We are inclined to agree. But what kind of story is it? The answers brings us, by way of a conclusion, back to where we began, with the persistent reality of capitalist crisis, and its most common stopgap remedy, fiscal austerity.

Austerity has been an important tool to preserve global capital accumulation and to protect the interests of the ruling class. It has emerged, in the words of economist Clara Mattei, as a "one-sided class warfare, led by the state and its economic experts and aimed at refurbishing the capital order in moments when it is crumbling."[2] Starting with the Nixon administration, this took the form of economic policies that sought to resolve the crisis of stagnation and inflation by drastically cutting back government spending on social welfare and other social programs. This state disinvestment from social reproduction resulted in working-class people finding it more difficult to access basic social services, including housing, employment, and welfare. These forms of economic insecurity, combined with the right-wing politics of law and order, enabled the unprecedented prison explosion that we today call mass incarceration.[3]

But this is not a sustainable state of affairs. Whereas in the recent past the state relied mostly, if not entirely, on "tough on crime" rhetoric to secure its legitimacy, today, amid the crisis of this order, we are witnessing the rise of carceral humanism as a framework for carceral expansion. It is potentially promising moment, as some scholars and activists insist that the fight against carceral expansion is "a frontline of antiracist class struggle" opposed to white supremacy, austerity, and even capitalism itself.[4] The Ferguson rebellion, the Black Lives Matter movement, and the George Floyd rebellion, in particular, have given us glimpses of how struggles that originated against police and carceral practices can possibly generalize into rejections of the entire capitalist order.

Yet so too have we seen how some of the issues animating these righteous movements have been incorporated into the progressive wing of the ruling class, emptying vital concepts, like antiracism, of their political meaning. To make matters more complicated, even some notable right-wingers have thrown in their lot against mass incarceration, like Newt Gingrich, who appears in Ava DuVernay's film *13th* professing his regrets about the role conservatives played in the prison buildup. Still more effective has been the involvement of carceral nonprofits in projects like the #CLOSErikers campaign, which have built brands around social justice and even abolitionist themes but ultimately serve the expansion of the punishment system and the perpetuation of capitalist social relations.

Austerity, the terrain on which we fight, furnishes the most common occasion for mass struggle, but it is merely a symptom of capitalist social relations—much the same as "neoliberalism" cannot be seriously opposed to any better forms of capitalism, but must be seen as an expression of its antihuman essence. Thus, while mass struggle is inevitable, constant, and always potentially anticapitalist, the power to define unfolding crises and orient movements toward its redress becomes a coveted political weapon in the hands of those who would happily keep capitalism for centuries to come. There is no guarantee that anti-austerity, or even seemingly anticapitalist, politics favor human liberation; just look at the historical scourge of anti-Semitism and the persistence of anti-system right-wing politics.[5]

The George Floyd rebellion in the summer of 2020 helped to mainstream abolitionist politics, and in the time since, important theorizing and reflection on antiprison organizing have been widely read.[6] For activists against the punishment system, the particular encroachment of ruling-class interests, and cage builders in particular, onto the rhetorical terrain of antiprison activism, and even abolitionism, should challenge us to sharpen our own analysis and develop better criteria by which to evaluate politics in the here and now. In this political climate, it is difficult to avoid the conclusion that *being against jails and prisons is simply not enough.* Abolitionism needs broader horizons and deeper guiding principles. Thankfully, much of this is contained within the rich history of the abolitionist tradition, waiting for us to put it to work.

THE FALSE PROMISE OF CARCERAL HUMANISM

The skyscraper jails are not just an isolated case of technocratic reforms aimed at "capitalism saving capitalism from capitalism," as the Gilmores put it.[7] Nor is this a story about incarceration alone; policing and prison reform, along with other promises of green capitalism and immigration reform, are the idioms of an emerging tendency of the US ruling class concerned with restoring legitimacy to the capitalist social order amid protracted crisis. In particular, scholars have argued that the Great Recession of 2008 introduced *technocratic Keynesianism* as an effort to revive the system, and it was reintroduced in response to the COVID-19 pandemic.[8] In 2008 this looked like the state bailing out the banking industry, and in 2020, expanding temporary welfare provisions to stave off the effects of the COVID-19 pandemic. We argue that similar technocratic reforms are currently being applied to the carceral state, cloaked in the language of building a *fairer*, more *humane*, and *cost-effective* punishment system. In this process, it is not just the usual suspects, such as liberal criminologists, who are pushing to reimagine a so-called humane system, but also the growing carceral nonprofit sector, and even conservatives as well.

In previous decades, the rhetoric of tough on crime was embraced by both sides of the political spectrum. While we continue to see this language deployed at the level of local politics, it does not have the national resonance it once did. On a local level, law-and-order politicians are slowly pushing out their more reform-minded counterparts as represented by the election of former police captain Eric Adams. Yet at the national level, *reform*, not tough on crime, is the main political messaging that is uniting conservatives, libertarians, and liberals around a common goal: to build popular legitimacy for various criminal justice institutions and to restore our faith in the capitalist order.

In the wake of a massive popular uprising against the carceral state, scholar and activist James Kilgore calls into question whether this new coalition "can deliver even enough change to calm the waters."[9] Looking at the spate of legislation passed on the heels of the George Floyd rebellion aimed at reforming police power, Naomi Murakawa argues that it was "a testament to crass opportunism," especially considering how Black death, namely the police murders of Sandra Bland, George Floyd, and Breonna Taylor, was used to further entrench the law and the carceral state into the lives of the people it purports to help.[10]

In decades past, jail boosters framed carceral construction as either the inevitable result of rising rates of crime or, in moments of honesty, an economic-development strategy for impoverished areas.[11] Today, against a backdrop of increased economic inequality and austerity that have obliterated the state's capacity to care for its citizens, jail boosters increasingly rely on the rhetoric of carceral humanism to promote jails and prisons as "caring social service providers."[12] Carceral humanism frames jails and prisons as the local fix to all kinds of social ills, from addiction to mental health to houselessness. The language of public safety, a long-standing, powerful discourse that has narrowed our ideas of victimization, harm, and violence, is now being replaced by the language of *care*—a shift in the politics of mass incarceration and the carceral state.

As Brett Story and Judah Schept remind us, the carceral state is very malleable, "allowing prisons, jails, and other constitutive parts to serve as solutions to very different kinds of communities navigating through different elements of neoliberal crisis."[13] We see this in the increased support for so-called justice campuses, gender-responsive jails and prisons, and mental health jails. These new forms of carceral humanism are dangerous because they justify treating social problems as criminal issues to be solved by warehousing people in allegedly nicer facilities. As we have shown with the case of Rikers, the culture of jails and prisons is not the fault of a few bad apples but an integral part of how jail authorities maintain control over prisoners. These facilities will not actually change, even if the justification for their existence does.

Since the dawn of the prison in the late eighteenth century, incarceration has, more often than not, been justified as a humanistic endeavor. Hence scholars Jack Norton, Lydia Pelot-Hobbs, and Judah Schept are correct to claim that "carceral humanism is a new expression of an older argument." Today's variant, they argue, is distinguished by the unique combination of neoliberalism, which has paired the racialized practices of mass incarceration and austerity, with "an emergent if shallow multicultural and bipartisan criminal justice effort."[14] This has in turn furnished the kind of social justice arguments for mass incarceration seen in the skyscraper jails and elsewhere across the United States. On a more basic level, the practices of carceral humanism, identified by abolitionist activist Rose Braz in California as early as 2006, some years before Kilgore coined the useful term, are becoming today far more sophisticated.[15] We believe the case study of the skyscraper jails represents a depth and scope of carceral humanism never before seen, and given its success, many of these tactics will likely be coming soon to a city or town near you.

Given that the rise, and transformation, of carceral humanism today is intimately bound up with the horrors of mass incarceration and an ongoing crisis of social reproduction, humanistic carceral projects can win political support by purporting to solve these scourges with the magic of jail construction. In ideological terms, austerity is the *only* context in which it would even make sense to open a mental health jail. The existing public health infrastructure has been discredited and dismantled to such an extent that bringing it back seems less possible or desirable than simply reinscribing its function into a jail. At the same time, communities that have been dismantled and sown with misery understandably seek redress, and it is important to emphasize the visceral power of virtually *any* solution presented as possible. But the promise of carceral humanism—that jails and prisons can be places where people can access "care" and can serve as a medicinal salve on the broader social crisis—cannot be fulfilled, despite the best intentions of reformers. The history of the prison and jail in the United States has shown us that innovations and reforms are destined to fail at their purported task, and that all such efforts leave in their wake are more wretched facilities.

#BEYONDROSIES

Carceral humanism nonetheless continues to pretend to solve the problems of austerity and mass incarceration with more jails. The rise of the gender-responsive jail model is a particularly troubling response to the damaging effects of incarceration on women and gender-marginalized people. As the statistics show, women are the fastest growing population in jails and prisons today.[16] New York City–based abolitionist Mon Mohapatra argues that the recent proposal to build a new women's jail in Harlem can only be understood as the latest effort in the much longer "genealogy" of reformist campaigns of the last two decades to remake the city as "the bastion of 'progressive punishment.'"[17] Reformers in New York have argued that building a gender-responsive jail to replace the Rose M. Singer Center on Rikers Island, commonly referred to as Rosie's, is the best solution for the unique problems that incarcerated women face.

One of the leading reformers advocating for a separate gender-responsive facility for women has been Sharon White-Harrigan, a formerly incarcerated woman who cut her teeth in various advocacy efforts involving incarcerated and formerly incarcerated women throughout New York State. Two years after joining the #CLOSErikers campaign, she helped found the nonprofit Women's Community Justice Association (WCJA) and, as its executive director, launched the #BEYONDrosies campaign for a new gender-responsive jail in Harlem.[18] The ongoing campaign is demanding that the city reduce Rosie's population to under one hundred, permanently close it before the 2027 timeline, and replace it with a "standalone, centralized, humane center, for those that remain."[19] But as abolitionist scholar Abby Cunniff deftly argues, #BEYON-Drosies willfully ignores that Rosie's, too, originally emerged as the centerpiece of rehabilitative reform efforts.[20]

The Rose M. Singer Center opened on Rikers Island in June 1988 as a new state-of-the-art facility dedicated to the rehabilitation of incarcerated women. On the eve of its opening, Rose M. Singer, the women's rights advocate and jail reform activist who, as a member of the New York City Board of Correction, pushed for its creation, boldly boasted its therapeutic role, saying, "The center will be a place of hope and renewal for all the women who come here."[21] To reflect the specific needs of incarcerated women, a nursery was built on its premises with a capacity to hold twenty-five infants. In contrast with the other drab facilities on Rikers, the new women's jail even included a garden, and its walls were painted in happy colors of rose, mauve, blue, and yellow.

But none of these architectural fixes proved effective to stem a culture of sexual violence and abuse from taking root inside Rosie's, as revealed by one lawsuit after another. In 2013, the US Department of Justice concluded that Rosie's was among the twelve worst carceral facilities in the country, largely because of its high rates of staff sexual misconduct and abuse.[22] Yet, despite government reports and lawsuits filed by incarcerated women against correction officers and the city itself, the abuse was continually swept under the rug. But following the 2023 passage of New York's Adult Survivors Act that extended the statute of limitations on reporting sexual abuse and assault, the abuse was finally out in the open and the general public could no longer ignore it. Nearly 20 percent of over 2,500 lawsuits filed under the new law were from women incarcerated at Rosie's.[23]

Today, Rosie's is far from the rehabilitative haven that Singer imagined. In fact, her granddaughter, Suzanne Singer, described it as "a torture chamber, where women are routinely abused, housed in unsanitary conditions, and denied medical and mental health services."[24] As the momentum to close Rikers grew, liberal reformers demanded a return to the therapeutic model of incarceration Rose Singer once supported in a new jail for women.[25]

The #BEYONDrosies campaign is a culmination of reform efforts that for years have tried to call attention to the specific needs of New York City's incarcerated women. A year prior to its launch, the New York Women's Foundation and the Prisoner Reentry Institute at John Jay College released a collaborative report, *Women InJustice: Gender and the Pathway to Jail in New York City*, which highlighted the specific pathways that lead women to jail, including the role of prior trauma and violence. The report made the case for gender-responsive reforms.[26] By this time, the New York Women's Foundation had become an experienced voice in matters of carceral expansion under the guise of reform. As readers may remember, the foundation was a key supporter of the Lippman Commission. The year 2017 was a busy one for the New York Women's Foundation, which also enlisted the help of the Vera Institute of Justice "to identify gender-informed strategies for getting New York City women disentangled from the criminal justice system."[27] Throughout that year, as part of its fact-finding mission, Vera met with various groups to discuss how to make this a reality. Their participatory research project even included site visits to Rosie's and focus groups with incarcerated women. Their 2018 collaborative report *A New Path to Justice: Getting Women Off of Rikers Island* put forth the idea that there should be "gender- and trauma-informed" programming and services tailored to meet the needs of incarceration women.[28]

Over the following four years, the campaign picked up new supporters, including liberal feminists ranging from actress Gina Belafonte to Gloria Steinem, who wrote public appeals in support of the proposed new jail. Belafonte went so far as to pen an op-ed in the *New York Times* highlighting the reform work of the Women's Community Justice Association and its founder, Sharon White-Harrigan, and inviting readers to imagine a "feminist jail" that is attentive to the needs of incarcerated women.[29] In May 2022, the WCJA partnered up with the Prison and Jail Innovation Lab at the University of Texas, Austin, and the Columbia Justice Lab, a university research center led by renowned sociologist Bruce Western and former commissioner of the New York City Department of Probation Vincent Schiraldi. They co-produced a white paper, *A Safer New York*, which made the case for a gender-responsive facility to replace Rosie's. The authors lambasted the city's plan to transfer incarcerated women to the new men's jail in Kew Gardens, calling it "an unsafe setback."[30] This report gave the #BEYONDrosies campaign the academic support it needed to push through its demands to repurpose the closed-down Lincoln Correctional Facility in Harlem into a new gender-responsive jail.

Boosters of the women's jail made the case that the Lincoln location would be built at a faster rate than would the Kew Gardens facility, and it would be cheaper and more easily accessible given the panoply of nonprofit social service providers in Harlem.[31] As the WCJA argued, the proposed new jail would also "operate using a new 'Reentry at Entry' model that focuses on therapeutic care, family unification, and skills building to break the cycle of incarceration."[32] Proponents of the new facility have argued that it will be responsive to the unique experiences of incarcerated women, especially in regard to the trauma and violence that often lead to criminal justice system involvement. To this end, reformers proposed that the new facility train all staffers in trauma-informed, culturally responsive, and gender-responsive care, reduce the number of correctional guards, and have social workers and nonprofit staffers manage the facility. These proposals emulate the newly reformed juvenile justice system.[33] Under Close to Home, New York's juvenile justice initiative, twenty-six juvenile prisons were closed throughout the state and the remaining youth were transferred "close to home" and into privately run facilities. While this has been heralded as a win by reformers, the results on the ground say otherwise.

When scholar Alexandra Cox visited some of these facilities in Upstate New York, she noticed that despite the rhetoric of reform, the facilities functioned as ordinary youth prisons. Young people were still locked in a facility where their day-to-day activities were monitored by staff and they had to complete therapeutic sessions as a condition of release. Furthermore, because of decarceration efforts, there were more staffers than youth, which led, ironically enough, to greater social control, namely through the use of mandatory therapeutic programming.[34] As in the case of gender-responsive jails, these so-called responsive-caging practices were ultimately responsive to the need for social control.

As abolitionists like Mon Mohapatra reflect, activists challenged the plan to build a new women's jail, relying on networks of abolitionists already in place. Mohapatra and other organizers, including the abolitionist collective Survived and Punished, penned a public letter to the Columbia Justice Lab calling out DOP commissioner Schiraldi and other staffers at the center for supporting the new women's jail. The letter did not receive a lot of public attention. But soon thereafter, a group of Columbia students successfully protested, demanding the university's disaffiliation with the center. Formerly incarcerated activists, including Laura Whitehorn, got involved to host conversations between abolitionists who opposed the plan and the activists who supported it, namely the WCJA. But these exchanges ultimately revealed that the differences between the two groups were too vast, for the time being at least.[35]

The fight to build a gender-responsive jail in Harlem continues to drum up support among reformers and jail boosters. In 2022, in response to the death of Mary Yehudah, an incarcerated woman at Rosie's who was found unresponsive in her cell, a coalition of reformers, including Michael Jacobson, former Manhattan district attorney Cyrus Vance Jr., former chair of the NYC Board of Correction Jennifer Jones Austin, and former director of the Mayor's Office for Criminal Justice Elizabeth Glazer, presented written testimony to the New York City Council Committee on Criminal Justice in support of the new women's jail.[36] The struggle against a nemesis of such sophistication requires, as Mohapatra concludes, a reconsideration of strategy and tactics.

AN ENTRY POINT

Reflecting on the lessons of No New Jails NYC, the fight against the Harlem women's jail, and ongoing organizing in the No New Jails national network, Mohapatra recounts,

> I now feel like a lot of these jail-expansion campaigns or campaigns to stop construction are more like entry points, rather than the ultimate goal. . . . Saying "Hey, there's a jail in your community, and you should care about that and you should try to get rid of it, or you should try to stop other ones from happening" is really an entry point into a much more expansive series of considerations about the world and life, because there are so many things that need to happen after that point to make sure that another

jail, another form of coercion or soft policing, does not emerge out of the organizing.

Crucially, she adds, "And I don't think I would have thought that four years ago."[37] We share this sentiment. In a moment defined by great uncertainty, two facts seem equally true: The first is that fights against the expansion of the carceral state are righteous and essential. The second is that these fights alone are not a sufficient political horizon for bringing into being the world abolitionists imagine.

A moment as decisive as ours calls for not only a diversity of tactics but, more broadly, a deepening of strategy. Jack Norton, Lydia Pelot-Hobbs, and Judah Schept urge abolitionists to "be adept at maneuvering the often mundane politics of land-use policy, from canvassing against new jail taxes to learning the county planning procedures to conducting political education about the false promise of jails as economic development or sites of care."[38] We agree that all of these tactics can be important politicizing moments and, quite practically, useful actions for preventing the kind of human misery found in prisons and jails. And if we want to create anticapitalist movements that regard jails and prisons as central aspects of class struggle, as these authors rightly prescribe, it is necessary to develop strategies that go beyond narrow and often defensive fights waged on our enemy's terms, and to move beyond the terrain of struggles inscribed within the law.

"The best way to think of the law," write radical labor lawyers Staughton Lynd and Daniel Gross, "is as a shield, not a sword. The law is not an especially good way to change things. But it can give you some real protection as you try to change things in other ways."[39] We believe that the present arsenal of US abolitionism is largely composed of shields, albeit ones being wielded as if they were swords. This mistaken assessment of the difference between defense and offense has led to a dearth of revolutionary abolitionist strategy. "Even if we had successfully stopped the city council from approving the construction of four new jails in NYC in 2019," reflects Mohapatra, "we would have still had to contend with all the jails on Rikers, the NYPD, the technocratic surveillance, the courts, and more."[40]

How can abolitionism respond to this stubborn fact? A fascinating glimpse of an answer comes to us today from Atlanta.

#STOPCOPCITY AND THE INSURRECTIONARY HORIZON

Just a year after the George Floyd rebellion and the local police killing of Rayshard Brooks, Atlanta city officials proposed a controversial new plan to build a sprawling police training center in a primarily Black working-class neighborhood, on the present site of one of the last green places left in the city, the Weelaunee Forest. For local activists, the political context was clear: the spectacular street militancy in Atlanta and elsewhere in 2020 had further delegitimized police forces already reeling from well-deserved public contempt, and these forces in turn found it increasingly difficult to maintain their rank and file's morale. Many cops walked away from their jobs, and in cities across America, law enforcement agencies continue to claim difficulty recruiting new officers.[41] Faced with a deepening legitimacy crisis within its own ranks and among the broader public, the Atlanta Police Foundation, a private-public consortium, found the answer in a shiny new police training complex, the Atlanta Public Safety Training Center, which activists have derisively called Cop City.[42]

In June of 2021, city council members approved the authorization for a development project that would lease the forest, an estimated 381 acres located in the unincorporated southwest part of

Dekalb County, to the Atlanta Police Foundation. The proposed site will serve as a $90 million police training facility, a third of which is being paid by the taxes of city residents. The rest is being funded by the Atlanta Police Foundation, a large US policing nonprofit, second only to its New York City equivalent, as well as by private corporations, including Home Depot and Chick-fil-A.[43] According to the center's website, the massive training complex will include an "auditorium for police/fire and public use," a "mock city for burn building training and urban police training," and an "Emergency Vehicle Operator Course for emergency vehicle driver training," as well as a gun range and a K-9 unit kennel.[44] Evoking the same rhetoric of *reimagining* the punishment system that we saw in the skyscraper jails and other projects of the carceral nonprofits, the Atlanta Police Foundation argued that the new training center would "reimagine law enforcement training, catapulting APD and Atlanta Fire Rescue to the vanguard of major urban law enforcement agencies."[45]

Nonetheless, Cop City, it seems, is quite unpopular in Atlanta. In a virtual Atlanta City Council meeting held on September 8, 2021, ahead of the city council vote, an estimated 70 percent of the callers opposed the proposal.[46] Nearly three hundred people had signed up for public comments, forcing council members to extend the meeting to two days. According to the *Atlanta Journal-Constitution*, the city council received 1,166 comments—totaling seventeen hours of audio.[47] Many residents opposed the plan on the grounds that it would lead to further police militarization in a predominantly Black city, the effects of which were fresh on their minds. Others argued that the Atlanta Police Department already receives a third of the city's budget, and the new proposed facility would just increase its power and scope.[48] Yet, against the wishes of Atlanta residents, in the summer of 2023, Atlanta's city council voted 10–4 to lease the land to the

Atlanta Police Foundation to build Cop City. As we write, the struggle continues.

Since the plan for Cop City was announced, activists have opposed its construction with a diversity of tactics. These have included the traditional mechanisms of working through local governing bodies like the city council and, most recently, employing an impressive petition campaign that gathered over 100,000 signatures.[49] But the movement has also been defined by rowdy street marches and protests in downtown Atlanta and at the construction company offices, raves and parties in the Weelaunee Forest, the sabotage of construction equipment, and protracted occupation of the forest itself by dedicated activists known as forest defenders. These actions have drawn in a large number of young people, many of whom are new to political organizing and seek to escape their low-wage jobs and find in Stop Cop City a struggle worthfighting.[50]

Weaving together movements for racial, economic, and environmental justice, "the Stop Cop City movement has made Atlanta an epicenter of abolitionist organizing," write organizers Micah Herskind and Kamau Franklin.

> The movement has no single unifying political framework; it includes abolitionists, anarchists, communists, liberals, libertarians, environmentalists, voting and civil rights activists, Indigenous and antisettler-colonialism organizers, and many more who may not identify with a particular political philosophy but who all choose trees over cops, transparency over backroom deals, and community resources over a burgeoning police state.[51]

Similarly, activist Hugh Farrell has recently noted,

The constellation of camps in the forest, as well as the various social segments that populate the movement— the elementary schoolchildren and their parents, visitors from outside Atlanta, the ravers, the community organizers and canvassers in the surrounding Black neighborhoods, trans activists and naturalists—are as marked by their connections and their relations as much as by their decentralization.[52]

Virtually anyone and everyone has been welcomed to join the fight against Cop City, leading to an impressive coalition that spans Atlanta, with solidarity organizing nationwide.

From the narrowly practical perspective of stopping Cop City from being built, each of these tactics stands equal to the rest, provided they get the desired result. But what is the real promise of the #StopCopCity campaign? Just as preventing the skyscraper jails would not end incarceration in New York City, stopping Cop City will not abolish the police, the prison system, or capitalism. Preventing the facility from being built will likely be counted by many as a step toward abolitionism, but this will remain an open question, as the cops would still get their training somewhere else, to the extent American cops need any more militarized training than they've already received, whether in their local department or a previous career in the military. A victory against Cop City would surely be a boon for progressives and radicals in Atlanta, and a political embarrassment for its boosters. But it is hard to imagine that simply stopping the facility would make the balance of forces much different from what it was in the years before—especially if this is accomplished by a ballot referendum that serves to legitimize the city government and integrate organizers into it.

What makes #StopCopCity the most important struggle of our moment, then, is not the possibility of stopping this monstrosity from being built. It is instead the tantalizing image of an abolitionist struggle oriented to an insurrectionary horizon. In particular, it is the movement's illegal tactics that have drawn the most attention and have captured imaginations all over the world, leading to thousands of people taking heroic risks together in Atlanta. The Weelaunee Forest has been the scene of brave and decisive actors striking *against* the carceral state, taking it as an external foe rather than as a terrain of technical intervention. The law is a shield. The forest defenders are our sword! Their courage and unwillingness to meet the capitalist state on its own terms is a guiding light in a moment defined by a dangerous impasse of leftist praxis.

The forest defenders are, of course, part of a long tradition of eco-defense tactics used against extractive and infrastructure projects and more recently aimed at carceral construction.[53] The enduring influence of the righteous struggle at Standing Rock, especially its rich diversity of tactics, is palpable as well.[54] The forest defenders also built off a tradition of insurrection seen across the United States, such as in the George Floyd rebellion, which in turn had used a set of practices developed in previous decades of struggle around the world.[55] But in the case of Stop Cop City, these tactics are on the verge of merging with the more traditional practices of abolitionism and community organizing to create the skeleton of the kind of formidable fighting force a successful revolution against capitalism requires.

Of course, Stop Cop City's illegal aspects have also made it vulnerable to harsh state repression. On January 18, 2023, state troopers descended on a forest defender encampment and murdered twenty-six-year-old Manuel "Tortuguita" Terán. The cops later alleged that Tortuguita fired first, but the report from the DeKalb County Medical Examiner's Office found no trace of gun residue powder on them.[56] Even more egregious was the fact, later disclosed, that Tortuguita evidently had their hands up.[57] And Tortuguita's murder was just the beginning of the state flexing its power to defeat the movement. Most recently, in September 2023, sixty-one activists were indicted by a Georgia grand jury under the Racketeer Influenced and Corrupt Organizations Act (RICO), deployed to treat the Stop Cop City movement as a "criminal enterprise" that the government traces back to the George Floyd rebellion of 2020.[58] The 109-page indictment reveals deep state surveillance of activists, including the monitoring of zine publications and flyers stating opposition to Cop City and internet accounts mentioning the coordination of mutual aid activities like buying food. The indictment accuses Atlanta Solidarity Fund activists of being the brains behind the "criminal enterprise," and the organization accordingly faces money laundering and racketeering charges for essentially raising money to bail protestors out. The state is using RICO as a tool to recast the activities of activist work and organizing (bailing people out of jail, writing letters to incarcerated people) as a criminal conspiracy.[59]

As many activists have noted, this legal maneuver by the state sets a dangerous precedent for movements against police and carceral power, including spreading fear to prevent further organizing. But it also means the state is taking notice. The example set in Atlanta, of bridging the ordinary toolbox of abolitionism and community organizing with the traditions of eco-defense and insurrectionary anarchism, offers a path forward, away from easily co-opted work undertaken within the halls of power, insular universities, and nonprofits beholden to the charity of elites. And given that so much of liberal activism revolves around demonizing and vilifying the brave militants who practice illegal protest tactics, it is particularly powerful to see that the movement in Atlanta has yet to be disorganized by the old racist trope of "outside agitators," shopworn privilege-baiting, and other weapons of the counterinsurgency seen in 2020.[60] To the extent that any struggle in the United States today shows the path forward, it is Atlanta, in all its rowdy, militant, and illegal glory.

Illegality cuts to the heart of the matter. "The central political issue/obstacle is the legitimacy of capital," argued Don Hamerquist in the midst of the Occupy Wall Street movement. Hamerquist emphasized illegality at a time when the movement risked shifting from a dynamic and formidable challenge to capitalist hegemony to a fairly predictable and landlocked exercise in speaking truth to power, as the progressive wing of the ruling class had already begun demonstrating its ability to subsume key ideological components of Occupy into a business-friendly variant of left populism. In contrast, large-scale illegality refuses to recognize the legitimacy of the capitalist state—standing as a visible rebuke to it—and cannot be welcomed inside. Moving forward, Hamerquist concluded, "the challenge must be embodied in a politics and culture of resistance that understands and embraces its 'illegality'—rather than its 'democracy,' or its 'representative' character, or even its 'militancy.'"[61] While this largely remained a road not taken for Occupy, the forest defenders have demonstrated the awesome power of unapologetic illegality in drawing hard political lines, resisting co-optation, and actually pulling people leftward.

The repression in Atlanta, therefore, does not discredit the illegality of the movement. Quite the opposite. This is the response that can be expected when the state begins to take us seriously. Repression of this scale, and worse, is inevitable as struggle deepens. The need for enduring community support in the face of repression, as well as for better communal practices of security and care, highlight the necessity of developing a robust revolutionary culture that builds on care work, mutual aid, and traditional community organizing.[62] The tantalizing combination of above-ground organization and clandestine activity seen in Stop Cop City has raised a number of important political questions, alongside very real dangers, both of which are equally unavoidable in moving forward toward any revolutionary horizon.[63]

We must particularly emphasize that the above-ground practices of mutual aid and care, which one could call the *social reproduction* of struggles, are sometimes wrongfully counterposed with street militancy, when they are in fact a necessary component of its success. Feminist philosopher Kelly Gawel invites us to conceptualize the practice of *militant care*, a communal "striving to cultivate a relational container capable of holding each other's pain, and of generating political power."[64] Many tasks that are vital to even a short-lived insurrectionary moment, such as jail support, antirepression work, mutual aid, and care for emotional and physical harm, are often carried out far from the spectacle of the street fight. It is necessary, therefore, to recognize and uplift this work, which is disproportionately done by women and femmes, and not allow it to become the foil for more confrontational tactics. These activities are not only valid in themselves, but indispensable to any successful revolution. Thankfully, the fusion of street militancy with practices of care and social reproduction is not a theoretical advancement we are proposing; it is already a vital component of revolutionary activity wherever it exists.

Atlanta may not have solved every problem facing the revolutionary left, but in many important ways, the struggle against Cop City helps show the way forward, beyond abolitionism as a politics in itself, and toward the necessity of communism.

REVOLUTIONARY ABOLITIONISM

Abolitionism in the United States today presents the possibility of a revolutionary alternative to the capitalist death cult presently driving life on our planet to the point of extinction. It simultaneously risks falling into the uncanny valley between reformism and revolution, inviting working-class people to imagine a world that actually isn't possible: a postrevolutionary society without the revolution required to get there. Without the central component of insurrectionary class struggle, the abolitionist vision is missing a giant step between its important praxis in the present day, and a decisively liberated future.

While the right-wing political enemies of campaigns like Defund the Police are effectively correct in saying that the campaign didn't find significant traction within the US working class, this perhaps isn't the smoking gun against radical politics they think it is.[65] It is just as likely that people who might be friendly to the ultimate aim of the movement simply cannot imagine a shift in municipal budgets delivering the kind of widespread social change necessary to dislodge the police from their central role in social reproduction. And are they wrong? Regardless, it is clear that until a critical mass of people believe that another world is possible, half measures like Defund the Police will continue to fall on deaf ears among a populace that has learned from experience to expect very little from its society. If anything, the experience of Defund the Police proves abolitionist conventional wisdom to be backward: instead of meeting reform-minded people where they were and slowly turning them into revolutionaries, the Defund campaign took putative revolutionaries, at a time of great upheaval, and turned them into reformists.

The simple fact is there will be no peaceful transition from our present mess of a society to one that upholds the values of abolitionism. The ruling class, large and small, who own the earth and are busily destroying it, will not surrender the reins of power without the greatest fight this planet has ever seen. Abolitionism, even in its most modest form, demands far more than the ruling class will ever give us of its own volition. Today's elites are so entrenched and recalcitrant that at this juncture in US history the imposition of even Bernie Sanders's presidential campaign platform would require strife equaling at least that of the French Revolution, guillotines and all—just as the abolition of slavery and realization of formal equality for Black people required a great, bloody civil war.

The present balance of power, within even liberal democratic states, which shifts the burden of social reproduction onto police and prisons, is an important cornerstone on which the entirety of wealth and power at the top of capitalist society rests. It represents a critical bloc of the ruling class's combined interest in fiscal austerity, which is itself imposed on them by the objective limits of capitalism, with the political imperative to keep working-class people in a position of extreme powerlessness. Why on earth would they give up this power voluntarily? The willingness of progressive elites to reconfigure the system of mass incarceration demonstrates not the disposability but the grave importance of their coercive power; they are trying to preserve control by tweaking its mechanisms, and perhaps making the mechanisms more "humane." A complete break from this order is necessary.

"Before abolitionism," writes scholar Joy James, "there was revolutionary struggle."[66] Revolutionary struggle is the grounds from which contemporary abolitionism sprang, and it must remain the imperative that animates it. As we have argued, contemporary US abolitionism counts among its many strengths an emphasis on the here and now. But this often comes at the expense of a strategic perspective that bridges these vital struggles in the present with a future communist society.[67] This is why we believe contemporary abolitionism must—in the spirit of Toussaint L'Ouverture, John Brown, Assata Shakur, the Black Panthers, and countless other abolitionists before us—orient its praxis toward the necessity of revolution.

"Abolitionism," writes Noel Ignatiev, "it has been shown, took shape not in direct opposition to overt proslavery ideas but to moderate elements within the antislavery camp."[68] Many within the US antislavery movement favored a gradualist approach, based on the assumption that emancipation could not be achieved overnight, and would instead be the product of slow, patient work across decades. One faction defined itself as "antislavery," as opposed to abolitionist, and limited its vision to attacking the power of slave states in the government, versus embracing the necessity to practically abolish the entire system by any means necessary. Moderate antislavery forces attempted technocratic fixes and political jockeying, unwilling to set their horizon on the violent and decisive break with the institution that was necessary to bring it to an end.

Abolitionists of this time engaged in many activities we could call lawful reforms: speaking out publicly, publishing, engaging with electoral politics, and more. These were tactics suitable for a broad-based struggle. Meanwhile, however, runaway slaves continued to take proactive, illegal steps to free and organize themselves, abolitionists agitated tirelessly in preparation for the coming break with legality, and, at last, John Brown and his multiracial band of insurrectionaries took a decisive step toward antislavery revolution, forever altering the political fault lines of the United States and sending the nation careening toward the glorious chaos of full abolition. "Slavery was abolished not through constitutional process but through war and revolution," Ignatiev concludes.[69] We believe, as Ignatiev never tired of arguing, that abolitionists today should closely study the tactics and strategies of their historical predecessors.

To say all this is not to call for political purism or sectarianism. The anticapitalist left is extremely weak in the United States, to whatever extent it can be said to even exist. And no programmatic solution, no matter how convincing on paper, has, as of yet, illuminated a way forward. In a situation so dire, we welcome experimentation and unorthodox thinking. On the most basic level, it is heartening to see anyone on our side winning *anything* and meeting *anyone* outside the usual activist circles. We are, therefore, very sympathetic to abolitionists and other activists who are testing out different strategies in important local fights, attempting to build power while simultaneously popularizing leftist ideas among people whose political consciousness largely proceeds from the inevitability of capitalism and the necessity of cutthroat competition for survival.

However, as many abolitionist organizers themselves are quick to point out, the challenges of co-optation are daunting.[70] What's more, even victories on the state's terrain are subject to revocation. For example, in cities where abolitionists have been successful at halting jail expansions, such as in Los Angeles and Sacramento, the nature of the actual victories is unclear. In 2019, in Los Angeles, abolitionists with the JusticeLA coalition shut down the city's plans to close down the Men's Central Jail and replace it with a mental health jail. This was an important victory that relied on abolitionists forming a broad-based coalition with other reformers and progressives, which also led to the push for important decarceration initiatives. But two years later, to the dismay of abolitionists, the jail remained open, and the County of Los Angeles Board of Supervisors voted in March 2023 to build a sixteen-bed facility for incarcerated people with mental health illness inside the decrepit facility.[71]

We have no intention of being glib about how serious a commitment it is to open a political horizon the likes of which we have glimpsed in Atlanta. Many forest defenders have suffered great consequences, including one who paid the ultimate price. It is instead, with great respect for the sacrifice of the Atlanta comrades, that we emphasize how heroic and necessary their work has been and highlight that the only possible victory for abolitionism will come through an *illegal* and highly *unsafe* confrontation with the capitalist state.

Abolitionism charting a revolutionary course will not necessarily mean extreme tactical militancy in situations that do not call for it, nor the addition of revolutionary rhetoric to the same old practices. Instead, a revolutionary abolitionism will mean evaluating present-day praxis based not simply on whether it abets the expansion of the carceral system but also on whether it prepares the ground for heightened struggles to come. We do not offer a magical bridge between isolated practices in the here and the realization of communism. But we believe that holding this goal aloft is the first step, from which future considerations will result.

In immediate practical terms, abolitionists would do well to interrogate more deeply our received ensembles of strategies and tactics. The criteria of "non-reformist reforms," then, could therefore be further clarified by engaging with a broader set of questions animating future praxis, such as the following:

- Does this action build the capacity of people, both individually and within broader organizations, to take initiative independent of the capitalist state and the nonprofit industrial complex, or does it further integrate our political work within these entities?
- Does this action prepare for independent, unlawful, pro-revolutionary intervention in moments of crisis such as the 2020 George Floyd rebellion, or does it foreclose the possibility of taking such action by binding politics to lawful, pro-system forms of political participation?
- Does this action challenge the racial order, or, alternatively, does it risk strengthening it?

- Will the success of this action detract from, or enhance, the legitimacy of one or more layers of state?
- Will this action promote loyalty to the liberal democratic process, or will it serve to further delegitimize these institutions and actors?
- Is this action leading people into the Democratic Party or smaller parties that ultimately support it, or does it help promote an extraparliamentary left?
- Does this action promote a reverence for, or stuckness within, the law, or does it encourage participants to treat the law with disdain and to strive toward tactics that break it?
- Will the success of this action potentially bolster the progressive wing of the ruling class, and if so, is that risk worth taking?
- Does this action encourage people to defer control over their lives to external powers and authorities, or does it encourage them to cultivate their ability to take direct control over these conditions?
- Does this action seek to give revolutionary leftist meaning to the widespread distrust of the political system and elites that predominantes today in the United States?
- Ultimately, how does this action relate to the self-emancipation of the working class, the abolition of race, patriarchy, and other modalities of oppression, and the decisive, extraparliamentary supersession of capitalism?

The list, of course, could go on and on. We do not pretend to have crafted the definitive criteria for taking action toward anticapitalist insurrection. Instead, debating and building such values communally must be an important process, entailing a complex, and likely contentious, engagement with vital political questions that are, in the abolitionism of today, largely glossed over in the name of specious unity. This work, no matter how uncomfortable, will be essential. Creating deeper and more dynamic standards for evaluating when and how to take action can help take us beyond the present morass and open up the possibility of what we call "prerevolutionary measures"—like those of the original abolitionists, who, through taking courageous actions within and outside of the law, "brought about a new situation, which led millions to think and act in new ways."[72]

NOTES

PROLOGUE

1. Jarrod Shanahan and Zhandarka Kurti, *States of Incarceration: Rebellion, Reform, and America's Punishment System* (London: Reaktion / Field Notes, 2022); See also Vortex Group, *The George Floyd Uprising* (Oakland: PM Press, 2023).

2. Jarrod Shanahan, *Captives: How Rikers Island Took New York City Hostage* (London and New York: Verso, 2022).

3. Zhandarka Kurti and Jarrod Shanahan, "Rebranding Mass Incarceration: The Lippman Commission and 'Carceral Devolution' in New York City," *Social Justice: A Journal of Crime, Conflict and World Order* 45, no. 2/3 (2018): 23–50; Zhandarka Kurti and Jarrod Shanahan, "Carceral Non-Profits and the Limits of Prison Reform," *ACME: An International Journal for Critical Geographies* 20, no. 6 (2022): 597–617; Zhandarka Kurti, Brinley Froelich, and Jarrod Shanahan, "From New York to Salt Lake City, There's No Such Thing as a Nice Prison," *Verso* (blog), March 13, 2020, www.versobooks.com/blogs/news/4595-from-new-york-to-salt-lake-city-there-s-no-such-thing-as-a-nice-prison; Zhandarka Kurti and Jarrod Shanahan, "Twice Stolen Wealth" *Kiteline Radio*, episode 281, December 11, 2021, https://www.kitelineradio.org/podcast/281-twice-stolen-wealth/.

4. Martha King, "Locked in a Vicious Cycle: How Past Is Prologue at Rikers," *Vital City*, February 15, 2023, www.vitalcitynyc.org/articles/rikers-captives-review.

5. Andy Newman and Emma G. Fitzsimmons, "New York Aims to Clear Streets of Mentally Ill," *New York Times*, November 29, 2022.

6. Judah Schept, *Coal, Cages, Crisis* (New York: New York University Press, 2022), 197–98. We appreciate the invaluable feedback Schept gave as part of the editorial process at Haymarket.

INTRODUCTION: HISTORY IN THE MAKING

1. Reuven Blau et al., "City Hall Still Planning for Shutdown of Rikers Island Jails, But Is Mayor All-In?" *The City,* December 29, 2002, https://www.thecity.nyc/2022/12/29/does-nyc-mayor-adams-support-rikers-shutdown.

2.　New York City Council, "Council Votes on Historic Legislation to Close Rikers Island," October 17, 2019, https://council.nyc.gov/press/2019/10/17/1818. The plan included an ill-defined financial commitment of $391 million to "address the root causes of mass incarceration" and reform the city's criminal justice system—a drop in the bucket compared with the cost of the new jails.

3.　Karen Matthews, "Plan to Close Notorious Rikers Jail Complex by 2026 Approved," Associated Press, October 17, 2019, https://apnews.com/article/bronx-us-news-ap-top-news-queens-new-york-city-6053d86faae6 4edbb315510e319c5a81; Matthew Haag, "N.Y.C. Votes to Close Rikers. Now Comes the Hard Part," *New York Times*, October 17, 2019, www.nytimes.com/2019/10/17/nyregion/rikers-island-closing-vote.html.

4.　"NYCLU Statement on Council Vote to Close Rikers Island," NYCLU, www.nyclu.org/en/press-releases/nyclu-statement-city-council-vote-close-rikers-island; Darren Walker, "In Defense of Nuance," Ford Foundation (blog), September 19, 2019, www.fordfoundation.org/news-and-stories/stories/posts/in-defense-of-nuance; Gabriel Sayegh, "Making Sense of the Fight over NYC Jails," Katal Center for Equity, Health, and Justice (blog), October 10, 2019, https://katalcenter.org/makingsenserikers.

5.　Matthews, "Plan to Close."

6.　No New Jails NYC (@nonewjails_nyc), "wowww @StephenLevin33 just used @prisonculture's name in his shameful justification for building $11 billion in new jails and cementing a future of incarceration. #closerikersnow #nonewjails," with video, Twitter, October 17, 2019, https://twitter.com/nonewjails_nyc/status/1184915381938466816.

7.　No New Jails NYC, "Nothing Has Changed. Together, We Will Win," *Medium*, October 18, 2019, https://medium.com/@nonewjails.ny/nothing-has-changed-together-we-will-win-4c843a24afe.

8.　The current population of Rikers hovers close to six thousand, down from its peak of twenty thousand in 1991.

9.　Sarah Monaghan, Michael Rempel, and Tao Lin, "Racial Disparities in the Use of Jails across New York City, 2016–2021," Data Collaborative for Justice at John Jay College, 2021, 6, https://datacollaborativeforjustice.org/wp-content/uploads/2023/02/DisparitiesReport-27.pdf.

10.　Monaghan, Rempel, and Lin, "Racial Disparities," 6.

11.　The New York City Department of Correction, Preliminary Mayor's Management Report, "Focus on Equity," 2023, https://www.nyc.gov/assets/operations/downloads/pdf/pmmr2023/doc.pdf.

12.　The New York City Comptroller's Office, "The State of New York City

Jails, One Year of Measuring Jail Operations and Management on the Comptroller's DOC Dashboard," August 9, 2023, https://comptroller.nyc. gov/reports/the-state-of-new-york-city-jails/#_ftn5.

13. Darren Mack, "I Know Rikers," April 11, 2019, Just Leadership USA, https://jlusa.org/2019/04/11/i-know-rikers.

14. Karl Marx, *Capital: A Critique of Political Economy*, vol. 1, *The Process of Production of Capital*, trans. Ben Fowkes (New York: Vintage Books, 1977), 875.

15. Dario Melossi and Massimo Pavarini, *The Prison and the Factory: Origins of the Penitentiary System*, trans. Glynis Cousin (London: Macmillan, 1981); Silvia Federici, *Caliban and the Witch: Women, the Body, and Primitive Accumulation* (Brooklyn: Autonomedia, 2003).

16. Georg Rusche and Otto Kirchheimer, *Punishment and Social Structure*, rev. ed. (New York: Columbia University Press, 1939; London: Routledge, 2003).

17. Gilmore Ruth Wilson, *Golden Gulag: Prisons, Surplus, Crisis, and Opposition in Globalizing California* (Berkeley, CA: University of California Press, 2007), 247.

18. Friedrich Engels, *The Conditions of the Working Class in England* (Oxford: Oxford University Press, 2009), 38.

19. John Irwin, *The Jail: Managing the Underclass in American Society* (Berkeley and Los Angeles: University of California Press, 2013).

20. Jack Norton, Lydia Pelot-Hobbs, and Judah Schept, eds., *The Jail Is Everywhere: Fighting the New Geography of Mass Incarceration* (London and New York: Verso, 2023).

21. Anat Rubin, "California's Jail Boom," Marshall Project, July 2, 2015, www.themarshallproject.org/2015/07/02/california-s-jail-building-boom.

22. Nicholas Turner, "Rural Communities Need More Healthcare, Not More Jails," Vera Institute of Justice, April 27, 2022, www.vera.org/news/rural-communities-need-more-health-care-not-more-jails.

23. Richard A. Oppel Jr., "'A Cesspool of a Dungeon': The Surging Population in Rural Jails," *New York Times,* December 13, 2019, https://www.nytimes.com/2019/12/13/us/rural-jails.html.

24. New York City Comptroller's Office, "The State of New York Jails."

25. In 2023, according to the Prison Policy Institute, an estimated 514,000 people were held in jail and 427,000 (83 percent) were not convicted of a crime. See Wendy Sawyer and Peter Wagner, "Mass Incarceration: The Whole Pie," Prison Policy, March 14, 2023, www.prisonpolicy.org/reports/pie2023.html.

26. Sawyer and Wagner, "Mass Incarceration"; Zhen Zeng, "Jail Report Series Preliminary Data Release (2023)" Bureau of Justice Statistics,

https://bjs.ojp.gov/library/publications/jails-report-series-preliminary-data-release-2023.

27. Jonathan Simon, foreword to Irwin, *The Jail*.

28. James Riker, *A Brief History of the Riker Family: From Their Emigration to this Country in 1638, to the Present Time* (New York: D. Fanshaw, 1851); Tom McCarthy, "Rikers: The Unwanted Island of the Unwanted?" (presentation, Greater Astoria Historical Society, June 25, 2017).

29. See, for instance, Mariya Moseley, "Rikers Island Was Named after a Judge Who Was Eager to Uphold Slavery," *Essence*, October 26, 2020, www.essence.com/culture/rikers-island-slavery-ties.

30. See Eric Foner, *Gateway to Freedom: The Hidden History of the Underground Railroad* (New York: W. W. Norton, 2015); For a deep historical dive into the activities of the Kidnapping Club, see Jonathan Daniel Wells, *The Kidnapping Club: Wall Street, Slavery, and Resistance on the Eve of the Civil War* (New York: Bold Type Books, 2020).

31. Jarrod Shanahan and Jayne Mooney, "New York City's Captive Workforce: Remembering the Prisoners Who Built Rikers Island," *International Journal of Law, Crime and Justice*, no. 56 (2019). 15. A representative argument, since removed from the internet, was #CLOSErikers, "Rikers Island: The Dark History of the City's Forgotten Neighborhood," 2016, formerly at www.closerikers.org.

32. "To Build a Bigger Jail," *New York Times*, September 20, 1886.

33. Shanahan and Mooney, "New York City's Captive Workforce," 13–26.

34. Jayne Mooney and Jarrod Shanahan, "Rikers Island: The Failure of a 'Model' Penitentiary," *Prison Journal* 100, no. 6 (2020): 687–708.

35. Quoted in Stacy Horn, *Damnation Island: Poor, Sick, Mad & Criminal in 19th-Century New York* (Chapel Hill, NC: Algonquin Books, 2018). Ironically, as Horn demonstrates, Blackwell's Island was built as a reform effort to relieve the notoriously overcrowded conditions at Bellevue Hospital, which at that point served not as the city's hospital but as a carceral network that included a penitentiary, an almshouse for the poor, and a workhouse for those convicted of petty offenses.

36. Jarrod Shanahan and Jack Norton, "A Jail to End All Jails," *Urban Omnibus*, December 6, 2017, urbanomnibus.net/2017/12/jail-end-jails; Mooney and Shanahan, "Rikers Island."

37. Kurti and Shanahan, "Rebranding Mass Incarceration."

38. Michel Foucault, *Discipline and Punish: The Birth of the Prison* (London: Allen Lane, 1977).

39. David Rothman, *The Discovery of the Asylum* (Boston: Little, Brown, 1971), xvi.

40. Stuart Hall et al., *Policing the Crisis: Mugging, the State and Law and*

Order, 2nd ed. (New York: Pelgrave Macmillan, 2013); Gilmore, *Golden Gulag*; Jordan Camp, *Incarcerating the Crisis: Freedom Struggles and the Rise of the Neoliberal State* (Berkeley: University of California Press, 2016); Tony Platt, *Beyond These Walls: Rethinking Crime and Punishment in the United States* (New York: St. Martin's, 2019); Orisanmi Burton, *Tip of the Spear: Black Radicalism, Prison Repression and the Long Attica Revolt* (Berkeley and Los Angeles: University of California Press, 2023).

41. John Herbers, "Violence; It Is as American as Cherry Pie," *New York Times*, June 8, 1969.

42. Joshua B. Freeman, *Working-Class New York: Life and Labor Since World War II* (New York: New Press, 2000), 179–200; Robert Brenner, *The Economics of Global Turbulence* (London and New York: Verso, 2006), 99–186; Thomas J. Sugrue, *The Origins of the Urban Crisis: Race and Inequality in Postwar Detroit* (Princeton: Princeton University Press, 2006), 125–77.

43. Antonio Gramsci, *Selections from the Prison Notebooks*, ed. and trans Quintin Hoare and Geoffrey Nowell Smith (New York: International Publishers, 1971).

44. Hall et al., *Policing the Crisis*, 214.

45. Hall et al., *Policing the Crisis*.

46. Tony Platt, "Managing the Crisis: Austerity and the Penal System," *Contemporary Marxism*, no. 4 (1981): 29–39; Naomi Murakawa, *The First Civil Right: How Liberals Built Prison America* (Oxford: Oxford University Press, 2014).

47. Lisa A. Kort-Butler, "Crime in Televised Presidential Campaign Ads: The Making of Visual Metaphor," *Deviant Behavior* 41, no. 5 (2020): 628–48.

48. Jeremy D. Mayer, "Nixon Rides the Backlash to Victory: Racial Politics in the 1968 Presidential Campaign," *The Historian* 64, no. 2 (2001): 361.

49. Dan Baum, "Legalize It All: How to Win the War on Drugs," *Harper's Magazine*, April 2016, https://harpers.org/archive/2016/04/legalize-it-all.

50. Hall et al., *Policing the Crisis*, 218.

51. Camp, *Incarcerating the Crisis*.

52. Michel Foucault, "Lemon and Milk," in *Power: The Essential Works of Michel Foucault 1954–1984* (New York: Penguin Classics, 2019), 438.

53. Jonathan Simon "Law's Violence, the Strong State, and the Crisis of Mass Imprisonment (for Stuart Hall)," *Wake Forest Law Review*, no. 49 (2014): 658.

54. Philip Jenkins, *Decade of Nightmares: The End of the Sixties and the Making of Eighties America* (Oxford: Oxford University Press, 2006), 249.

55. Murakawa, *The First Civil Right*.

56. Jonathan Simon, *Governing through Crime: How the War on Crime*

Transformed American Democracy and Created a Culture of Fear (Oxford: Oxford University Press, 2007).

57. Jack Norton and David Stein, "Materializing Race: On Capitalism and Mass Incarceration," *Spectre*, October 22, 2020, https://spectrejournal. com/materializing-race.

58. Gilmore, *Golden Gulag*, 88–127.

59. Ruth Wilson Gilmore and Craig Gilmore, "Beyond Bratton," in *Policing the Planet: Why the Policing Crisis Led to Black Lives Matter*, ed. Jordan T. Camp and Christina Heatherton (London and New York: Verso, 2016), 173.

60. David Ranney, *New World Disorder: The Decline of U.S. Power* (Charleston, SC: CreateSpace, 2014), 8–9.

61. Ranney, *New World Disorder*, 38.

62. Nassim Nicholas Taleb, *The Black Swan: The Impact of the Highly Improbable*, 2nd ed. (New York: Random House, 2010).

63. Phil A. Neel, "The Knife at Your Throat," *Brooklyn Rail*, October 2022, https://brooklynrail.org/2022/10/field-notes/The-Knife-At-Your-Throat.

64. CUNY Struggle, "CUNY at the Crossroads," 2016, https://cunystruggle. org/cuny-at-the-crossroads.

65. The idea that we could potentially be living in the collapse of the liberal democratic order has been popularized by the journalist Robert Evans on the popular podcast *It Could Happen Here*, www.iheart.com/podcast/105-it-could-happen-here-30717896.

66. Shanahan and Kurti, *States of Incarceration*.

67. Sarah Jaffe, "Social Reproduction and the Pandemic, with Tithi Bhattacharya," *Dissent*, April 2, 2020, https://www.dissentmagazine. org/online_articles/social-reproduction-and-the-pandemic-with-tithi-bhattacharya.

68. Mimi Abramovitz, "From the Welfare State to the Carceral State: Whither Social Reproduction?," *Afflia: Feminist Inquiry in Social Work* 38, no. 1 (2023): 33–34.

69. Reuben Miller, "Devolving the Carceral State: Race, Prisoner Reentry, and the Micro-politics of Urban Poverty Management," *Punishment and Society* 16, no. 3 (2014): 305–35; Abramovitz, "Welfare State," 20–39, 23.

70. Brenner, *The Economics of Global Turbulence*; Alex Callinicos, "Contradictions of Austerity," *Cambridge Journal of Economics* 36, no. 1 (January 2012): 65–77.

71. Gilmore and Gilmore, "Beyond Bratton."

72. Zhandarka Kurti, "Living through the Perfect Storm: Interview with William I. Robinson," *Brooklyn Rail*, April 2024, https://brooklynrail. org/2024/04/field-notes/Living-through-the-Perfect-Storm-William-Robinson-with-Zhandarka-Kurti.

73. William I. Robinson and Jerry Harris, "Towards a Global Ruling Class: Globalization and the Transnational Ruling Class," *Science and Society* 64, no. 1 (2000): 11–54.

74. Don Hamerquist, "Withering," in *A Brilliant Red Thread: Revolutionary Writings from Don Hamerquist*, ed. Luis Brennan (Montreal: Kersplebedeb, 2022), 304.

75. Dom Hamerquist, "Ferguson," in Brennan, *Brilliant Red Thread*, 275–92.

76. James Kilgore, "Repackaging Mass Incarceration," *Counterpunch*, June 6, 2014, www.counterpunch.org/2014/06/06/repackaging-mass-incarceration.

77. Jasmine Heiss, "A Quiet Jail Boom," in Norton, Pelot-Hobbs, and Schept, *Jail Is Everywhere*, 23.

78. Dave Ranney and Don Hamerquist, email exchanges with the authors (May 27, 2023).

79. Norton, Pelot-Hobbs, and Schept, "Introduction," in *Jail Is Everywhere*, 4–7.

80. Jonathan Lippman and Melissa Mark-Viverito, "Closing Rikers Island Is a Moral Imperative," *New York Times*, March 31, 2017.

81. Many progressives also had cause to laud the council's support of reducing the city jail population to 3,500, increasing investment in so-called alternatives to incarceration, and making small investments toward abating homelessness and other "root causes" of incarceration. The cost of these, again, was new jails. See Office of New York City Council Member Farah N. Louis, "New York City Council Votes to Close Rikers," news release, October 18, 2019, https://council.nyc.gov/farah-louis/2019/10/18/new-york-city-council-votes-to-close-rikers.

82. Bill Parry, "Nearly a Thousand Protesters March through Astoria Calling for Close of Rikers Island," *QNS*, September 29, 2016, https://qns.com/2016/09/nearly-a-thousand-protesters-march-through-astoria-calling-for-close-of-rikers-island.

83. Dan Gallagher et al., *Justice in Design: Toward a Healthier and More Just New York City Jail System* (New York: Van Alen Institute and the Independent Commission for New York City Criminal Justice and Incarceration Reform, 2017), https://past.vanalen.org/content/uploads/2017/07/Justice-in-Design-Report.pdf. We treat this and other early jail plans extensively in Kurti and Shanahan, "Rebranding Mass Incarceration."

84. No New Jails NYC, "On the False Guarantee to Close Rikers," *Medium*, September 25, 2019, https://medium.com/@nonewjails.ny/no-new-jails-nyc-on-the-false-guarantee-to-close-rikers-66f20115344e; Asha Ramachandran, "The False Promise of Closing Rikers Island," *Washington Square News*, October 27, 2019, https://nyunews.com/opinion/2019/10/28/rikers-closure-nyc-prison-activism.

85. Matthews, "Plan to Close."

86. Matthews, "Plan to Close."
87. Editorial Board, "How to Close Rikers," *New York Times*, October 15, 2019; Haag, "N.Y.C. Votes." For a survey of the *Times*' long history of carceral boosterism, see Jarrod Shanahan and Nadja Eisenberg-Guyot, "All Jails Fit to Build," *The Brooklyn Rail*, February 2020, https:// brooklynrail.org/2020/02/field-notes/All-Jails-Fit-to-Build.
88. Public land use hearings attended by the authors were dramatic affairs characterized by constant interruptions from nearby residents and abolitionist opponents of the jails.
89. Kurti and Shanahan, "Rebranding Mass Incarceration."
90. New York City Council, "Council Votes to Pass the 'Renewable Rikers' Act," news release, February 11, 2021, https://council.nyc.gov/ press/2021/02/11/2069.
91. Rachel Vick and Jacob Kaye, "DOC Two Months Late on Deadline to Transfer Part of Rikers Island," *Queens Daily Eagle*, August 11, 2022, https://queenseagle.com/all/no-plan-for-future-of-rikers-transfers.
92. Jake Lahut, "NYC Mayoral Candidate Eric Adams Says 'Young White Affluent People' Lead the 'Defund the Police' Movement," *Business Insider*, April 27, 2021, www.businessinsider.com/eric-adams-defund-the-police-young-white-affluent-people-2021-4.
93. Liam Stack, "Mayor Adams to New York City Shoppers: Drop That Mask" *New York Times*, March 6, 2023, https://www.nytimes.com/2023/03/06/ nyregion/eric-adams-theft-masks-nyc.html.
94. Elizabeth Kim, "Adams Says He Plans to Recreate 2011 Video Showing How to Search Child's Belongings for Contraband," *Gothamist*, April 4, 2022, https://gothamist.com/news/adams-says-he-plans-to-recreate-2011-video-showing-how-to-search-childs-belongings-for-contraband.
95. Erin Durkin, "Adams' Solitary Confinement Stance Sets Up Fight with City Council," *Politico*, January 7, 2022, https://www.politico.com/ news/2022/01/13/adams-solitary-confinement-stance-sets-up-fight-with-city-council-527051.
96. Jacob Kaye, "Mayor Casts Doubt on Plan to Close Rikers," *Queens Daily Eagle*, August 31, 2022, https://queenseagle.com/all/2022/8/31/mayor-casts-doubt-on-plan-to-close-rikers.
97. Reuven Blau et al, "City Hall Still Planning for Shutdown of Rikers Island Jails, But Is Mayor All-In?," *The City,* December 29, 2022, https://www. thecity.nyc/2022/12/29/does-nyc-mayor-adams-support-rikers-shutdown/.
98. Theodore Hamm, "Eric Adams Embraces Big Real Estate. What's in It for the Rest of Us?," *The Independent*, October 13, 2021, https:// indypendent.org/2021/10/eric-adams-embraces-big-real-estate-whats-in-it-for-the-rest-of-us.

99. Karl Marx and Friedrich Engels, "Manifesto of the Communist Party," in *The Marx-Engels Reader*, ed. Robert C. Tucker (New York: W. W. Norton, 1978), 496.

100. Kathleen Woodroofe, *From Charity to Social Work in England and the United States* (Toronto: University of Toronto Press, 1968), 77–100; Barry Kaplan, "Reformers and Charity," *Social Service Review* 52, no. 2 (1978): 202–14; Michael Katz, *Poverty and Policy in American History* (Cambridge, MA: Academic Press, 1983); Stephen Pimpare, *The New Victorians: Poverty, Politics, and Propaganda in Two Gilded Ages* (New York: New Press, 2004).

101. Martha Branscombe, *The Courts and the Poor Laws in New York State, 1784–1929* (Chicago: University of Chicago Press, 1942).

102. Michael Katz, *Poverty and Policy in American History.*

103. Adam Smith, *An Inquiry into the Nature and Causes of the Wealth of Nations*, vol. 1, ed. Edwin Cannan (Chicago: University of Chicago Press, 1977), 18.

104. Adam Smith, *The Theory of Moral Sentiments* (New York: Clarendon, 1976), 190.

105. Andrew Carnegie, *The Gospel of Wealth, and Other Timely Essays* (Garden City, NY: Doubleday, Doran, 1933).

106. Ruth Wilson Gimore, "In the Shadow of the Shadow State," in *The Revolution Will Not Be Funded*, ed. INCITE! Women of Color Against Violence (Cambridge, MA: South End, 2007), 46.

107. Paul Arnsberger, Melissa Ludlum, Margaret Riley, and Mark Stanton, "A History of the Tax-Exemption Sector: An SOI Perspective," Internal Revenue Service, *Statistics of Income Bulletin*, Winter 2008, www.irs.gov/pub/irs-soi/tehistory.pdf.

108. Nicole P. Marwell, "Privatizing the Welfare State: Nonprofit Community-Based Organizations as Political Actors," *American Sociological Review*, no. 69 (2004): 265–91; Andrew J. F. Morris, *The Limits of Voluntarism: Charity and Welfare from the New Deal through the Great Society* (Cambridge: Cambridge University Press, 2011).

109. Barbara Howe, "The Emergence of Scientific Philanthropy, 1900–1920, Origins, Issues, and Outcomes," and Sheila Slaughter and Edward T. Silva, "Looking Backwards: How Foundations Formulated Ideology in the Progressive Period," in *Philanthropy and Cultural Imperialism: Foundations at Home and Abroad*, ed. Robert F. Arnove (Bloomington: Indiana University Press, 1982).

110. Rothman, *Discovery of the Asylum*; David Rothman, *Conscience and Convenience: The Asylum and Its Alternatives in Progressive America* (New York: Taylor & Francis, 1980).

111. Zhandarka Kurti and Jarrod Shanahan, "Carceral Non-Profits and the Limits of Prison Reform," *ACME: An International Journal for Critical*

Geographies 20, no. 6 (2022): 597–617.

112. Nancy Kriplen, "Stingy Founder of 'Genius Grants' Was No Fan of Charity," *Chicago Tribune*, October 4, 2012.

113. Andrea Smith, "Introduction," in *The Revolution Will Not Be Funded: Beyond the Non-Profit Industrial Complex*, ed. INCITE! Women of Color Against Violence (Cambridge, MA: South End, 2007), 3–6.

114. Karen Ferguson, *Top Down: The Ford Foundation, Black Power, and the Reinvention of Racial Liberalism* (Philadelphia: University of Pennsylvania Press, 2013), 24–38.

115. Ferguson, *Top Down*, 5–7.

116. Inderjeet Parmar, "The 'Big 3' Foundations and American Global Power," *American Journal of Economics and Sociology* 74, no. 4 (2015): 676–703.

117. Robert L. Allen, *Black Awakening in Capitalist America* (Garden City, NY: Doubleday, 1969; Trenton, NJ: Africa World, 1990), 70–76.

118. Sam Collings-Wells, "From Black Power to Broken Windows: Liberal Philanthropy and the Carceral State," *Journal of Urban History* 48 no. 4 (2022): 739–59.

119. Portions of this section have been amended from our essay: Kurti and Shanahan, "Carceral Non-Profits."

120. Malcolm M. Feeley, "How to Think about Criminal Court Reform," *Boston University Law Review*, no. 98 (2018): 673–730; Mary T. Phillips, *A Decade of Bail Research in New York City* (New York: New York City Criminal Justice Agency, 2012), www.prisonpolicy.org/scans/DecadeBailResearch12.pdf.

121. Laurie Johnston, "Louis J. Schweitzer Dead; Founder of Vera Institute," *New York Times*, September 21, 1971.

122. Jarrod Shanahan and Zhandarka Kurti, "Managing Urban Disorder in the 1960s: The New York City Model," Gotham Institute for New York City History, January 7, 2020, www.gothamcenter.org/blog/managingurbandisorder.

123. Katherine Beckett and Naomi Murakawa, "Mapping the Shadow Carceral State: Toward an Institutionally Capacious Approach to Punishment," *Theoretical Criminology* 16, no. 2 (2012): 221–44.

124. The latter argument is made compellingly in Feeley, "Criminal Court Reform."

125. Michael Barker, *Under the Mask of Philanthropy* (Evington, Leicester: Hextall, 2017), 67.

CHAPTER 1: SHUT DOWN RIKERS

1. Graham Rayman, "Rikers Violence Out of Control," *Village Voice*, May 9, 2012.

2. US Attorney's Office, Southern District of New York, "Manhattan U.S. Attorney Finds Pattern and Practice of Excessive Force and Violence at NYC Jails on Rikers Island That Violates the Constitutional Rights of Adolescent Male Inmates," news release, August 4, 2014, www.justice. gov/usao-sdny/pr/manhattan-us-attorney-finds-pattern-and-practice-excessive-force-and-violence-nyc-jails.

3. *Nunez v. City of New York*, 11 Civ. 5845 (LTS) (JCF). The Nunez Monitor reports drip with frustration. See DOC, Nunez Monitor Reports, 2023, www.nyc.gov/site/doc/media/nunez-reports.page.

4. Jennifer Gonnerman, "Before the Law," *New Yorker*, September 29, 2014, www.newyorker.com/magazine/2014/10/06/before-the-law.

5. Jennifer Gonnerman, "Kalief Browder Learned How to Commit Suicide on Rikers," *New Yorker*, June 2, 2016, www.newyorker.com/news/news-desk/kalief-browder-learned-how-to-commit-suicide-on-rikers.

6. *State of Missouri v. Darren Wilson*, Grand Jury, volume 4, September 10, 2014, 45.

7. Mark Follman, "Michael Brown's Mom Laid Flowers Where He Was Shot—and Police Crushed Them," *Mother Jones*, August 27, 2014, www.motherjones.com/politics/2014/08/ferguson-st-louis-police-tactics-dogs-michael-brown.

8. "The New Ghettos Burning," *Ultra*, August 17, 2014, www.ultra-com.org/project/new-ghettos-burning; Barbara Ransby, *Making All Black Lives Matter: Reimagining Freedom in the 21st Century* (Berkeley and Los Angeles: University of California Press, 2018); Keeanga-Yamahtta Taylor, *From #BlackLivesMatter to Black Liberation* (Chicago: Haymarket Books, 2016), 151–90; "Brown v. Ferguson," *Endnotes*, no. 4 (2017) 11–40; JF and friends, "The Old Mole Breaks Concrete: The Ongoing Rupture in New York City," *Unity and Struggle*, December 11, 2014, www.unityandstruggle.org/2014/12/the-old-mole-breaks-concrete.

9. David Ranney, *Global Decisions, Local Collisions: Urban Life in the New World Order* (Philadelphia: Temple University Press, 2003), 34–70.

10. Joshua B. Freeman, *Working-Class New York: Life and Labor Since World War II* (New York: New Press, 2000), 55.

11. William K. Tabb, *The Long Default: New York City and the Urban Fiscal Crisis* (New York: Monthly Review, 1982); Eric Lichten, *Class, Power, and Austerity: The New York City Fiscal Crisis* (South Hadley, MA: Bergin and Garvey, 1986).

12. Jamie Peck, *Constructions of Neoliberal Reason* (Oxford: Oxford University Press, 2012), 135.

13. Independent Commission on New York City Criminal Justice and Incarceration Reform (Lippman Commission), *A More Just New York*

      City, 2017, n.p., https://nycitylens.com/wp-content/rikers/wp-content/ uploads/2017/05/IndependentCommissionFinalReport.pdf.

14. Ranney, *Global Decisions*, 43–45.

15. John Hull Mollenkopf, *A Phoenix in the Ashes: The Rise and Fall of the Koch Coalition in New York City Politics* (Princeton: Princeton University Press, 1992); Rebecca Hill, "'The Common Enemy Is the Boss and the Inmate': Police and Prison Guard Unions in New York in the 1970s–1980s," *Labor* 8, no. 3 (September 2011): 65–96.

16. George Jackson, *Soledad Brother: The Prison Letters of George Jackson* (Chicago, 1970); Robert T. Chase, "We Are Not Slaves: Rethinking the Rise of Carceral States through the Lens of the Prisoner Rights' Movement," *Journal of American History* 102, no. 1 (June 2015): 73–86; Dan Berger and Toussaint Losier, *Rethinking the American Prison Movement* (New York: Routledge, 2017); Orisanmi Burton, *Tip of the Spear: Black Radicalism, Prison Repression and the Long Attica Revolt* (Berkeley: University of California Press, 2023).

17. Harold Baer Jr. and Arminda Bepko, "A Necessary and Proper Role for Federal Courts in Prison Reform: The Benjamin v. Malcolm Consent Decrees," *New York Law School Review* 52, no. 1 (2007): 3–64.

18. Hill, "'Common Enemy'"; Jarrod Shanahan, *Captives: How Rikers Island Took New York City Hostage* (London and New York: Verso, 2022).

19. Shanahan, *Captives*, 267–70. Herbert Sturz served on the Lippman Commission.

20. Tom Goldstein, "The City and the State May Soon Formalize a Prison Swap," *New York Times*, March 11, 1979.

21. Stuart Marquez, "Riots, Rebellion and the City's Attempt to 'Sink' Rikers Island," NYC Department of Records and Information Services (blog), April 19, 2019, www.archives.nyc/blog/2019/4/19/riots-rebellion-and-the-citys-second-attempt-to-sink-rikers-island.

22. Jarrod Shanahan and Pilar Maschi, "There Are Abolitionists All around Us," *Commune*, no. 5 (Winter 2020); plans for the new jails, in possession of the authors, courtesy of Martin Horn.

23. Neil Smith, "Giuliani Time: The Revanchist '90s," *Social Text*, no. 57 (Winter 1998): 1–20.

24. Jarrod Shanahan, "Every Fire Needs a Little Bit of Help," *Endnotes*, May 2022, https://endnotes.org.uk/posts/jarrod-shanahan-every-fire-needs-a-little-bit-of-help.

25. Michael Barbaro and David W. Chen, "De Blasio Wins Mayor's Race in Landslide," *New York Times*, November 5, 2013.

26. David Freedlander, "Dante de Blasio's Killer Ad May Have Won NYC Primary for His Dad," *Daily Beast*, April 20, 2017, www.thedailybeast.

com/dante-de-blasios-killer-ad-may-have-won-nyc-primary-for-his-dad.

27. Jonathan Lippman and Melissa Mark-Viverito, "Closing Rikers Island Is a Moral Imperative," *New York Times*, March 31, 2017.

28. Ransby, *Making All Black Lives Matter*, 2.

29. "Brown v. Ferguson," 40–46; Sean Campbell, "The BLM Mystery," *New York Magazine*, January 31, 2022, https://nymag.com/ intelligencer/2022/01/black-lives-matter-finances.html; Karen Ferguson, "The Perils of Liberal Philanthropy," *Jacobin*, November 26, 2018, https://jacobin.com/2018/11/black-lives-matter-ford-foundation-black-power-mcgeorge-bundy.

30. "Shaped by a broad, sophisticated understanding of the interplay of multiple identities, race, and power in the US," Brook Kelly-Green of the Ford Foundation argued in 2016, "the leaders of this decentralized movement are nimble and networked," operating "in relationship to more established and easily identifiable civil rights and social justice organizations, while transcending their boundaries." See Brook Kelly-Green, "Why Black Lives Matter to Philanthropy," Ford Foundation, July 19, 2019, www.fordfoundation.org/news-and-stories/stories/posts/why-black-lives-matter-to-philanthropy.

31. Daniel Roberts, "Nike Is Setting the Tone for Sports Brands in its Response to the George Floyd Protests," *Yahoo Finance*, June 1, 2020, https://finance.yahoo.com/news/nike-is-setting-the-tone-for-sports-brands-in-its-response-to-the-george-floyd-protests-180707761.html.

32. Karl Marx, *Capital: A Critique of Political Economy*, vol. 3, trans. Ben Fowkes (New York: Penguin Books, 1981), 736.

33. Taylor, *#BlackLivesMatter*, 180.

34. Olúfẹ́mi O. Táíwò, *Elite Capture: How the Powerful Took Over Identity Politics (and Everything Else)* (Chicago: Haymarket Books, 2022).

35. Sarah Kendzior, "Ferguson Inc.," *Politico Magazine*, March 4, 2015, www.politico.com/magazine/story/2015/03/ferguson-inc-115765.

36. Kenneth P. Vogel and Sarah Wheaton, "Major Donors Consider Funding Black Lives Matter," *Politico*, November 13, 2015, www.politico.com/ story/2015/11/major-donors-consider-funding-black-lives-matter-215814.

37. Ellen McGirt, "Who Is Funding Black Lives Matter," *Fortune*, August 8, 2016, https://fortune.com/2016/08/08/funding-black-lives-matter-ford.

38. Kendzior, "Ferguson Inc."

39. "Black Lives Matter 2020 Impact Report," Black Lives Matter Global Network, 2021, 18, https://blacklivesmatter.com/2020-impact-report.

40. Michael A. Memoli, "Black Lives Matter Playing a Prominent Role at Democratic Convention," *Los Angeles Times*, July 26, 2016.

41. Proponents of this view struggle to explain how, when visits were

abruptly curtailed during the first wave of the COVID-19 pandemic, the amount of drugs smuggled into Rikers actually went *up*. "Mayor de Blasio, Commissioner Ponte Announce 14-Point Rikers Anti-Violence Agenda," New York City Office of the Mayor, March 12, 2015, www. nyc.gov/office-of-the-mayor/news/166-15/mayor-de-blasio-commissioner-ponte-14-point-rikers-anti-violence-agenda; George Joseph and Reuven Blau, "When Visitors Were Banned from Rikers Island, Even More Drugs Showed Up," *The City*, February 9, 2022, www.thecity.nyc.

42. Raven Rakia and Ashoka Jegroo, "How the Push to Close Rikers Went from No Jails to New Jails," *The Appeal*, May 28, 2018.

43. "Reflections and Lessons from the First Two Phases of the #CLOSErikers Campaign: August 2015–August 2017," Katal Center for Equity, Health and Justice, January 2018, 8, https://katalcenter.org/wp-content/uploads/2022/06/Katal_CLOSErikers_Campaign_Report_PRINT_-_final.pdf.

44. Katal, "Reflections," 11; "Rally October 18, 2014," Resist Rikers, October 16, 2014, https://resistrikers.wordpress.com/2014/10/16/resistrikers-rally-on-saturday-october-18.

45. Rakia and Jegroo, "No Jails to New Jails"; Michael Winerip, "De Blasio Setting Up a Test: Prison Reformer vs. Rikers Island," *New York Times*, April 5, 2014.

46. "Here Are City Documents on 'Effort' to Close Rikers That de Blasio Denies," DNAinfo, April 14, 2016, www.dnainfo.com/new-york/20160414/college-point/here-are-city-documents-on-effort-close-rikers-that-de-blasio-denies.

47. Neil Barsky, "Shut Down Rikers Island," *New York Times*, July 19, 2015.

48. Ed Morales, "Behind the Growing Calls to Close Rikers Island," *City Limits*, November 24, 2015, https://citylimits.org/2015/11/24/behind-the-growing-calls-to-close-rikers-island.

49. Ryan Brady, "Stringer Joins Calls to Shut Down Rikers," *Gotham Gazette*, November 20, 2015, www.gothamgazette.com/government/5998-stringer-joins-calls-to-shut-down-rikers.

50. Ashoka Jegroo, "Protesters Carrying Coffin Demand Rikers Island Be Shut Down," *Waging Nonviolence*, February 24, 2016, https://wagingnonviolence.org/2016/02/protesters-carrying-coffin-demand-rikers-island-be-shut-down; Campaign to Shut Down Rikers, "ShutDownRikers," Change.org, October 13, 2015, www.change.org/p/bill-de-blasio-andrew-cuomo-joseph-ponte-shut-down-rikers.

51. Christina Sterbenz and Sarah Jacobs, "This Man's Youngest Brother Killed Himself after Spending 3 Years at One of the Country's Most Notorious Jails—Now He Wants to Shut It Down," *Business Insider*,

July 30, 2016, www.businessinsider.com/akeem-browder-rikers-shut-down-2016-7.

52. Jeff Mays, "East Harlem Councilwoman Melissa Mark-Viverito Arrested at OWS Protest," *DNAinfo*, November 18, 2011, www.dnainfo. com/new-york/20111118/harlem/east-harlem-councilwoman-melissa-markviverito-arrested-at-ows-protest; Anonymous, "The 1% of the 99%," *Libcom*, December 27, 2011, https://libcom.org/article/1-99.

53. New York City Council, "Speaker Mark-Viverito Delivers 2016 State of the City Address," news release, February 11, 2016, https://council. nyc.gov/press/2016/02/11/47; Gloria Pazmino, "Lippman Announces Members of Criminal Justice Commission," *Politico*, March 17, 2016, www.politico.com/states/new-york/city-hall/story/2016/03/lippman-announces-members-of-criminal-justice-commission-032484.

54. Julian Guerrero, "The Call to Close Rikers Gets Louder," *Socialist Worker*, February 25, 2016, https://socialistworker.org/2016/02/25/the-call-to-close-down-rikers-gets-louder (emphasis ours).

55. Jegroo, "Protesters Carrying Coffin."

56. Lippman and Mark-Viverito, "Closing Rikers Island."

57. Katal, "Reflections," 15–16.

CHAPTER 2: #CLOSERiKERS

1. "Our Grantees," Tow Foundation, n.d., www.towfoundation.org/ grantee-partners/our-grantees; "JustLeadershipUSA (JLUSA)," Cause IQ, n.d., www.causeiq.com/organizations/justleadershipusa,901019268; "JustLeadershipUSA," MacArthur Foundation, n.d., www.macfound. org/grantee/justleadershipusa-10084075; "About Us," More Just NYC, n.d., www.morejustnyc.org/about-us; Nikita Stewart, "A Report of Sexual Misconduct, a $25,000 Payment and an Activist's Abrupt Exit," *New York Times*, February 2, 2018. Our initial research into the jail boosters' network benefited immensely from a No New Jails NYC visual map entitled *Follow the Money*, which is, unfortunately, no longer available online.

2. Caroline Preston, "A Thirtysomething Billionaire Couple Take on Tough Issues via Giving," *Chronicles of Philanthropy*, October 16, 2011, www. philanthropy.com/article/a-thirtysomething-billionaire-couple-take-on-tough-issues-via-giving; David Barboza, "Enron Trader Had a Year to Boast of, Even If . . .," *New York Times*, July 9, 2022; Arnold's activist investment is chronicled in great detail at the website *The Truth about John D. Arnold*, www.truthaboutjohnarnold.com; "Reform in Action: Fact Sheets on Initial Findings by Area," ISLG, September 13, 2023, https://islg.cuny.edu/resources/reform-in-action.

3. "Progress Report and Legislative Agenda," A More Just NYC, December

2018, 18, https://static1.squarespace.com/static/5b6de4731aef1de914f43628/t/5c198f9af950b7863cd60bac/1545179066057/Progress+Report.pdf; "List of Grants: Social Justice Program," J.M. Kaplan Fund, 2021, https://jmkfund.org/wp-content/uploads/2015/04/SJ-GRANTS-LIST_12.2021-1.pdf; More Just NYC, "About Us."

4.   Zhandarka Kurti and Jarrod Shanahan, "Rebranding Mass Incarceration: The Lippman Commission and 'Carceral Devolution' in New York City," *Social Justice: A Journal of Crime, Conflict and World Order* 45, no. 2/3 (2018).

5.   "JustLeadershipUSA Inc.," *ProPublica Nonprofit Explorer*, https://projects.propublica.org/nonprofits/organizations/901019268; "Katal Center for Health, Equity, and Justice, Inc.," *ProPublica Nonprofit Explorer*, https://projects.propublica.org/nonprofits/organizations/811323278.

6.   "#CLOSErikers," JustLeadershipUSA, n.d., https://jlusa.org/campaign/closerikers.

7.   Campaign to Shut Down Rikers, "Resistance in the Face of Co-optation," *Medium*, May 19, 2016, https://medium.com/@ShutDownRikers/campaign-to-shut-down-rikers-official-statement-7e773a4fc0c4.

8.   Campaign to Shut Down Rikers, "Resistance in the Face of Co-optation"; "Join the Campaign to Close Rikers and Build Communities," #CLOSERikers, April 17, 2017, https://web.archive.org/web/20170913181023/http://www.closerikers.org/take-action, accessed via the Internet Archive Wayback Machine.

9.   Ben Norton, "Black Lives Matter Activists Launch Abolition Square Encampment, Demanding Reparations, End to Broken Windows Policing," *Salon*, August 5, 2016, www.salon.com/2016/08/05/black-lives-matter-activists-launch-abolition-square-encampment-demanding-reparations-end-to-broken-windows-policing.

10.   "Reflections and Lessons from the First Two Phases of the #CLOSErikers Campaign: August 2015–August 2017," Katal Center for Equity, Health and Justice, January 2018, 15–16, https://katalcenter.org/wp-content/uploads/2022/06/Katal_CLOSErikers_Campaign_Report_PRINT_-_final.pdf.

11.   *Propublica Nonprofit Explorer*, "JustLeadershipUSA Inc."

12.   Glenn E. Martin, "Those Closest to the Problem Are Closest to the Solution," *The Appeal*, September 22, 2017.

13.   "Katal Center for Equity Health and Justice," Cause IQ, n.d., www.causeiq.com/organizations/katal-center-for-health-equity-and-justice,811323278.

14.   "About Us," Katal Center for Equity Health and Justice, n.d., https://katalcenter.org/about.

15. Manuel Pastor, Jennifer Ito, and Rachel Rosner, *Transactions, Transformations, Translations: Metrics That Matter for Building, Scaling, and Funding Social Movements* (Los Angeles: University of Southern California Dornsife Program for Environmental and Regional Equity, 2011), 9, http://dornsife.usc.edu/assets/sites/242/docs/transactions_transformations_translations_web.pdf.

16. Felipe De La Hoz, "Activists Launch #CLOSErikers Campaign to Close Rikers Island," *Observer*, April 15, 2016, https://observer.com/2016/04/activists-launch-closerikers-campaign-to-close-rikers-island.

17. Katal, "Reflections," 15–16; Ryan Brady, "Stringer Joins Calls to Shut Down Rikers," *Gotham Gazette*, November 20, 2015, www.gothamgazette.com/government/5998-stringer-joins-calls-to-shut-down-rikers.

18. De La Hoz, "Activist Launch #CLOSErikers"; #CLOSERikers, "Join the Campaign."

19. Katal, "Reflections," 18.

20. Kim Fyke and Gabriel Sayegh, "Anarchism and the Struggle to Move Forward," *Perspectives on Anarchist Theory* 5, no. 2 (Fall 2001): 1, 10–13.

21. Katal, "Reflections," 18.

22. The authors are in possession of an internal #CLOSErikers white paper from the fall of 2016—the period when Katal insists "no one had to answer that question"—in which the pivot to advocacy for new jails, albeit euphemized as "Public Health and Safety Centers," is already clearly anticipated.

23. Katal, "Reflections," 18–22.

24. Having already begun study of nonprofits and business unions through a Marxist lens, Jarrod cannot pretend to have been innocent to the workings of such organizations, and he came to these conclusions, which fit his prior understanding of how they function, very quickly. Nonetheless, he found this glimpse at the inside of such a novel campaign to be too valuable to pass up—until #CLOSErikers began advocating for skyscraper jails, and it was time to say goodbye.

25. Katal, "Reflections," 23–25; Bill Parry, "Nearly a Thousand Protesters March through Astoria Calling for Close of Rikers Island," *QNS*, September 29, 2016, https://qns.com/2016/09/nearly-a-thousand-protesters-march-through-astoria-calling-for-close-of-rikers-island.

26. Independent Commission on New York City Criminal Justice and Incarceration Reform (Lippman Commission), *A More Just New York City*, 2017, 15, 39–40, https://nycitylens.com/wp-content/rikers/wp-content/uploads/2017/05/IndependentCommissionFinalReport.pdf; Zhandarka Kurti and Jarrod Shanahan, "Rebranding Mass Incarceration: The Lippman Commission and 'Carceral Devolution' in New York City,"

Social Justice: A Journal of Crime, Conflict and World Order 45, no. 2/3 (2018): 23–50.

27. Lippman Commission, *More Just*, 17.

28. The Mayor's Office of Criminal Justice (MOCJ), *Smaller, Safer, Fairer: A Roadmap to Closing Rikers Island*, 2017, 12, https://criminaljustice. cityofnewyork.us/reports/smaller-safer-fairer-copy.

29. Lippman Commission, *More Just*, 39.

30. MOCJ, *Smaller, Safer, Fairer*, 13–15.

31. MOCJ, *Smaller, Safer, Fairer*, 4–5.

32. "Funders Summit on Justice Reform: The Nation's Eyes on Rikers," Philanthropy New York, n.d., https://philanthropynewyork.org/event-calendar/funders-summit-justice-reform-nation-s-eyes-rikers.

33. The organizers also acknowledge, "Our colleagues at the Vera Institute of Justice, Columbia Justice Lab, JustLeadershipUSA, Katal Center for Health, Equity & Justice, Center for Court Innovation, Fortune Society, and More Just NYC [Lippman Commission] provided their input in the development of the Summit." This is especially interesting because the summit came after Katal had formally severed itself from #CLOSErikers. See Funders Summit on Justice Reform, *The Nation's Eyes on Rikers: A Report on Community Leader-Identified Priorities, Opportunities for Funders and Key Organizing Objectives*, Philanthropy New York, June 2018, 7–9, https://philanthropynewyork.org/sites/default/files/resources/PNY_Funders%20Summit%20Report.pdf.

34. Funders Summit, *Nation's Eyes on Rikers*, 11, 13, 22.

35. Funders Summit, *Nation's Eyes on Rikers*.

36. Katal, "Reflections," 27.

37. Funders Summit, *Nation's Eyes on Rikers*, 12.

38. "ULURP Explained," *City Limits*, n.d., https://citylimits.org/zonein/ulurp-explained.

39. Jack Norton, Lydia Pelot-Hobbs, and Judah Schept, eds., *The Jail Is Everywhere: Fighting the New Geography of Mass Incarceration* (London and New York: Verso, 2023).

40. Katal, "Reflections," 7.

41. Audrey Wachs, "City Taps Perkins Eastman to Research Alternatives to Rikers," *Architect's Newspaper*, January 26, 2018, www.archpaper.com/2018/01/city-taps-perkins-eastman-study-alternatives-rikers.

42. City of New York, *New York City Borough-Based Jail System Draft Scope of Work to Prepare a Draft Environmental Impact Statement CEQR No. 18DOC001Y*, August 15, 2018.

43. Anna Sanders, "No New Jail for Staten Island, de Blasio Now Says," *SILive*, April 3, 2017, www.silive.com/news/2017/04/no_new_jail_for_

staten_island.html.

44. Lauren Cook, "Plans to Close Rikers Island and Open Borough-Based Jails Underway," *AM New York*, June 7, 2019, www.corrections1.com/facility-design-and-operation/articles/plans-to-close-rikers-island-and-open-borough-based-jails-underway-0l8eGipkX2OyokFX.

45. "Staten Island," NYU Furman Center, 2019, https://furmancenter.org/neighborhoods/view/staten-island; Alex Bell, "Your Neighborhood NYPD Officer Isn't Likely to Be Your Neighbor," *Labs Bell Blog*, 2016, https://blog.labsbell.com/blog/NYPDHomeZip.

46. Caroline Spivack, "Rikers Island Closure and Borough-Based Jail Plan, Explained," *Curbed New York*, February 26, 2020.

47. Maurice Carroll, "Action on Chinatown Jail Put Off after Protest," *New York Times*, November 19, 1982.

48. Yoav Gonen, "Plans to Build High-Rise Jail in Lower Manhattan Nixed," *New York Post*, November 28, 2018, https://nypost.com/2018/11/28/plans-to-build-high-rise-jail-in-lower-manhattan-nixed.

49. "First Requests for Proposal for Borough-Based Jails Program to Be Released in Early 2020," New York City Department of Design and Construction, November 14, 2019, www.nyc.gov/site/ddc/about/press-releases/2019/pr-111419-jails-rfp.page.

50. Jarrod Shanahan, *Captives: How Rikers Island Took New York City Hostage* (London and New York: Verso, 2022), 338–40.

51. Eva Fedderly, *These Walls: The Battle for Rikers Island and the Future of America's Jails* (New York: Avid Reader Press, 2023), 133.

52. All written responses submitted during the EIS process are collected, alongside the city's highly selective responses, in the 3,167-page document City of New York, *New York City Borough-Based Jail System Final Scope of Work to Prepare a Draft Environmental Impact Statement CEQR No. 18DOC001Y* (New York City, 2019), appendix B.

53. Brian Kavanagh and Nydia M. Velázquez, comments in City of New York, *Final Scope of Work*, appendix B.

54. These voices will be explored at length in chapter 4.

55. Rob Bryan "Closing Rikers Island: A Step Beyond Prison Reform," *Dissent*, May 18, 2017, https://www.dissentmagazine.org/online_articles/close-rikers-campaign-prison-reform-abolition-de-blasio.

56. Given the stenographic nature of the source article, it is unclear where Martin's words end and the author's begin. The reader is left guessing whether Martin used the term "non-reformist reform" or the author simply added this to augment his argument. In either case, the argument is the same. See Bryan, "Closing Rikers Island."

57. Jonathan Sperling, "Three Distinct Viewpoints Emerge at Raucous

Kew Gardens Jail Hearing," *Queens Daily Eagle*, April 25, 2019, https://queenseagle.com/all/kew-gardens-jail-hearing; Stewart, ""A Report of Sexual Misconduct."

58. No New Jails NYC, *Close Rikers Now, We Keep Us Safe*, 2019, www.nonewjailsnyc.com/no-new-jails-close-rikers-now-we-keep-us-safe-guide#:~:text=A%20New%20Yorker's%20Guide%20to,without%20building%20any%20new%20jails.; Osha Oneeka Daya Brown et al., "$11 Billion for What?! Incarcerated Organizers with No New Jails NYC Explain How to Shut Down Rikers without Building New Jails," *CUNY Law Review* 23, no. 1 (January 2020): 1–24.

59. "Bronx Defenders' Revised Statement on the Closing of Rikers Island and the Creation of Borough-Based Jails," Bronx Defenders, September 4, 2019, www.bronxdefenders.org/bronx-defenders-revised-statement-on-the-closing-of-rikers-island-and-the-creation-of-borough-based-jails.

60. Vocal-NY (@VOCALNewYork), "BREAKING: @VOCALNewYork Releases Letter to @NYCMayor Demanding Major Community Investments as a Part of Any Plan to Close Rikers Island," X image, September 4, 2019, https://twitter.com/vocalnewyork/status/1169265793676259330.

61. "No New Jails NYC Legal Staff Letter," June 17, 2019, https://sites.google.com/view/nnjattorneysletter.

62. "Open Letter from the Legal Aid Society: False Binary of the Close Rikers Plan," Legal Aid Society, October 17, 2019, https://legalaidnyc.org/news/legal-aid-society-false-binary-close-rikers-plan.

63. "National Lawyers Guild Supports NoNewJails NYC Campaign," National Lawyers Guild, September 4, 2019, www.nlg.org/national-lawyers-guild-supports-nonewjails-nyc-campaign; Janaki Chadha, "AOC Jumps into Rikers Fray, Opposing de Blasio's Jail Replacement Plan," *Politico*, October 2, 2019, www.politico.com/states/new-york/city-hall/story/2019/10/02/aoc-jumps-into-rikers-fray-opposing-de-blasios-jail-replacement-plan-1217360.

64. Glenn Martin has since attempted to distance himself from the campaign, dubbing it "a liberal reform space" that "lost its way" in its advocacy for the new jails. See Fedderly, *These Walls.*

65. "The Justice Fund," New York Women's Foundation, n.d., https://www.nywf.org/the-justice-fund.

66. Office of the Mayor, "Mayor de Blasio Announces 'Smaller, Safer, Fairer: A Roadmap to Closing Rikers Island,'" news release, June 22, 2017, www.nyc.gov/office-of-the-mayor/news/427-17/mayor-de-blasio-smaller-safer-fairer—roadmap-closing-rikers-island.

67. Soffiyah Elijah, "'No New Jails' Means Same Old Jails," *New York Daily*

News, October 11, 2019.

68. James Kilgore and Judah Schept, "The Long Fight against Jail Expansion in Champaign-Urbana, Illinois: An Interview with James Kilgore of Build Programs, Not Jails," in Norton, Pelot-Hobbs, and Schept, *Jail Is Everywhere*.

69. Soffiyah Elijah, "To the mud slingers, haters & folks who are upset that I told the truth about the Rikers situation & think they're capable of challenging me—forget about it. I only debate my peers, all others . . . I TEACH! Later," Twitter post, https://twitter.com/SoffiyahElijah/status/1183050004916817920.

70. Gabriel Sayegh, "Making Sense of the Fight over NYC Jails," Katal Center for Equity, Health, and Justice, October 10, 2019, https://katalcenter.org/makingsenserikers.

71. CURB, "How to Stop a Jail in Your Town: A Compilation of Resources from Fights against Jail Expansion," Critical Resistance, May 31, 2019, https://criticalresistance.org/resources/placeholder-resource-3.

72. Maurice Chammah, "Inside the Mayor's Plan to Close Rikers," *New Yorker*, March 22, 2019, www.newyorker.com/news/dispatch/inside-mayor-bill-de-blasio-plan-to-close-rikers-island.

73. Rachel Foran, Mariame Kaba, and Katy Naples-Mitchell, "Abolitionist Principles for Prosecutor Organizing: Origins and Next Steps," *Stanford Journal of Civil Rights and Civil Liberties* 16, no. 496 (2021): 516.

74. CB1 Community Board hearing, April 8, 2019.

75. Rachel Holliday Smith et al., "Local Boards Reject Rikers Replacement Jails, but Council Reps Hold the Key," *The City*, May 28, 2019, www.thecity.nyc/2019/5/28/21211070/local-boards-reject-rikers-replacement-jails-but-council-reps-hold-the-key.

76. Hundreds of such testimonials appear in City of New York, *Final Scope of Work*, appendix B.

77. "Hit Pause on Borough-Based Jails Process," Municipal Art Society of New York, July 22, 2019, www.mas.org/news/hit-pause-on-borough-based-jails-process.

78. "About," Neighbors United Below Canal, n.d., www.nubcnyc.com/about-nubc.

79. Amy Plitt and Caroline Spivack, "Rikers-Replacing Borough-Based Jails Will Drastically Shrink," *Curbed New York*, October 15, 2019, https://ny.curbed.com/2019/10/15/20915614/rikers-island-new-york-city-council-borough-jails-smaller.

80. Mayor's Office of Criminal Justice, "Projected City Jail Population Falls to 3,300 by 2026," news release, October 14, 2019, https://criminaljustice.cityofnewyork.us/press-release/projected-city-jail-

population-falls-to-3300-by-2026.

81. Chammah, "Inside the Mayor's Plan."

82. NYC Mayor's Office of Criminal Justice, Letter to Hon. Margaret S. Chin, September 27, 2018, in City of New York, *Final Scope of Work*, appendix B.

83. David Brand, "New Queens Jail Would House All Detained Women in NYC," *Queens Daily Eagle*, March 22, 2019, https://queenseagle.com/all/2019/3/22/new-queens-jail-would-house-only-women.

84. Office of the Mayor, City of New York, "Borough-Based Jail Plan Points of Agreement," October 18, 2019, http://council.nyc.gov/data/wp-content/uploads/sites/73/2019/10/BBJ_Points_of_Agreement_Rikers.pdf.

85. Ayana Smith and Mariela Mariano, "Deep Disagreements Ahead of Key Hearing on Bronx Jail Site," *City Limits*, https://citylimits.org/2019/05/22/deep-disagreements-ahead-of-key-hearing-on-bronx-jail-site/.

86. Chammah, "Inside the Mayor's Plan."

87. Eric L. Adams to Howard Judd Fiedler, October 29, 2018, in City of New York, *Final Scope of Work*, appendix B.

88. Sarita Daftary-Steel to the City of New York, in City of New York, *Final Scope of Work*, appendix B.

89. Representative Jo Anne Simon to Howard Fiedler, October 29, 2018, in City of New York, *Final Scope of Work*, appendix B.

90. Lippman Commission, "Closing the Chapter on Rikers," October 2019, 3, https://static1.squarespace.com/static/5b6de4731aef1de914f43628/t/5da60eb59dac4376675bfe93/1571163845478/AMJNYC+-+Closing+the+Chapter+on+Rikers+%28Oct.+2019%29.pdf.

91. Morales, "Behind the Growing Calls."

92. Darren Walker, "In Defense of Nuance," Ford Foundation, September 19, 2022, www.fordfoundation.org/news-and-stories/stories/posts/in-defense-of-nuance.

93. "'No New Jails' Activists Protest at Ford Foundation," *Artforum*, September 27, 2019, www.artforum.com/news/no-new-jails-activists-protest-at-ford-foundation-80907.

94. We discuss this tension, as it played out in 2020 street activity, in Jarrod Shanahan and Zhandarka Kurti, "The Shifting Ground: A Conversation on the George Floyd Rebellion," *Ill Will*, September 20, 2020, https://illwill.com/the-shifting-ground-a-conversation-on-the-george-floyd-rebellion.

95. Matthew Haag, "N.Y.C. Votes to Close Rikers. Now Comes the Hard Part.," *New York Times*, October 17, 2019, www.nytimes.com/2019/10/17/nyregion/rikers-island-closing-vote.html; "Mayor Announces Outposted Therapeutic Housing Units," NYC Health and Hospitals, November 26, 2019, www.nychealthandhospitals.org/

pressrelease/mayor-announces-outposted-therapeutic-housing-units-to-serve-patients-in-custody-with-serious-health-needs.

96. Martin Z. Braun, "Bond Investors Largely Ignore NYC's $7 Billion Deficit," *Bloomberg*, November 23, 2023, www.bloomberg.com/news/articles/2023-11-21/nyc-s-7-billion-deficit-is-largely-ignored-by-muni-investors.

97. Ruth Wilson Gilmore, "Foreword," in Norton, Pelot-Hobbs, and Schept, *Jail Is Everywhere*, xi.

98. As quoted in Dashiell Allen, "Is It Possible to Close Rikers without Building a New Jail in Chinatown?," *Village Sun*, February 20, 2022, https://thevillagesun.com/is-it-possible-to-close-rikers-without-building-a-new-jail-in-chinatown.

99. "The Closing of Rikers: A Survival Strategy of the Carceral State," Oakland Abolition & Solidarity, April 13, 2017, https://oaklandabosol.org/2017/04/13/the-closing-of-rikers-a-survival-strategy-of-the-carceral-state. "

100. New York City Department of Design and Construction (NYC DDC), *Design Principles & Guidelines, NYC Borough-Based Jails Program, A Design-Build Program, Manhattan Facility*, January 2022, 5. Identical verbiage appears in the plans for Brooklyn (January 2022), Queens (April 2022), and the Bronx (August 2022), alongside such Orwellian chestnuts as "required security enclosures should not evoke a sense of cages."

101. Katal, "Reflections," 26.

CHAPTER 3: "JUSTICE HUBS"

1. Stanley Richards, "Opinion: Planned Borough-Based Jails Are a Chance for a 'Radically Different' System," *City Limits,* May 11, 2022, https://citylimits.org/2022/05/11/opinion-planned-borough-based-jails-are-a-chance-for-a-radically-different-system.

2. "Reflections and Lessons from the First Two Phases of the #CLOSErikers Campaign: August 2015–August 2017," Katal, January 2018, 14, https://katalcenter.org/wp-content/uploads/2022/06/Katal_CLOSErikers_Campaign_Report_PRINT_-_final.pdf.

3. James Kilgore, "Repackaging Mass Incarceration," *Counterpunch*, June 6, 2014, www.counterpunch.org/2014/06/06/repackaging-mass-incarceration.

4. See Jack Norton, Lydia Pelot-Hobbs, and Judah Schept, eds., *The Jail Is Everywhere: Fighting the New Geography of Mass Incarceration* (London and New York: Verso, 2023)

5. Judah Schept, *Progressive Punishment: Job Loss, Jail Growth, and the Neoliberal Logic of Carceral Expansion* (New York: New York University Press, 2015), 52.

6.   Dan Gallagher et al., *Justice in Design: Toward a Healthier and More Just New York City Jail System* (New York: Van Alen Institute and the Independent Commission for New York City Criminal Justice and Incarceration Reform, 2017), 10, https://past.vanalen.org/content/uploads/2017/07/Justice-in-Design-Report.pdf.

7.   Reuben Jonathan Miller and Forrest Stuart, "Carceral Citizenship: Race, Rights and Responsibility in the Age of Mass Supervision," *Theoretical Criminology* 21, no. 4 (2017): 533.

8.   "Reimagining Prisons," Vera Institute of Justice, 2023, https://www.vera.org/reimagining-prison; "Reimagining Criminal Justice," #CLOSErikers, 2017, www.closerikers.org/reimagining-criminal-justice, accessed via the Internet Archive Wayback Machine.

9.   Independent Commission on New York City Criminal Justice and Incarceration Reform (Lippman Commission), *A More Just New York City*, 2017, 76, https://nycitylens.com/wp-content/rikers/wp-content/uploads/2017/05/IndependentCommissionFinalReport.pdf.

10.   Katie Wilson, "Carceral Camouflage: Inscribing and Obscuring Neoliberal Penality through New York City's Borough-Based Jail Plan" (honors thesis, Oberlin College, 2019), 71, https://digitalcommons.oberlin.edu/honors/139.

11.   Gallagher et al., *Justice in Design*, 16.

12.   Gallagher et al., 9.

13.   Gallagher et al., 42.

14.   Lippman Commission, *More Just*, 76.

15.   New York City Department of Design and Construction (NYC DDC), *Design Principles & Guidelines, NYC Borough-Based Jails Program, A Design-Build Program, Manhattan Facility*, January 2022, 12. Identical verbiage appears in the plans for Brooklyn (January 2022), Queens (April 2022), and the Bronx (August 2022).

16.   NYC Criminal Justice, *Borough Based Jails Master Plan*, 2018, www.nysenate.gov/sites/default/files/article/attachment/bk_community_engagement_9.14_pop_reduction_program_slides.pdf.

17.   Gallagher et al., *Justice in Design*, 29.

18.   Wilson, "Carceral Camouflage," 41.

19.   Kenneth Ricci, Frank Greene, and Rosalie Genevro, "What Jail Can't Do," *Urban Omnibus*, December 6, 2017, https://urbanomnibus.net/2017/12/what-jail-cant-do.

20.   Max Wylie, *400 Miles from Harlem: Courts, Crime, and Correction* (New York, MacMillan, 1972), 15.

21.   State Commission of Prisons, *Twenty-Sixth Annual Report* (Albany, 1921), 35–36.

22. Malcolm M. Feeley, *The Process Is the Punishment: Handling Cases in a Lower Criminal Court* (New York: Russell Sage, 1979), 5.

23. Feeley, *Process Is the Punishment*.

24. Center for Court Innovation, Bureau of Justice Assistance, *Community Courts: An Evolving Model* (Washington, DC: US Department of Justice, Office of Justice Programs, 2000), www.ojp.gov/pdffiles1/bja/183452.pdf.

25. Robin Steinberg and Skylar Albertson, "Broken Windows Policing and Community Courts: An Unholy Alliance," *Cardozo Law Review* 37, no. 3 (2015): 995–1024.

26. See Greg Berman and John Feinblatt, *Good Courts: The Case for Problem Solving Justice* (New York: New Press, 2005).

27. Stanley Cohen, "The Punitive City: Notes on the Dispersal of Social Control," *Contemporary Crises*, no. 3 (1979): 339–63.

28. "Rethinking Rikers Island," Center for Justice Innovation, n.d., www.innovatingjustice.org/rethinking-rikers-island.

29. US Department of Justice, Civil Rights Division, *Investigation of the Ferguson Police Department*, March 4, 2015, www.justice.gov/sites/default/files/opa/press-releases/attachments/2015/03/04/ferguson_police_department_report.pdf.

30. Alexandra Natapoff, "Criminal Municipal Courts," *Harvard Law Review* 134, no. 3 (2021): 973.

31. Natapoff, "Criminal Municipal Courts," 1046.

32. See Brendan D. Roediger, "Abolish Municipal Courts: A Response to Professor Natapoff," *Harvard Law Review* 134, no. 4 (2021): 213–27.

33. Gallagher et al., *Justice in Design*, 12, 53.

34. Gallagher et al., 49.

35. Gallagher et al., 6.

36. Gallagher et al., 50.

37. "Polis Station," Studio Gang, 2015, https://studiogang.com/project/polis-station.

38. Spencer Ackerman, "Homan Square Revealed: How Chicago Police 'Disappeared' 7,000 People," *The Guardian*, October 19, 2015, https://www.theguardian.com/us-news/2015/oct/19/homan-square-chicago-police-disappeared-thousands.

39. Zach Stafford, "Chicago Protestors Occupy Homan Square for Eighth Day to Demand Closure," *The Guardian*, July 29, 2016, www.theguardian.com/us-news/2016/jul/29/chicago-protestors-occupy-homan-square-police-black-lives-matter.

40. Shana Agid, "How What We Ask Shapes What We Can Imagine: Decoupling Design and Punishment," *Space and Culture* 25, no. 3 (2022): 447–462.

41. Studio Gang, "Polis Station."

42. Agid, "What We Ask," 451–61.

43. Agid, 448.

44. Gallagher et al., *Justice in Design*, 20.

45. Gallagher et al., 19.

46. Richard E. Wener, *The Environmental Psychology of Prisons and Jails* (Cambridge: Cambridge University Press, 2012), 46–68.

47. Gallagher et al., *Justice in Design*, 20.

48. Ricci, Greene, and Genevro, "What Jail Can't Do."

49. US Attorney's Office, Southern District of New York, "Manhattan U.S. Attorney Finds Pattern and Practice of Excessive Force and Violence at NYC Jails on Rikers Island That Violates the Constitutional Rights of Adolescent Male Inmates," news release, August 4, 2014, www.justice.gov/usao-sdny/pr/manhattan-us-attorney-finds-pattern-and-practice-excessive-force-and-violence-nyc-jails.

50. Gallagher et al., *Justice in Design*, 79; Reuven Blau, "City Jails Other Than Rikers See Surge in Violence," *New York Daily News*, May 20, 2018; Office of New York Comptroller Scott Stringer, "Comptroller Stringer 2015 Analysis: Violence at City Jails Spikes Dramatically and Cost Per Inmate Explodes Even as Inmate Population Declines," news release, October 16, 2015, https://comptroller.nyc.gov/newsroom/comptroller-stringer-2015-analysis-violence-at-city-jails-spikes-dramatically-and-cost-per-inmate-explodes-even-as-inmate-population-declines.

51. Gallagher et al., *Justice in Design*, 19.

52. Maurice Chammah, "Inside the Mayor's Plan to Close Rikers," *New Yorker*, March 22, 2019, www.newyorker.com/news/dispatch/inside-mayor-bill-de-blasio-plan-to-close-rikers-island.

53. Wylie, *400 Miles*, 74; DOC, *Saga of the Women's House of Detention*, n.d., 2, Box 4, Folders 6–7, p. 16, Anna M. Kross Archives, Smith College.

54. Gallagher et al., *Justice in Design*, 51–52.

55. Gallagher et al., 21.

56. Gallagher et al., 57.

57. Leah Meisterlin, "Not Yet #AfterRikers: Looking for #JusticeInDesign," *Avery Review*, June 2018.

58. Gallagher et al., *Justice in Design*, 30.

59. Olivia Ahn, EIS comment sheet in City of New York, *New York City Borough-Based Jail System Final Scope of Work to Prepare a Draft Environmental Impact Statement CEQR No. 18DOC001Y* (New York City, 2019), appendix B.

60. Gallagher et al., 32–39.

61. Meisterlin, "Not Yet #AfterRikers."

62. Gallagher et al., *Justice in Design*, 28.
63. Wilson, "Carceral Camouflage," 26.
64. NYC DDC, *Design Principles & Guidelines, Manhattan*, 14.
65. New York City Office of the Mayor, *Beyond Rikers, Towards a Borough-Based System (Confidential)*, 2018, 35, www.nyc.gov/html/mancb3/downloads/calendar/2018/CB1%20CB3_090618.pdf.
66. Meisterlin, "Not Yet #AfterRikers."
67. Gallagher et al., *Justice in Design*, 11.
68. Meisterlin, "Not Yet #AfterRikers."
69. William Shakespeare, *Henry V*, act 1, scene 1, in *The Complete Works of William Shakespeare* (New York: Crown, 1975), 490.
70. Arrian of Nicomedia, *The Anabasis of Alexander*, trans. E. J. Chinnock (London: Hodder and Stoughton, 1884), 84 (emphasis ours).
71. Meisterlin, "Not Yet #AfterRikers." In a distinctly postmodernist lexicon, Meisterlin refers to the design of the new jails as "a process so easily hijacked by power," as if "power," however this abstraction is to be understood, would be otherwise absent from a project funded and promoted by some of the richest and most powerful political actors in the city, working together to design a network of skyscraper jails.
72. Meisterlin, "Not Yet #AfterRikers."
73. Zhandarka Kurti and Jarrod Shanahan, "Rebranding Mass Incarceration: The Lippman Commission and 'Carceral Devolution' in New York City," *Social Justice: A Journal of Crime, Conflict and World Order* 45, no. 2/3 (2018): 28–29.
74. Rebecca M. Bratspies, "Renewable Rikers: A Plan for Restorative Environmental Justice," *Loyola Law Review*, no. 66 (2020): 372.
75. Bratspies, "Renewable Rikers," 383 (emphasis in original).
76. Todd Levon Brown, "Evaluating Correctional Environments: A Critical Psychosociospatial Approach," in *The Palgrave Handbook of Prison Design*, ed. Dominique Moran, Yvonne Jewkes, Kwan-Lamar Blount-Hill, and Victor St. John (London: Palgrave Macmillan, 2022), 283–86.
77. Brown, "Evaluating Correctional Environments," 290–95.
78. Brown, 294–96. The article Brown cites approvingly is Jean-François Couturier, "Door & Window Design Solutions Improve Security, Efficiency," *Correctional News*, December 30, 2015, https://correctionalnews.com/2015/12/30/door-window-design-solutions-improve-security-efficiency.
79. Richards, "Planned Borough-Based Jails."
80. Lippman Commission, *More Just*, 86–88; Gallagher et al., *Justice in Design*, 19, 51; The Mayor's Office of Criminal Justice (MOCJ), *Smaller, Safer, Fairer: A Roadmap to Closing Rikers Island*, 2017, 9, 31, 37–39, 46, 48,

https://criminaljustice.cityofnewyork.us/reports/smaller-safer-fairer-copy.

81. Gallagher et al., *Justice in Design*, 19.

82. Lippman Commission, "Closing the Chapter on Rikers," October 2019, 13, https://static1.squarespace.com/static/5b6de4731aef1de914f43628/t/5 da60eb59dac4376675bfe93/1571163845478/AMJNYC+-+Closing+the+C hapter+on+Rikers+%28Oct.+2019%29.pdf.

83. Richards, "Planned Borough-Based Jails."

84. Blau, "City Jails."

85. Chammah, "Inside the Mayor's Plan."

86. Liz Blum, "Decarcerating Sacramento: Confronting Jail Expansion in California's Capital," in *The Jail Is Everywhere: Fighting the New Geography of Mass Incarceration*, ed. Jack Norton, Lydia Pelot-Hobbs, and Judah Schept (London and New York: Verso, 2023), 68.

87. Don Mitchell, "There's No Such Thing as Culture: Towards a Reconceptualization of the Idea of Culture in Geography," *Transactions of the Institute of British Geographers* 20, no. 1 (1995): 102–16.

88. Michael Jacobson et al., "Beyond the Island: Changing the Culture of New York City Jails," *Fordham Urban Law Journal* 45, no. 2 (2018): 379.

89. This is a central argument of Jarrod Shanahan, *Captives: How Rikers Island Took New York City Hostage* (London and New York: Verso, 2022).

90. The two references to COBA to be found in this text are both favorable. See Jacobson et al., "Beyond the Island," 384, 429.

91. Reuven Blau, "Adams' Ties to Lobbying Firm That Represents Jail Workers Raises Questions on Rikers Island Future," *The City*, October 31, 2021, www.thecity.nyc/2021/10/31/22756037/eric-adams-rikers-island-ties-to-correction-officer-lobbyist.

92. Shanahan, *Captives*, 306–33.

93. Jacobson et al., "Beyond the Island," 403–7.

94. Lippman Commission, *More Just*, 88; Benjamin Heller, "Why New York City Needs a Blueprint to Rightsize the Department of Correction," Vera Institute of Justice, May 2020, www.vera.org/publications/rightsize-nyc-department-of-correction.

95. Cindy Rodriguez, "Unions Call Plan to Close Rikers Laughable," WNYC News, April 4, 2017, www.wnyc.org/story/unions-call-plan-close-rikers-laughable.

96. Jacobson et al., "Beyond the Island," 417–18.

97. Jacobson et al., 411–12.

98. Jacobson et al., 405.

99. Jacobson et al., 415–34.

100. "Our Approach," CUNY Institute for State and Local Governance, n.d., https://islg.cuny.edu/our-approach.

101. Raoul Vaneigem, "Basic Banalities, Part II," in *Situationist International Anthology*, ed. and trans. Ken Knabb (Berkeley: Bureau of Public Secrets, 2006), 161.

CHAPTER 4: ANOTHER WORLD IS POSSIBLE

1. City of New York, *New York City Borough-Based Jail System Final Scope of Work to Prepare a Draft Environmental Impact Statement CEQR No. 18DOC001Y* (New York City, 2019), appendix A, 106–7; Daniel McCarthy to Howard Fiedler, City of New York, *Final Scope of Work*, appendix B.

2. Crystal Hoyte-Miguel to Howard Fiedler, *Final Scope of Work*, appendix B; Eric Horn, Borough-Based Jail System Comment Sheet, *Final Scope of Work*, appendix B, 2018; Bill Gati to Howard Fiedler, *Final Scope of Work*, appendix B; Jessica Katz to Howard Fiedler, *Final Scope of Work*, appendix B; KP to Howard Fiedler, *Final Scope of Work*, appendix B; Neil, Lisa, and Nathan Duncan to Howard Fiedler, *Final Scope of Work*, appendix B; Benjamin D. Sampson, Borough-Based Jail System Comment Sheet, *Final Scope of Work*, appendix B; "Concerned Resident" to Howard Fiedler, *Final Scope of Work*, appendix B; "Concerned Resident" to Howard Fiedler, *Final Scope of Work*, appendix B; Thomas Warns to Howard Fiedler, *Final Scope of Work*, appendix B; Matthew Nadelson to Howard Fiedler, *Final Scope of Work*, appendix B.

3. City of New York, *Final Scope of Work*, appendix B.

4. See, for instance, City of New York, *Final Scope of Work*, appendix A, 39–48, 53–54.

5. City of New York, *Final Scope of Work*, appendix A, 42.

6. City of New York, *Final Scope of Work*, appendix B.

7. Diego Beekman Neighborhood Plan, Diego Beekman, 2017, www.diegobeekman.org/the-plan.

8. Amanda M. Philip, "The Closing of Rikers Island: The Opening of Possibilities in the Bronx" (master's thesis, Pratt Institute, 2019), 60–61.

9. We have included the location and affiliation (e.g., NNJ) of respondents when they offered this information in their remarks.

10. Lucia Cappuccio to Howard Fiedler, *Final Scope of Work*, appendix B.

11. Zoe Alexander to Mayor's Office of Environmental Coordination and the Department of Correction, *Final Scope of Work*, appendix B.

12. Enid Braun to Howard Fiedler, *Final Scope of Work*, appendix B.

13. Sivan Amar to Howard Fiedler, *Final Scope of Work*, appendix B.

14. Gaurav Jashnani, "Statement against NYC's Roadmap to Closing Rikers Island," *Final Scope of Work*, appendix B.

15. Kate Winkelstein-Duveneck to Howard Fiedler, *Final Scope of Work*,

appendix B.

16. Sharon Hughes to Howard Fiedler, *Final Scope of Work*, appendix B.

17. M. J. Williams, "Statement against NYC's Roadmap to Closing Rikers Island," *Final Scope of Work*, appendix B (emphasis in original).

18. Linda Banta to Howard Fiedler (1) *Final Scope of Work*, appendix B.

19. Zoe Alexander to Mayor's Office of Environmental Coordination and the Department of Correction, *Final Scope of Work*, appendix B.

20. Jarrod Shanahan and Jack Norton, "A Jail to End All Jails," *Urban Omnibus*, December 6, 2017, urbanomnibus.net/2017/12/jail-end-jails.

21. Scott H. Jacobs to Howard Fiedler, *Final Scope of Work*, appendix B.

22. Brian Kelly to Howard Fiedler, October 15, 2018, *Final Scope of Work*, appendix B.

23. Carolyn Yao, Borough-Based Jail Comment Sheet, *Final Scope of Work*, appendix B.

24. Allison Brown to Mayor's Office of Environmental Coordination and the Department of Correction, *Final Scope of Work*, appendix B, 2018.

25. Frank Braio to Howard Fiedler, *Final Scope of Work*, appendix B, 2018.

26. Tristan Beach to Mayor's Office of Environmental Coordination and the Department of Correction, *Final Scope of Work*, appendix B, 2018.

27. Jessica Ngok to Howard Fiedler, *Final Scope of Work*, appendix B, 2018.

28. Nadja Eisenberg Guyot to Howard Fiedler, *Final Scope of Work*, appendix B, n.d.

29. Bryan Welton to Howard Fiedler, *Final Scope of Work*, appendix B, 2018.

30. Fabio Sborea to Howard Fiedler, *Final Scope of Work*, appendix B, 2018.

31. Jorky Badillo to the City of New York, *Final Scope of Work*, appendix B, 2018.

32. Sivan Amar to Howard Fiedler, *Final Scope of Work*, appendix B, 2018.

33. Linda Banta to Howard Fiedler (2), *Final Scope of Work*, appendix B, 2018.

34. Tanya Nguyen to Howard Fiedler, *Final Scope of Work*, appendix B, 2018.

35. Elaine Cao to Mayor's Office of Environmental Coordination and the Department of Correction, *Final Scope of Work*, appendix B, 2018.

36. Jose Rodriguez to Howard Fiedler, *Final Scope of Work*, appendix B, 2018.

37. Rowena Chodkowski to Howard Fiedler, *Final Scope of Work*, appendix B, 2018.

38. Sylvia Morse to Howard Fiedler, *Final Scope of Work*, appendix B, 2018.

39. Dr. Jim Fairbanks, "Saving Justice," *Final Scope of Work*, appendix B, October 29, 2018 (emphasis in original).

40. Nadja Eisenberg-Guyot to Howard Fiedler, *Final Scope of Work*, appendix B, 2018.

41. "Students Criticize APS for Funding Police in Schools," *Atlanta Progressive News*, February 22, 2015, https://atlantaprogressivenews.

com/2015/02/22/students-criticize-aps-for-funding-police-in-schools.

42. No New Jails NYC (NNJ), *Close Rikers Now, We Keep Us Safe,* 2019, 3, www.nonewjailsnyc.com/no-new-jails-close-rikers-now-we-keep-us-safe-guide.

43. NNJ, *Close Rikers Now,* 5.

44. Osha Oneeka Daya Brown et al., "$11 Billion for What?! Incarcerated Organizers with No New Jails NYC Explain How to Shut Down Rikers without Building New Jails," *CUNY Law Review* 23, no. 1 (January 2020): 13.

45. NNJ, *Close Rikers Now,* 6. These claims are cited in the original. See, for instance, Alliance for Safety and Justice, *Crime Survivors Speak: The First Ever National Survey of Victims' Views on Safety and Justice,* n.d., https://allianceforsafetyandjustice.org/wp-content/uploads/documents/Crime%20Survivors%20Speak%20Report.pdf.

46. Daya Brown et al., "$11 Billion for What?!," 7.

47. Of course, capital projects like the skyscraper jails are not financed the same way as direct public spending is. However, they constitute large debts to be paid off over a long period of time. Therefore, while NNJ isn't quite correct that the city was in the position of "freeing $11 billion for the needs of the people" (Daya Brown et al., 5) by canceling the skyscraper jails plan, the actual amount these jails will cost over time is actually much, much more.

48. NNJ, *Close Rikers Now,* 28.

49. Odilka Santiago, "Regulating Time and Space: The Disciplining of Latina and Black Sheltered Homeless Women in NYC," *Critical Dialogues in Latinx Studies,* ed. Mérida Rúa and Ana Ramos-Zayas, (New York: NYU Press, 2021), 379–91.

50. NNJ, *Close Rikers Now,* 28–29.

51. NNJ, *Close Rikers Now,* 29–31.

52. NNJ, *Close Rikers Now,* 32–44.

53. Daya Brown et al., "$11 Billion for What?!," 19.

54. Dee Squalé, "Shut Down Rikers, and Then What?," *City Limits,* February 16, 2016, https://citylimits.org/2016/02/16/cityviewsshut-down-rikers-and-then-what; Campaign to Shut Down Rikers, "Resistance in the Face of Co-optation," *Medium,* May 19, 2016, https://medium.com/@ShutDownRikers/campaign-to-shut-down-rikers-official-statement-7e773a4fc0c4.

55. Keeanga-Yamahtta Taylor, "Until Black Women Are Free, None of Us Will Be Free," *New Yorker,* July 20, 2020, www.newyorker.com/news/our-columnists/until-black-women-are-free-none-of-us-will-be-free.

56. Combahee River Collective, "'The Combahee River Collective Statement' (1977)," in *Available Means: An Anthology Of Women's Rhetoric(s),* ed. Joy Ritchie and Kate Ronald (Pittsburgh: University of Pittsburgh

Press, 2001), 292–300, https://doi.org/10.2307/j.ctt5hjqnj.50; Keeanga-Yamahtta Taylor, *How We Get Free: Black Feminism and the Combahee River Collective* (Chicago: Haymarket Books, 2017).

57. Black Freedom Studies, "Black and Red: Black Liberation and Socialism," April 1, 2021, www.blackfreedomstudies.org/events/spring-2021/black-and-red-black-liberation-and-socialism.

58. Olúfẹ́mi O. Táíwò, *Elite Capture: How the Powerful Took Over Identity Politics (and Everything Else)* (Chicago: Haymarket Books, 2022), 68–74.

59. "States of Incarceration: Zhandarka Kurti and Jarrod Shanahan with Tobi Haslett," *Brooklyn Rail*, October 2022, https://brooklynrail.org/2022/10/field-notes/States-of-Incarceration-Zhandarka-Kurti-and-Jarrod-Shanahan-with-Tobi-Haslett.

60. James Forman Jr., *Locking Up Our Own: Crime and Punishment in Black America* (New York: Farrar, Straus and Giroux, 2017).

61. Ruth Wilson Gilmore and Craig Gilmore, "Beyond Bratton," in *Policing the Planet: Why the Policing Crisis Led to Black Lives Matter*, ed. Jordan T. Camp and Christina Heatherton (London and New York: Verso, 2016).

62. Much of this assessment is consistent with an anonymous critique circulated by former NNJ members "Authenticity and Abolition," *It's Going Down*, July 20, 2020, https://itsgoingdown.org/authenticity-and-abolition.

63. Mia Mingus, "Transformative Justice: A Brief Description," *Leaving Evidence* (blog), January 9, 2019, https://leavingevidence.wordpress.com/2019/01/09/transformative-justice-a-brief-description.

64. Sidney Franklin, "Rikers Replacement Plan Moves Forward with Reduced Jail Tower Heights," *Architect's Newspaper*, October 23, 2019, www.archpaper.com/2019/10/city-council-approves-rikers-jails.

65. "Jail Update: The First Stage of a 30-Story Jail for White Street Is Underway," *Tribeca Citizen Community News*, August 23, 2023, https://tribecacitizen.com/2023/08/23/jail-update-demolition-has-begun-in-earnest-and-local-bjsinesses-are-alraedy-feeloing-the-pain.

66. Coalition to Protect Chinatown and LES, "No Towers No Compromise," 2021, https://peoplefirstnyc.org/no-towers.

67. Linda Poon, "Rikers Jail Replacement Plan Pits Chinatown against New York City," *Bloomberg*, June 17, 2022, www.bloomberg.com/news/articles/2022-06-17/nyc-plan-to-replace-rikers-spurs-protest-in-chinatown.

68. Maurice Carroll, "Action on Chinatown Jail Put Off after Protest," *New York Times*, November 19, 1982.

69. Fan Jiao, "New York City Jail Reform and Chinese New Yorkers Civil Rights Movement," *Historical Record of Chinese Americans*, April 11, 2021, https://usdandelion.com/archives/3797.

70. "Open Letter to the Museum of Chinese in America: Reject Jails," https://docs.google.com/forms/d/e/1FAIpQLSfNXkjd2vOd_7NV3yXaL YA7K_mhHAeYahVrrBtJRHV1sislkQ/viewform.

71. Dashiell Allen, "Ten Arrested Trying to Block Start of Demolition Work for Chinatown 'Megajail,'" *Village Sun*, October 1, 2023, https://thevillagesun.com/nine-arrested-trying-to-block-start-of-demolition-for-chinatown-megajail.

72. Commission on Community Reinvestment and the Closure of Rikers Island Report, 2021, www.nyc.gov/assets/hra/downloads/pdf/hra-docs/Commission-Community-Reinvestment-Report.pdf.

CHAPTER 5: WHAT'S AT STAKE?

1. Eva Fedderly, *These Walls: The Battle for Rikers Island and the Future of America's Jails* (New York: Avid Reader Press, 2023), 120.

2. Clara Mattei, "The Dawn of Austerity," interview by Nick Serpe, *Dissent*, February 13, 2023, www.dissentmagazine.org/online_articles/the-dawn-of-austerity.

3. Tony Platt, "Managing the Crisis: Austerity and the Penal System," *Contemporary Marxism*, no. 4 (1981): 29–39.

4. Jack Norton, Lydia Pelot-Hobbs, and Judah Schept, eds., *The Jail Is Everywhere: Fighting the New Geography of Mass Incarceration* (London and New York: Verso, 2023), 180.

5. Xtn Alexander and Matthew N. Lyons, Foreword by Janeen Porter, *Three Way Fight: Revolutionary Politics and Antifascism* (Oakland, CA: PM Press, 2024).

6. Mariame Kaba *We Do This 'Til We Free Us: Abolitionist Organizing and Transforming Justice* (Chicago: Haymarket 2021); Derecka Purnell, *Becoming Abolitionists* (New York: Verso, 2021); Angela Davis, Gina Dent, and Erica Meiners, *Abolition. Feminism. Now* (Chicago: Haymarket, 2022); Ruth Wilson Gilmore *Abolition Geography: Essays Towards Liberation* (New York: Verso, 2022); Rachel Herzing and Justin Piché, *How to Abolish Prisons: Lessons from the Movement against Imprisonment* (Chicago: Haymarket, 2024).

7. Gilmore and Gilmore, "Beyond Bratton," 189–90.

8. James Wood, Valentina Ausserladscheider, and Matthew Sparkes, "'COVID-Keynesianism' Was a Short-Term Crisis Management Tactic. Neoliberal Policymaking Is Back," *LSE British Politics and Policy* (blog), September 28, 2022, https://blogs.lse.ac.uk/politicsandpolicy/covid-keynesianism-was-a-short-term-crisis-management-tactic-neoliberal-policymaking-is-back.

9. James Kilgore, "Repackaging Mass Incarceration."

10. Naomi Murakawa, "Say Their Names, Support Their Killers: Police Reform in the 2020 Black Lives Matter Uprisings," *UCLA Law Review*, no. 69 (September 2023): 1432.

11. Jack Norton, "Why Are There So Many People in Jail in Scranton, PA?" Vera Institute of Justice, January 4, 2017, www.vera.org/in-our-backyards-stories/why-are-there-so-many-people-in-jail-in-scranton-pa.

12. Kilgore, "Repackaging Mass Incarceration."

13. Brett Story and Judah Schept, "Against Punishment: Centering Work, Wages, and Uneven Development in Mapping the Carceral State," *Social Justice: A Journal of Crime, Conflict and World Order* 45, no. 4 (2018): 10.

14. Jack Norton, Lydia Pelot-Hobbs, and Judah Schept, "Introduction," in Norton, Pelot-Hobbs, and Schept, *The Jail Is Everywhere*, 5–7.

15. Rose Braz, "Kinder, Gentler, Gender Responsive Cages: Prison Expansion Is Not Prison Reform," *Women, Girls, and Criminal Justice* 7, no. 6 (2006): 87–91.

16. Wendy Sawyer, "The Gender Divide: Tracking Women's Incarceration Growth," Prison Policy Initiative, January 9, 2018, www.prisonpolicy.org/reports/women_overtime.html.

17. Mon Mohapatra, "Lessons from the No New Jails Network," in Norton, Pelot-Hobbs, and Schept, *Jail Is Everywhere*, 171.

18. "About WCJA," Women's Community Justice Association, n.d., www.womenscja.org/about_wcja.

19. Women's Community Justice Association (WCJA) et al., *A Safer New York City: The Women's Center for Justice; A Nation-Leading Approach on Women & Gender-Expansive People*, May 2022, 29, https://justicelab.columbia.edu/sites/default/files/content/Womens%20Center%20for%20Justice.pdf.

20. Abby Cunniff, "NYC Activists Push Back against Proposed 'Feminist' Jail in Harlem," *Truthout*, July 2, 2022, https://truthout.org/articles/nyc-activists-push-back-against-proposed-feminist-womens-jail-in-harlem/.

21. "Rose M. Singer Center Opens on Rikers Island," *Corrections News*, July 1988, www.correctionhistory.org/html/searches/cnwsrosie.html.

22. Allen J. Beck, US Department of Justice Programs, Bureau of Justice Statistics, *Sexual Victimization in Prisons and Jails Reported by Inmates, 2011–12, National Inmate Survey, 2011–12*, May 2013, https://bjs.ojp.gov/content/pub/pdf/svpjri1112.pdf.

23. Char Adams, "Hundreds of Lawsuits Allege Decades of Sexual Abuse at Rikers Island," NBC News, December 5, 2023, www.nbcnews.com/news/nbcblk/sexual-abuse-lawsuits-rikers-island-new-york-adult-survivors-act-rcna126898.

24. Suzanne Singer, "The Women's Jail at Rikers Island Is Named for My Grandmother. She Would Not Be Proud," op-ed, *New York Times*, May

12, 2020, www.nytimes.com/2020/05/12/opinion/womens-jail-rikers-island-covid.html.

25. Cunniff, "NYC Activists Push Back."

26. New York Women's Foundation and Prisoner Reentry Institute at John Jay, *Women InJustice: Gender and the Pathway to Jail in New York City*, 2017, https://justiceandopportunity.org/wp-content/uploads/2017/08/John_Jay_WIJ-Report_FINAL.pdf-secure.pdf.

27. New York Women's Foundation and Vera Institute of Justice, *A New Path to Justice: Getting Women Off Rikers Island*, November 2018, www.vera.org/downloads/publications/A-New-Path-to-Justice-v.5.pdf.

28. New York Women's Foundation and Vera Institute of Justice, *New Path to Justice.*

29. Gina Belafonte, "What Would a Feminist Jail Look Like," *New York Times*, May 14, 2022, www.nytimes.com/2022/05/14/nyregion/jail-women.html.

30. WCJA et al., *Safer New York City*, 2.

31. WCJA et al., 4.

32. WCJA et al., 3.

33. WCJA et al., 5.

34. Alexandra Cox, *Trapped in a Vice: The Consequences of Confinement for Young People* (New Brunswick: Rutgers University Press, 2018).

35. Mohapatra, "Lessons."

36. New York City Council Committee on Criminal Justice, June 28, 2022, https://justicelab.columbia.edu/sites/default/files/content/Joint%20Testimony%20Women's%20Center%20for%20Justice.pdf.

37. Mohapatra, "Lessons," 170.

38. Norton, Pelot-Hobbs, and Schept, "Conclusion," in *Jail Is Everywhere*, 185–86.

39. Staughton Lynd and Daniel Gross, *Labor Law for the Rank and Filer: Building Solidarity while Steering Clear of the Law* (Oakland: PM Press, 2008), 15.

40. Mohapatra, "Lessons," 177.

41. Associated Press, "The U.S. Is Experiencing a Police Hiring Crisis," NBC News, *US News*, September 6, 2023, www.nbcnews.com/news/us-news/us-experiencing-police-hiring-crisis-rcna103600.

42. Micah Herskind, "This Is the Atlanta Way: A Primer on Cop City," *Scalawag*, May 1, 2023, https://scalawagmagazine.org/2023/05/cop-city-atlanta-history-timeline.

43. George Chido, "George on Georgia: Why Is Atlanta Rushing to Build Cop City in Dekalb County," February 6, 2023, https://decaturish.com/2023/02/george-on-georgia-why-atlanta-is-rushing-to-build-cop-

city-in-dekalb-county/.

44. "About," Atlanta Public Safety Training Center, www.atltrainingcenter.com/the-training-center.

45. "Public Safety Training Center," Atlanta Police Foundation, https://atlantapolicefoundation.org/programs/public-safety-training-center.

46. Micah Herskind, "Cop City and the Prison Industrial Complex in Atlanta," *Mainline*, February 7, 2022, www.mainlinezine.com/cop-city-and-the-prison-industrial-complex-in-atlanta.

47. J. D. Capelouto, Anjali Huynh, and Wilborn P. Nobles III, "17 Hours of Comments Continue to Play before Tonight's Vote on Atlanta Police Training Center," *Atlanta Journal Constitution*, updated September 8, 2021, www.ajc.com/news/atlanta-news/17-hours-of-public-comment-pour-in-ahead-of-police-training-center-vote.

48. Herskind, "Primer on Cop City."

49. Timothy Pratt, "Outcry as Atlanta Refuses to Handle Petitions Over 'Cop City' Police Campus," *The Guardian*, September 11, 2023, www.theguardian.com/us-news/2023/sep/11/atlanta-petition-police-cop-city-georgia.

50. Hugh Farrell, "The Strategy of Composition," *Ill Will*, January 14, 2023, https://illwill.com/composition.

51. Micah Herskind and Kamau Franklin, "The Struggle to Stop Cop City—By Any Means Necessary," *The Forge*, September 7, 2023, https://forgeorganizing.org/article/struggle-stop-cop-city-any-means-necessary.

52. Farrell, "Strategy of Composition."

53. *Decompositions*, "The Fate of Composition," April 3, 2024, https://decompositions.noblogs.org/post/2024/04/03/the-fate-of-composition.

54. Nick Estes, *Our History Is the Future: Standing Rock Versus the Dakota Access Pipeline* (London and New York: Verso, 2019).

55. Vortex Group, *The George Floyd Uprising* (Oakland: PM Press, 2023).

56. Natasha Lennard, "Police Shot Atlanta Cop City Protester 57 Times, Autopsy Finds," *The Intercept*, April 20, 2023, https://theintercept.com/2023/04/20/atlanta-cop-city-protester-autopsy.

57. R. J. Rico, "Autopsy: 'Cop City' Protester Had Hands Raised When Killed," *AP News*, March 13, 2023, https://apnews.com/article/cop-city-protest-tortguita-shooting-autopsy-d49cf387b9496d769ca4421f90ff530b.

58. Rick Rojas and Sean Keenan, "Dozens of 'Cop City' Activists Are Indicted on Racketeering Charges," *New York Times*, September 5, 2023, www.nytimes.com/2023/09/05/us/cop-city-atlanta-indictment.html.

59. Micah Herskind, "The Stop Cop City Indictment Is An Act Of Desperation," *The Defector*, September 12, 2023, https://defector.com/the-stop-cop-city-indictment-is-an-act-of-desperation.

60. Shemon and Arturo, "The Return of John Brown: White Race Traitors in

the 2020 Uprising," *Ill Will*, September 4, 2020, https://illwill.com/the-return-of-john-brown-white-race-traitors-in-the-2020-uprising.

61. Don Hamerquist, "Email on the Historical Situation," in *A Brilliant Red Thread: Revolutionary Writings from Don Hamerquist*, ed. Luis Brennan (Montreal: Kersplebedeb, 2022), 108.

62. Dean Spade, *Mutual Aid: Building Solidarity during this Crisis (and the Next)* (London and New York: Verso, 2020).

63. A provocative engagement with the strategic questions around generalizing a movement like Stop Cop City into a broader, sustained revolt recently appeared in *Ill Will*, an important publication offering serious revolutionary perspectives around Stop Cop City and a variety of other struggles. See: Anonymous, "States of Siege," *Ill Will*, February 19, 2024, https://illwill.com/states-of-siege.

64. Kelly Gawel, "Radical Care: Seeking New and More Possible Meetings in the Shadows of Structural Violence," *Krisis: Journal for Contemporary Philosophy* 43, no. 1 (2023): 16.

65. Matthew Yglesias, "Defund Police Is a Bad Idea, Not a Bad Slogan," *Slow Boring*, December 7, 2020, www.slowboring.com/p/defund-police-is-a-bad-idea-not-a.

66. Joy James, "Airbrushing Revolution for the Sake of Abolition," *Black Perspectives*, July 20, 2020, www.aaihs.org/airbrushing-revolution-for-the-sake-of-abolition.

67. Jarrod Shanahan and Zhandarka Kurti, *States of Incarceration: Rebellion, Reform, and America's Punishment System* (London: Reaktion / Field Notes, 2022), 142–83.

68. Noel Ignatiev, "Introduction," in *The Lesson of the Hour: Wendell Phillips on Abolition & Strategy*, ed. Wendell Phillips (Chicago: Charles H. Kerr, 2001), 17.

69. Ignatiev, "Introduction," in Phillips, *Lesson of the Hour*, 17–26.

70. Rachel Herzing and Justin Piché, *How to Abolish Prisons: Lessons from the Movement against Imprisonment* (Chicago: Haymarket, 2024).

71. Steve Scauzillo, "LA County to Treat Severely Mentally Ill Inmates in the Twin Towers Jail," *Los Angeles Daily News*, May 16, 2023, www.dailynews.com/2023/05/16/la-county-to-treat-severely-mentally-ill-inmates-in-the-twin-towers-jail.

72. Ignatiev, "Introduction," 26.

INDEX

ABOUT THE AUTHORS

ZHANDARKA KURTI is an Assistant Professor of Criminal Justice and Criminology at Loyola University, Chicago. She researches and writes about race, class, policing, incarceration, and mass supervision. She is the co-author of *States of Incarceration: Rebellion, Reform and the Future of America's Punishment System* and editor of *Treason to Whiteness is Loyalty to Humanity.* She lives in Chicago.

JARROD SHANAHAN is the author of *Captives: How Rikers Island Took New York City Hostage*, coauthor of *States of Incarceration: Rebellion, Reform, and America's Punishment System*, and *City Time: On Being Sentence to Rikers Island*, and editor of *Treason to Whiteness Is Loyalty to Humanity.* He lives in Chicago and works as an assistant professor of Criminal Justice at Governors State University in University Park, IL.

ABOUT HAYMARKET BOOKS

Haymarket Books is a radical, independent, nonprofit book publisher based in Chicago. Our mission is to publish books that contribute to struggles for social and economic justice. We strive to make our books a vibrant and organic part of social movements and the education and development of a critical, engaged, and internationalist Left.

We take inspiration and courage from our namesakes, the Haymarket Martyrs, who gave their lives fighting for a better world. Their 1886 struggle for the eight-hour day—which gave us May Day, the international workers' holiday—reminds workers around the world that ordinary people can organize and struggle for their own liberation. These struggles—against oppression, exploitation, environmental devastation, and war—continue today across the globe.

Since our founding in 2001, Haymarket has published more than nine hundred titles. Radically independent, we seek to drive a wedge into the risk-averse world of corporate book publishing. Our authors include Angela Y. Davis, Arundhati Roy, Keeanga-Yamahtta Taylor, Eve Ewing, Aja Monet, Mariame Kaba, Naomi Klein, Rebecca Solnit, Olúfẹ́mi O. Táíwò, Mohammed El-Kurd, José Olivarez, Noam Chomsky, Winona LaDuke, Robyn Maynard, Leanne Betasamosake Simpson, Howard Zinn, Mike Davis, Marc Lamont Hill, Dave Zirin, Astra Taylor, and Amy Goodman, among many other leading writers of our time. We are also the trade publishers of the acclaimed Historical Materialism Book Series.

Haymarket also manages a vibrant community organizing and event space in Chicago, Haymarket House, the popular Haymarket Books Live event series and podcast, and the annual Socialism Conference.